John Lande

Lawyering with Planned Early Negotiation

How You Can Get Good Results for Clients and Make Money

ABA
AMERICAN BAR ASSOCIATION
Defending Liberty
Pursuing Justice

D1394538

Cover design by ABA Publishing.

Page layout by Quadrum Solutions.

The materials contained herein represent the opinions and views of the author and/ or the editors, and should not be construed to be the views or opinions of the law firms or companies with whom such persons are in partnership with, associated with, or employed by, nor of the Section of Dispute Resolution of the American Bar Association unless adopted pursuant to the bylaws of the Association.

No thing contained in this book is to be considered as the rendering of legal advice for specific cases, and readers are responsible for obtaining such advice from their own legal counsel. This book and materials contained herein are intended for educational and informational purposes only.

14 13 12 11   5 4 3 2

Library of Congress Cataloguing-in-Publication Data is on file with the Library of Congress.

ISBN 978-1-61632-101-7

Discounts are available for books ordered in bulk. Special consideration is given to state bars, CLE programs, and other bar-related organizations. Inquire at Book Publishing, ABA Publishing, American Bar Association, 321 North Clark Street, Chicago, Illinois 60654.

www.ababooks.org

May 2012

Best,

John Lande

Contents

CHAPTER 1
Planned Early Negotiation and How Lawyers and
Clients Can Benefit from It

CHAPTER 2
Establishing Good Lawyer-Client Relationships

CHAPTER 3
Billing Systems: Managing the Financial Relationship
between Lawyers and Clients

BIBLIOGRAPHY

Introduction

This book is written for lawyers who negotiate in their work and who want to improve their legal skills and effectiveness. Sooner or later, most lawyers negotiate in their cases. You are likely to spend much of your time negotiating about substantive and procedural issues regardless of whether you have a transactional or litigation practice; whether you work for a big firm, serve as inside counsel, or are a solo practitioner; whether you have a specialized practice or are a general practitioner. And although this book is geared toward civil practitioners, even lawyers who practice criminal law could benefit from some of the ideas and techniques presented here.

In litigation, many negotiations occur late in the case, when trial or other deadlines are bearing down. The conventional wisdom is that settlement "on the courthouse steps" is necessary to force the other side to be more reasonable. Similarly, lawyers negotiating deals often delay making concessions until the last possible minute to gain negotiating leverage.

This book explains why *planned early negotiations* (PEN)—rather than unplanned late negotiations—can be more effective and can increase your success in practice. It also provides specific techniques and forms to help you skillfully use PEN when appropriate.

The truth is that settling sooner is usually better than later for parties. They would generally prefer to resolve their legal matters as soon as possible, especially if this reduces the cost and produces an acceptable result.

Many parties feel agonized when they are in a legal dispute. By the time they consult lawyers, parties are likely to feel distrustful, angry, and/or afraid. Even though many parties and lawyers are not normally adversarial, they may act that way when they believe that the other side is being unreasonable. When both sides feel this way, it takes only one apparently hostile act to set off a cycle of escalating conflict that is hard to stop. Each action, or even just a disrespectful tone, can be used as justification for a counteraction that perpetuates the conflict.

Parties normally benefit from a process that treats them respectfully, de-escalates conflict, efficiently obtains the information needed to resolve disputes, minimizes legal costs, and promptly produces a result that satisfies their most important goals—or at least provides a result that they can live with. Satisfying your clients' interests should lead to more referrals, job satisfaction, and income.

Most lawyers would actually prefer to resolve cases sooner as long as it wouldn't hurt their clients' cases. I believe that most lawyers sincerely care about their clients and want to do the best they can for them, including resolving matters efficiently when it would be in their clients' interests to do so.

One can't suggest negotiation—especially early negotiation—without raising understandable fears that clients would be harmed and that lawyers will lose money compared to what they would earn if they litigated cases fully. Chapter 1 describes a "prison of fear" that can trap parties and lawyers into avoiding negotiation even though it would be in their interest to pursue it. That chapter suggests ways you can escape from this prison. Of course, early negotiation is not appropriate in every case, and you should use various approaches in different cases. You should carefully assess all your cases and consult with clients about what approaches make the most sense in each case. Thus you can use early negotiation in some cases and vigorous, lengthy litigation in others.

Although the potential benefits of early negotiation for clients are obvious, the benefits for *lawyers* may not be as clear. Perhaps the most important benefit is your sense of professional pride in more deeply satisfying clients' interests and doing a good, efficient job. Lawyering can be hard work, and it takes highly skilled professionals to do it well. Constantly dealing with hostile conflict is emotionally draining, and you can relieve your stress in working cooperatively with the other side, when appropriate, to advance the parties' interests. Satisfying your clients generates good will, which can translate into repeat business and referrals of new clients. In addition, you can increase your effective billing rates by using creative compensation arrangements (described in Chapter 3). And increasing clients' satisfaction is likely to increase your fee *collection* rate as well.

As the world economy becomes more competitive, using smart, efficient, and early negotiation when appropriate may not be an optional luxury for many lawyers. Instead, it may become a necessity—as well as a savvy strategy—for lawyers to successfully manage their practices, particularly as sophisticated clients expect more engagement in decision-making and control over legal costs. This strategy may not work for large firms whose business model depends *exclusively* on maximizing the number of billable hours from an army of associates doing litigation as usual. However, for most other lawyers and firms, including enlightened big firms, incorporating PEN techniques into your practices could be a good way to increase your clients' satisfaction (as well as your own) and make more money.

Of course, there is no guarantee that by using the techniques described in this book you will get early and favorable settlements in every case; however, if you generally follow these suggestions, you are likely to get good results overall.

This approach does not require you to use PEN procedures in every case. As described in Chapters 6 and 10, these techniques are not always appropriate, so you should assess when they might be in your clients' interests and discuss this with them.

Although this book focuses particularly on PEN processes, the philosophy and many of the specific skills and strategies can be used in most types of legal representation at any stage of a case. So this book is not just about negotiation, it really reflects a general approach to practicing law—and in virtually every case you should benefit from at least some of the techniques described here.

Inspirations for this Book

This book grows out of two threads of my work: (1) my research and practice about (alternative) dispute resolution, and (2) my teaching a lawyering course to law students.

I received my first mediation training in 1982 and then had a solo practice in Oakland, California, for several years where I practiced both mediation and representation. I found that mediation was generally very satisfying for me and my clients. We were able to focus sharply on both parties' interests and usually find ways to efficiently satisfy them. (This is called "interest-based negotiation," or IBN, and is described in Chapter 5.) Freed from the adversarial structure of litigation, my clients often felt comfortable, and even liberated, to speak openly, respectfully, and caringly to each other. In many cases, they were more than just comfortable, they felt *wonderful* about the mediation. It gave them the chance to act like the good people they were and affirm the worth of the other at the same time. It helped them tailor their agreements to work well for both parties. It also felt natural for me to care about both parties in mediation and help them find a solution they both would feel comfortable with.

In the mid-1990s, I directed a child protection mediation program at the University of Arkansas–Little Rock. Despite very challenging situations, I was able to manage a mediation process where all the participants were respected. In many cases, people made very good decisions that would not have been possible without it.

As a law professor, I have studied mediation, watching with pride as it became widely accepted in many parts of the United States and around the world. I never believed that mediation is a panacea or that it should be used in all cases, but I knew that it offers great potential benefits for parties, professionals, and society. I was also well aware that mediation is imperfect, like all human processes.

Like many others in the dispute resolution field, I had mixed feelings about court-ordered mediation. On one hand, these orders forced lawyers to try mediation, and many found that they really liked it. Without the mandates, many lawyers would have remained unduly skeptical, and the mediation field would not have grown as much as it has.

On the other hand, I was uneasy about courts ordering parties to participate in a process that was supposed to be voluntary (even though the parties did not have to settle in mediation). Moreover, the mandates that forced lawyers to participate in mediation led them to dominate the process and focus on legal issues, often ignoring parties' interests. In some places, mediation became a normal part of the litigation process, which I called "liti-mediation."[1] Many lawyers valued mediation as a way to end litigation, but only late in the process, usually after discovery had been completed. Although many lawyers appropriately embraced the benefits of mediation, others viewed it as just another venue for adversarial contest, and they learned how to "game" the system. In an article on bad-faith negotiation in mediation, I quoted a lawyer who described his approach to mediation:

> [I]f . . . I act for the Big Bad Wolf against Little Red Riding Hood and I don't want this dispute resolved, I want to tie it up as long as I possibly can, and mandatory mediation is custom made. I can waste more time, I can string it along, I can make sure this thing never gets resolved because . . . I know the language. I know how to make it look like I'm heading in that direction. I make it look like I can make all the right noises in the world, like this is the most wonderful thing to be involved in when I have no intention of ever resolving this. I have the intention of making this the most

expensive, longest process but is it going to feel good. It's going to feel so nice, we're going to be here and we're going to talk the talk but we're not going to walk the walk.[2]

Thinking about how to deal with abuse of mediation, I focused on the field of "dispute system design" (DSD). I thought that rules punishing alleged "bad faith" in mediation were likely to make the problem worse. If people didn't want to be in mediation, the big-bad-wolf lawyers could still find ways to abuse the system, including abusing the rules prohibiting bad faith. Rather than trying to force them to behave properly in mediation, I suggested that court planners use DSD methods to reduce problems by designing court mediation programs so that the parties and lawyers would generally *want* to use the process.

DSD involves analyzing a system for handling an ongoing series of disputes. Planners convene a group of stakeholders interested in the system, analyze how well it is working, and agree on how to improve it. To make a system work well, participants need appropriate education and training, and the system needs to be reviewed periodically to make any needed adjustments. DSD is an incredibly flexible set of techniques that has been applied to a wide range of situations, including systems in businesses, government agencies, nonprofit organizations, and many others. This book applies DSD concepts to legal practice.

My thinking was also influenced by serving on the Task Force on Improving Mediation Quality of the ABA Section of Dispute Resolution. The Section created the task force to develop a strategy for promoting quality as an alternative to certification, as there has been a long-standing, unresolved controversy within the mediation field about whether certification of mediators would improve mediation quality. In addition, the issue of quality is related to the controversy about whether it is appropriate for mediators to express their opinions and pressure the parties to settle. Mediators define this issue as whether mediators can be "evaluative" (i.e., express opinions) or must be "facilitative" (i.e., only ask questions and not express opinions). Informed by focus groups and surveys of experienced mediators and lawyers who used mediation in civil cases, the task force recommended careful advance planning of mediation to tailor the process in each case to fit the needs of the parties. It finessed the facilitative-evaluative debate by analyzing various types of opinions that mediators might express and by encouraging parties, lawyers, and mediators to have explicit discussions about what mediator interventions were or were not desired. Rather than making general recommendations of best practices based on particular models of mediation, the task force recognized that people had different conceptions of mediation quality and thus recommended that parties and professionals establish their own standards of quality by customizing the mediation process in each case.

I have also studied Collaborative Practice, which has many features addressing problems of mandatory mediation. Collaborative Practice involves an agreement between lawyers and parties to use interest-based negotiation, typically from the outset of a matter. Thus it represents a marked contrast with much mediation, which often occurs late in a case and where lawyers continue to rely on adversarial and legal approaches to negotiation. Moreover, in the Collaborative process, the lawyers have the professional responsibility to initiate and manage the negotiation process, whereas with mediation, the lawyers often wait until they are ordered to mediate. In the mediation process itself, they typically respond to the mediator's moves rather than take the initiative.

The "disqualification agreement" (DA) is an essential feature of Collaborative Practice; a process isn't considered Collaborative without it. The DA is a provision in a "participation agreement," which parties sign at the beginning of a case to establish procedures for negotiation. The DA provides that if the parties decide to litigate the matter, the Collaborative lawyers are disqualified from representing the parties in litigation. If the parties want to be represented in litigation, they must hire new lawyers to do so. The DA creates incentives for the parties and lawyers to remain in negotiation, considering that termination of the process would mean that parties would presumably incur additional expense in hiring new lawyers and Collaborative lawyers would stop receiving fees when the Collaborative process ended. The DA also helps everyone focus on negotiation, since the lawyers wouldn't think about what they would do if the case wouldn't settle and the parties don't worry that the Collaborative lawyers will become their adversaries in litigation. Research and anecdotal reports suggest that the DA often produces these effects.

Although I could see the benefits of the DA, I was also concerned that it creates risks that parties would get stuck in a Collaborative process in some cases because they had invested too much money in it, or that one party could abuse the process to take advantage of the other. There is evidence that these risks are real, though it is not clear how often they materialize. Considering the risks, I recommended that lawyers experiment with what is called "Cooperative" Practice, which is similar to Collaborative Practice but does not involve the DA. Ethical rules require that lawyers get clients' informed consent to use a Collaborative process, part of which involves consideration of reasonable alternatives (as described in Chapter 10). I believe that offering both Collaborative and Cooperative processes would increase clients' choice and enhance the quality of their decision making.[3]

Thus my practice and research led me to focus on encouraging lawyers to *generally* take the initiative to manage cases from the outset rather than wait to negotiate until late in a negotiation process, often in response to initiatives by courts or mediators. Given the proliferation of dispute resolution processes, clients now have more choices. To be most effective in representing clients, lawyers must understand the different processes and be competent in advising about and representing clients in the processes. In a recent article, I noted a variety of initiatives in the courts and private practice encouraging lawyers to take more responsibility for early handling of cases rather than rely on litigation as usual or unplanned late negotiation.[4]

The second experience informing this book is my teaching a course on lawyering since 2004. This is a required course for University of Missouri first-semester law students, and it prompts me to consider what I think is essential for law students to know about the profession they are preparing to enter. Over the years, I have focused primarily on what the 2007 "Carnegie Report" calls the "apprenticeship of professional identity and purpose," which complements "apprenticeships" of intellect and skills.[5] The course leads students to consider the following questions:

- What is the lawyer's job?
- What should be the relationship between lawyers and their clients?
- How should the fact that only a small fraction of cases go to trial (let alone go up on appeal) affect how lawyers handle legal disputes?
- What interests do clients have in addition to protecting their financial positions?
- How can lawyers assess and protect their clients' interests?
- How can lawyers most effectively represent clients in negotiation and mediation?

- How can lawyers help clients choose and shape appropriate dispute resolution processes?
- Regardless of the kinds of cases they want to handle, what kind of lawyer do they want to be?[6]

This course teaches students about traditional and client-centered approaches to lawyering (regarding the balance of decision making between lawyers and clients), positional and interest-based approaches to negotiation (described in Chapter 5), and facilitative and evaluative approaches to mediation. I firmly believe that there is no single correct approach for dealing with any of these issues. Instead, I teach that all lawyers should reflect on their own general philosophies and, most important, be open to their various clients' preferences about these issues. I believe that lawyers should consider that clients often have important non-monetary interests, that they are likely to ultimately settle most of their cases, and that litigation itself is often expensive, time-consuming, frustrating, and sometimes the cause of new problems. This does not mean that clients should *always* engage in early negotiation or settle their cases. But I do teach that lawyers should carefully assess cases early in an engagement and discuss with clients whether negotiation or some other process would best serve the clients' interests. In some cases, clients wisely choose to pursue litigation full-steam ahead. Choosing to litigate is a better decision if clients have first carefully considered their real interests and options for satisfying them.

Endnotes

1. John Lande, *How Will Lawyering and Mediation Practices Transform Each Other?,* 24 Fla. St. U. L. Rev. 839, 846 (1997).

2. John Lande, *Using Dispute System Design Methods to Promote Good-Faith Participation in Court-Connected Mediation Programs,* 50 UCLA L. Rev. 69, 70-71 (2002) (quoting Julie Macfarlane, *Culture Change? Commercial Litigators and the Ontario Mandatory Mediation Program,* 2002 J. Disp. Resol. 241, 267).

3. John Lande, *Possibilities for Collaborative Law: Ethics and Practice of Lawyer Disqualification and Process Control in a New Model of Lawyering,* 64 Ohio St. L.J. 1315 (2003); John Lande & Forrest S. Mosten, *Collaborative Lawyers' Duties to Screen the Appropriateness of Collaborative Law and Obtain Clients' Informed Consent to Use Collaborative Law,* 25 Ohio St. J. on Disp. Resol. 437 (2010).

4. John Lande, *The Movement Toward Early Case Handling in Courts and Private Dispute Resolution,* 24 Ohio St. J. on Disp. Resol. 81 (2008).

5.   WILLIAM   M.   SULLIVAN   ET   AL.,   EDUCATING   LAWYERS: PREPARATION FOR THE PROFESSION OF LAW (2007).

6.   The syllabus is available at http://www.law.missouri.edu/aalsadr/ Syllabi/lande_syllabus_lawyering.htm.

Overview of this Book

Chapter 1 analyzes why parties and lawyers are often afraid to negotiate even if they very much want to reach agreement. It describes a "prison of fear" that keeps people paralyzed in adversarial processes even when they want to "change the game" to be more cooperative. It contrasts key PEN processes— Settlement Counsel, Cooperative Practice, and Collaborative Practice—with "litigation as usual," where negotiation often is unplanned and occurs late in a case. Chapter 1 summarizes how PEN processes can help you and your clients escape from the prison of fear in appropriate cases.

Lawyers generally need to establish good working relationships with clients to negotiate effectively and, indeed, represent them effectively in any process. Chapter 2 describes typical interests that clients and lawyers have in their relationships. Understanding these interests can help you maintain productive and profitable relationships with your clients. Part of your job is to understand clients' fears and help clients manage them. Chapter 2 shows how you can help clients develop realistic expectations (and thus relieve anxiety) by using "decision analysis," setting the stage for later negotiations. This chapter also describes how limiting the scope of representation to negotiation, in Settlement Counsel or Collaborative processes, can help you develop good relationships with clients in appropriate cases. Finally, this chapter suggests that you develop a philosophy of practice to help you make difficult decisions, and it offers several examples of such philosophies.

Clients' anxiety about legal bills compounds their worries and can create problems in their relationships with their lawyers. Chapter 3 describes different billing arrangements that give your clients a greater feeling of control as well as provide mutually beneficial incentives, including billing premiums, for you to satisfy your clients' interests.

Chapter 4 focuses on lawyers' relationships with "opposing" counsel. Even in adversarial litigation, you have an interest in maintaining a good working relationship with your counterpart who represents the other party. Normally, you have a mutual interest in focusing on the merits of the matter and avoiding unnecessary disputes, delays, and expenses. In an adversarial environment, it is very easy to get crossways with your counterpart, and it can take some planning and initiative to prevent unnecessary disputes. The main advice is to develop a personal relationship with your counterpart at the outset and reach an understanding that you will consult each other before taking adverse actions. Although this strategy won't always work, it can be effective more often than you might think. Chapter 4 also addresses the special relationship between Settlement Counsel and Litigation Counsel who are simultaneously representing the same client in a matter. Obviously, there is potential for conflict in these situations, which would harm the clients' interests, and this chapter suggests ways to develop good relationships between the respective lawyers.

Chapter 5 is a basic primer on the two main approaches to negotiation. In "positional" negotiation, parties exchange a series of offers and counteroffers, where each side is trying to end up with the most favorable result from its perspective. In "interest-based" negotiation, the parties try to develop and reach agreements that satisfy both parties' interests. For both approaches, this chapter provides an overview, description of assumptions and typical tactics, and summary of general advantages and disadvantages. This chapter also describes how the perceived alternatives to a negotiated agreement affect negotiation.

Chapter 6 focuses specifically on how you can plan and conduct planned early negotiations. It discusses the first, critical step of assessing whether negotiation is appropriate. This assessment may be more difficult than you might expect, and this chapter describes how to do such an assessment. If you determine that your client and the other side are interested in using a PEN process, you should plan the process so that it is likely to be successful. This involves careful preparation of your client and coordination with the other lawyer. This chapter sets out procedures for conducting the negotiation, and it concludes with a description of a successful case.

Chapter 7 analyzes why lawyers regularly have difficulty in negotiation and suggests a general approach, including a checklist of techniques. It then provides suggestions for dealing with uncooperative behavior by your client or the other side. In addition, it suggests ways to deal with lawyers with whom you have recurring problems.

Chapter 8 discusses the use of additional professionals in negotiation, which can be very helpful and is sometimes essential. It addresses some preliminary issues, such as whether to jointly engage neutral professionals and/or separately engage various professionals. It also discusses whether to engage professionals from the outset to work as a team or to engage them during the process as needed. It then describes various types of professionals and considerations in engaging them. These include mediators, financial professionals and appraisers, technical experts, mental health professionals, neutral evaluators, private adjudicators, and public adjudicators. This chapter also addresses issues of confidentiality and use of professionals' work product as well as continued engagement after the negotiation ends.

Chapter 9 describes how you can improve the quality of your services to clients. In addition to using procedures discussed in the preceding chapters, lawyers should continue to develop their skills. This includes receiving training, participating in continuing education programs, and getting regular feedback on your performance. This chapter describes various methods for getting feedback, including client surveys or interviews, comments from other professionals with whom you worked on particular cases, and participation in expert or peer consultation groups.

Chapter 10 addresses key ethical issues relevant to planned negotiation. These include diligence and loyalty in representing clients' interests, client decision making and informed consent, discussion of ADR options, screening cases for appropriateness, avoiding impermissible conflicts of interest, confidentiality, truthfulness to others, membership in a negotiation practice organization, advertising, and withdrawal from representation.

This book is a general guide and not a comprehensive treatise on any of the issues it discusses. A bibliography of useful resources is included so that you may explore these issues in more depth. The appendixes provide forms that you can use or adapt in your practice. Some readers will be familiar with some parts of the book, but hopefully you will find new, valuable material in other parts.

Reviewing this summary of the book, you can see that it analyzes legal practice as a system for handling a continuing series of cases. Borrowing concepts from the field of dispute system design, it suggests an approach for handling individual cases as well as your practice overall. On the individual-case level, it recommends engaging the stakeholders in conducting a careful analysis of the matter, starting with your primary stakeholders—your clients—and including the other lawyer and party, as well as other professionals whom you engage. It suggests jointly selecting and designing a process for handling issues and making periodic adjustments as appropriate. It emphasizes the importance of educating the parties, especially your clients, as appropriate so that they can participate in the process as effectively as possible and get the best possible outcomes.

On the level of your practice overall, it invites you to add planned early negotiation processes to the set of services you offer. To do this, you would implement flexible protocols for effective handling of your cases, receive training in practice theory and skills, get feedback from various sources to assess your performance, and make appropriate adjustments. While this book focuses particularly on incorporating planned early negotiation into your practice, it is really about improving your practice generally.

This book is written particularly for lawyers in private practice, although others may find it valuable as well. Corporate and government inside counsel may find it useful in managing their legal dockets. Legal clients may read it to understand lawyers' perspectives and how they can improve their lawyers' work. Law school instructors may find it useful for teaching negotiation and lawyering courses. Law students may want to read it for a practical perspective about how they may work in the future. Professionals who work with lawyers in negotiation, especially mediators, may find it helpful for cases in which they work with lawyers and may want to refer lawyers to the techniques described in this book. Bar associations and courts may use this book in continuing legal education programs to promote good professional behavior.

For simplicity, this book is written as if the reader were a lawyer representing clients in disputes, though most of the same principles would apply to transactional work. It assumes that there are only two parties in the dispute, each with a lawyer, though much of this can be applied in multiparty cases and even if one or more parties is not represented. The term "client" may include both actual and prospective clients, depending on the context. "Party" may include the party's lawyer. "Negotiator" may refer to a lawyer or party or both. Similarly, the "other side" may refer to a lawyer or party or both. The terms "Collaborative," "Cooperative," "Settlement Counsel," and "Litigation Counsel" are capitalized when referring to formal processes to distinguish them from the generic uses of these terms.

This book benefits from interviews with practitioners who generously shared their time, experience, insights, and wisdom, for which I am extremely grateful. These include Kathy Bryan, President and CEO, International Institute for Conflict Prevention and Resolution, New York, New York; Sevilla C.P. Claydon, Of Counsel, Garvey Schubert Barer, Seattle, Washington; Marilyn J. Endriss, Principal/Owner, Sound Conflict Solutions LLC, Edmonds, Washington; Sheldon (Shelly) E. Finman, Attorney at Law and Mediator, Fort Myers, Florida; Eric Galton, Lakeside Mediation Center, Austin, Texas; David A. Hoffman, Mediator, Arbitrator, Attorney, Boston Law Collaborative, LLC, Boston, Massachusetts; Holly M. Hohlbein, Counselor at Law, Kirkland, Washington; James E. McGuire, JAMS, Boston, Massachusetts; Forrest S. ("Woody") Mosten, Mediator and Collaborative Attorney, Los Angeles, California; Bennett G. Picker, Senior Counsel, Stradley Ronon Stevens & Young LLP, Philadelphia, Pennsylvania; Anne F. Preston, Owner and Chair, Garvey Schubert Barer, Seattle, Washington; Douglas C. Reynolds, The New Law Center, LLC, Cambridge, Massachusetts; James R. Skirbunt, Partner, Skirbunt, Skirbunt & Wirtz LLC, Cleveland, Ohio; R. Bruce Whitney, former Chief Litigation Counsel, Air Products & Chemicals, Inc., Allentown, Pennsylvania; Thomas R. Woodrow, Partner, Holland & Knight, Chicago, Illinois; P. Marshall Yoder, Attorney & Counsellor at Law, Wharton Aldhizer & Weaver, PLC, Harrisonburg, Virginia. These lawyers have given permission to use the references to them in this book (sometimes without attribution). Other than that, the statements in this book do not necessarily represent their views.

I am grateful for the support of a research fellowship from the University of Missouri School of Law that permitted me to write this book. Steve Lambson and other Law School librarians provided helpful research. I especially appreciate the thoughtful comments and suggestions of Shelly Finman, Holly Hohlbein, Jim McGuire, Woody Mosten, and Bruce Whitney on a draft of this book.

Dedication

To my dear wife, Ann.

About the Author

John Lande is the Isidor Loeb Professor and Director of the LLM Program in Dispute Resolution at the University of Missouri School of Law. He received his J.D. from Hastings College of Law and Ph.D. in sociology from the University of Wisconsin-Madison. He began mediating professionally in 1982 in California. He was a fellow in residence at the Program on Negotiation at Harvard Law School and the Director of the Mediation Program at the University of Arkansas at Little Rock Law School. His work focuses on various aspects of dispute systems design, including publications analyzing how lawyering and mediation practices will transform each other, business lawyers' and executives' opinions about litigation and ADR, designing court-connected mediation programs, improving the quality of mediation practice, the "vanishing trial," and "planned early negotiation." The International Institute for Conflict Prevention and Resolution gave him its award for best professional article in 2007 for "Principles for Policymaking about Collaborative Law and Other ADR Processes," 22 Ohio State Journal on Dispute Resolution 619 (2007).

Planned Early Negotiation and How Lawyers and Clients Can Benefit from It

1

Getting Trapped in a Prison of Fear
Planned Early Negotiation Processes
Escaping the Prison of Fear
    Careful Case Assessment
    Planned Exchange of Information
    Protection from Exploitation
    Escape Hatches
    Protection against Legal Malpractice
    Appropriate Compensation for Legal Services

Although most legal disputes eventually settle without trial, the negotiation usually is not a pretty picture. If negotiation was always easy, we would never need trials—or even careful negotiation strategies. Negotiation often *is* very hard, even when parties and lawyers sincerely want to be reasonable. Cognitive biases lead people to systematically misjudge the facts and merits of a dispute. Disputes often touch deeply held beliefs and values, and they stimulate strong emotions. Conflict—and how it is handled—can affect people's perceptions of their identity, casting them as worthy of sympathy or condemnation. The mere process of disputing can compound the original conflict by adding new grievances based on the way that the lawyers and parties interact with each other. Sometimes lawyers, in particular, aggravate conflicts for various reasons, including expectations about their role as vigorous advocates, their desires to maintain clients' confidence by fighting for them, their personalities and habits, and interests in increasing their fees. If one person perceives that the other side has acted offensively, the offended individual can justify a retaliatory reaction, which can set off a cycle of escalation.

In an all-too-common pattern in "litigation as usual," settlement comes only after the lawyers engage in adversarial posturing, the litigation process escalates the original conflict, the parties' relationship deteriorates, the process takes a long time and a lot of money, and none of the parties is particularly happy with the settlement. Although some lawyers enjoy this process and make a good living from it, many would prefer to use a more productive and efficient process, but they feel stuck in playing the adversarial "game." The New Law Center's Doug Reynolds says that "the much-maligned lawyers aren't bad as some people think. In some situations, they get goaded into being adversarial. If the other side starts out adversarial, they feel they have to respond in kind." This happens even for lawyers who use negotiation whenever possible. For example, Marshall Yoder, of Wharton Aldhizer & Weaver, who does Collaborative Practice as well as litigation, says that he "can get pulled into an adversarial mode really easily if someone else starts it."

Of course, it doesn't always happen this way. Sometimes the process is relatively cooperative, quick, and easy, and the parties are satisfied with the results. But litigation isn't designed to produce a satisfying negotiation process, and this normally isn't the result.

Lawyers and other dispute resolution experts have been working for decades to create "a better way" to resolve legal disputes, in the words of former Chief Justice Warren Burger. The alternative dispute resolution (ADR) field reflects a continuing effort to improve dispute resolution processes and provide more options for parties and their lawyers to "fit the forum to the fuss." Historically, ADR has involved alternatives to litigation, such as arbitration, mediation, and neutral evaluation, as well as improving negotiation within the litigation process. ADR processes, including negotiation, offer many potential benefits for parties, including better results, less time and cost invested in disputing, protection of privacy, and an opportunity to choose and shape dispute resolution processes to fit their needs. Although parties do not always realize these benefits from using ADR processes, they often do find them to be very valuable.

The book *Getting to Yes*[1] popularized interest-based negotiation as an alternative to the traditional positional approach used in litigation, where each side makes extreme offers and counteroffers to gain partisan advantage or to protect against being taken advantage of. (These two approaches to negotiation are described in Chapter 5.) Although cases are often settled through positional negotiation, this process often creates incentives to withhold or misrepresent information, stimulates mistrust, leads to gaming tactics to gain advantage, increases hostility, harms relationships, produces agreements that do not satisfy parties' most important interests, and prolongs the process. In legal cases, the parties often settle "on the courthouse steps" without a careful analysis of options that could satisfy both parties' interests.

Kathy Bryan, president and CEO of the CPR Institute and former head of worldwide litigation for Motorola, says that when disputes occur in businesses, "groupthink" or conventional wisdom takes over. People think, "We're good. The other side is bad. We have a good case so, 'Lawyers, you go beat them over the head.'" Her reading of research about negotiation as well as her own experience in litigation indicates that taking polar positions and trying to "stick it to the other side" is the least successful strategy. People are more successful when they offers things to the other side and create a reciprocal desire to offer something back. But by and large, lawyers normally use an adversarial approach.

Even when you win in litigation, this doesn't necessarily satisfy your clients. One lawyer described such a case. She represented the plaintiff in a sexual harassment suit. Her client (who we will call Jane Smith) was one of only two women in the workplace in a field traditionally dominated by men. Smith had been subjected to egregious sexual harassment: a co-worker "leaned up against her" a number of times, employees watched pornographic movies depicting violent rapes, and there were pinup posters in the workplace. The parties engaged in a fruitless negotiation where they "weren't even in the same country, let alone the same ballpark."

After a three-week trial, the jury found for the plaintiff on all counts, and although there were no economic damages, the jury returned a huge verdict for emotional distress. After the trial, jurors came out and hugged Smith. The verdict was front-page news, and the newspaper ran an editorial chastising the employer. This was the best day in court that any plaintiff could have. Several years later, Smith's lawyer asked if she would go to trial if she if had to do it all over again. Smith said she would have settled instead. She compared it to when she was a little girl and her mother would tell her to apologize to her sister. She would apologize, but it was a hollow apology because it wasn't sincere. Even though Smith won at trial, she never had the feeling that the employer took responsibility for its actions, which was what she really wanted. Although plaintiffs don't always get that satisfaction from negotiation, well-conducted negotiations and mediations sometimes produce remarkable results (for both plaintiffs and defendants) that would be impossible to achieve at trial.

This case suggests that lawyers can do a valuable service for their clients by helping them consider what is most important to them and anticipate how they would feel about different results. Even if you get a blowout win in court, it may not satisfy your client. And, of course, you aren't going to get a blowout win in court in every case. You can often satisfy your clients' interests better in negotiation while eliminating the risk of an unfavorable trial result, saving time and money from additional litigation, and protecting their privacy. Most cases eventually settle without trial anyway, so why not negotiate early in a case or even before filing suit?

Getting Trapped in a Prison of Fear

Although people often like the idea of negotiation *in theory*, many are afraid to use it in their own situations. Parties may have unsuccessfully tried to work out problems on their own, leading them to doubt the other side's sincerity and to feel unsure that they can negotiate a satisfactory resolution. If a corporate transactional lawyer negotiated unsuccessfully, the client and litigation counsel might feel that there is no point in even trying further negotiation.

Sometimes people worry that even suggesting it would make them look weak and lead the other side to try to take advantage. Sometimes people doubt that the others in the dispute would negotiate honestly and are afraid to even explore this possibility. Thus, out of fear, parties often seek help from lawyers and courts to protect themselves. These actions can reinforce fears by the other side and justify adversarial approaches, leading to a cycle of escalating conflict. Given an atmosphere of fear and mistrust, it can be hard just to get people to suggest or consider negotiation, especially early in a case.

When people first consult lawyers about a dispute, they often have an adversarial mind-set and want the lawyers to act tough to protect them from the other side, which they perceive as unreasonable. Lawyers often feel that they can get the best results for clients by starting with an extreme position and later making concessions as necessary. Although lawyers often mention negotiation in an initial consultation, they often do so as part of a discussion that demonstrates their loyalty and willingness to fight if needed. They may fear—sometimes quite accurately—that if they seem too interested in negotiation, prospective clients will not retain them or will worry whether the lawyers will really protect them.

Some lawyers may fear that an early negotiation process will force them to resolve their cases before they are ready. Litigators are used to collecting as much information as they can and analyzing it over a period of time. Some may worry that an early negotiation process would require them to make hasty decisions based on partial information, potentially jeopardizing their clients' interests. Anne Preston, of Garvey Schubert Barer, said that some lawyers are reluctant to negotiate early in a case because the process would force them get to the core of the case before they know "what's going on," and they would worry about the information they would never get to see.

This is a "prison of fear" that keeps parties and lawyers from negotiating early in a dispute. Although lawyers know that most cases will eventually settle—often only after a process that takes too long and costs too much—they often feel powerless to steer clients toward a more productive path. If you and your clients can overcome the fear of entering negotiation, you stand a good chance of reaching an agreement satisfying your clients' interests. Table 1 describes the prison of fear and ways to escape from it, which are discussed in more detail below.

Table 1. Getting Trapped in—and Escaping from—the Prison of Fear

Parties' and Lawyers' Fears of Negotiation	Ways to Deal with the Fears
You are negotiating because you don't have a good case and you will look weak to the other side.	Tell the other side that you routinely consider negotiation whenever it might be appropriate.
The other side will try to take advantage of you.	Carefully assess the benefits and risks of negotiation and proceed only if the potential benefits outweigh the risks.
The other side will not share information or be honest.	Negotiate only when you have some confidence that the other side will mutually exchange information; use mechanisms to provide confidence that you have sufficient and accurate information before settling.
Your story will not be heard and validated.	Negotiate only when you have some confidence that the other side will seriously consider your perspective and interests.
You will "give away" too much to the other side.	Assert your legitimate interests, don't "give away" too much to the other side, and be prepared to use an "escape hatch" if necessary.

Your client will lose confidence in you and the other side will not respect you as an aggressive advocate.	You can negotiate powerfully *and also* communicate to your clients and the other side that you and your client are prepared to litigate vigorously if necessary.*
You will risk malpractice liability if you settle without full discovery.	Much discovery has little value, and your malpractice risk will not increase if you get your client's informed consent for settlement.
You will lose revenue if you negotiate early in a case.	You can maintain or increase your revenue by using creative compensation arrangements and generating good will by satisfying clients' interests in negotiation.

* In Settlement Counsel and Collaborative Practice processes described below, Settlement Counsel and Collaborative lawyers would not represent clients in litigation, but the clients should be prepared to litigate if necessary.

People sometimes express these fears indirectly. They may sincerely believe in the value of negotiation or ADR generally, and their firms may have even signed a pledge to regularly consider it, but somehow their cases generally don't seem quite right for it—at least not until late in litigation. They think that they might be ready after the next event in litigation, such as finding the "smoking gun," completing the next deposition, getting a ruling on a motion to compel discovery or summary judgment, etc. Although these may be valid considerations in particular cases, this general pattern reflects an underlying fear about losing something important in negotiation.

This book is designed to help you help your clients use effective ways to handle disputes and avoid getting trapped in a prison of fear. Instead of reacting defensively out of fear, you can build trust with the other side so that you can negotiate with more confidence. Instead of relying only on ad hoc negotiation processes (which are initiated and developed for each case), you can also provide procedures that have general structures so that you don't have to "re-invent the wheel" for each negotiation, but that are also flexible and can be adapted for each case. Instead of waiting until both sides are worn down by litigation before suggesting negotiation, you can offer a negotiation process at the beginning of a case—a planned early negotiation (PEN). This book describes how you can design a PEN process to fit the parties' preferences.

Planned Early Negotiation Processes

This book describes three PEN processes: Settlement Counsel, Cooperative negotiation, and Collaborative negotiation. David Hoffman, of the Boston Law Collective, notes that these processes are ways for lawyers to help their clients "get to yes" sooner rather than later.

A Settlement Counsel is hired solely to negotiate, and the party may (or may not) simultaneously retain Litigation Counsel. If Settlement and Litigation Counsel are involved simultaneously, they operate in parallel with each other. This arrangement permits both Settlement and Litigation Counsel to focus on their respective tasks without confusion of goals of negotiation and litigation. One party in a dispute can unilaterally use a Settlement Counsel without the other side using separate Settlement and Litigation Counsel.[2] Sometimes lawyers serve as private negotiation advisors, without disclosure to Litigation Counsel and/or the other side. In these situations, the lawyers do not represent the clients in negotiation, and this activity is not covered in this book.

Cooperative negotiation involves an explicit agreement by the parties to use a planned negotiation process. Typically, this occurs at the beginning of a case, and the lawyers focus exclusively on negotiation. If needed, the lawyers can represent the parties in litigation and later return to negotiation, if appropriate. In a Cooperative negotiation, lawyers focus on only one procedure at a time—negotiation or litigation.[3] The process agreement may include a procedure for resolving disputes, such as mediation or arbitration.

Collaborative negotiation also involves an explicit agreement to negotiate, typically at the outset of a matter. The distinctive feature of a Collaborative negotiation is the "disqualification" provision in the agreement, which precludes the Collaborative lawyers from representing parties in litigation. If the parties decide to litigate the matter, the Collaborative lawyers must withdraw from the case, and if the parties want legal representation, they must hire litigation counsel who may not be in the same firm as the Collaborative lawyers. You can think of Collaborative negotiation as a process where both parties agree to hire Settlement Counsel and refrain from contested litigation during negotiation.[4]

Figure 1 compares general patterns of negotiation in Cooperative and Collaborative Practice and litigation. In a common pattern of litigation, the parties begin in the litigation process and may negotiate in that context, often after an extended period of litigation. In this situation, the lawyers typically negotiate directly with each other, conveying messages between the parties, who may never meet to negotiate. In Cooperative and Collaborative Practice, the parties generally begin with negotiation and typically participate actively in the process. With Collaborative practitioners, virtually all of the negotiation is done in joint meetings with the parties and lawyers together. Cooperative practitioners use joint meetings selectively based on whether they think it would be productive. Figure 1 shows that Cooperative lawyers can participate in litigation but Collaborative lawyers cannot. In practice, there are variations in each model. For example, the negotiation processes may involve mediators and other professionals to help resolve disputes. In litigation, parties may or may not negotiate. In Cooperative and Collaborative models, parties may or may not litigate. Some parties negotiate in other ways, such as without lawyers, without filing suit, or in mediation.

Figure 1. Negotiation in Litigation, Cooperative, and Collaborative Models of Lawyering.

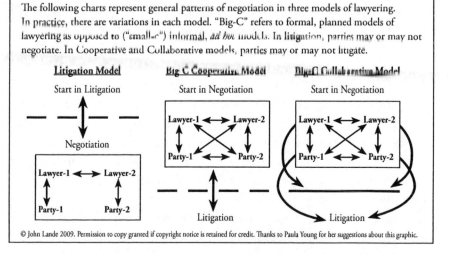

Negotiation in Litigation, Cooperative, and Collaborative Models of Lawyering

The following charts represent general patterns of negotiation in three models of lawyering. In practice, there are variations in each model. "Big-C" refers to formal, planned models of lawyering as opposed to ("small-c") informal, *ad hoc* models. In litigation, parties may or may not negotiate. In Cooperative and Collaborative models, parties may or may not litigate.

Litigation Model **Big-C Cooperative Model** **Big-C Collaborative Model**

Start in Litigation   Start in Negotiation   Start in Negotiation

Negotiation

Lawyer-1 ◄──► Lawyer-2   Lawyer-1 ◄──► Lawyer-2   Lawyer-1 ◄──► Lawyer-2

Party-1   Party-2   Party-1 ◄──► Party-2   Party-1 ◄──► Party-2

Litigation   Litigation

© John Lande 2009. Permission to copy granted if copyright notice is retained for credit. Thanks to Paula Young for her suggestions about this graphic.

Each of the PEN processes focuses primarily on negotiation, using different mechanisms to separate negotiation and potential litigation procedures. Many of the issues and dynamics are similar for all three processes, and thus much of this book would apply to any of them, though it will note differences when relevant. Each process has advantages and disadvantages, and your clients may prefer one over another in a given case.

These processes have been used in virtually every type and size of civil case. These include family, business, employment, environmental, intellectual property, product liability, professional negligence, personal injury, insurance, and many other issues. Clients range from working-class couples with low-asset divorces to huge corporations in business disputes with more than $100 million at stake. Because you do these processes privately, they are particularly appropriate when your clients want to protect their privacy, such as in family, business, and law firm dissolutions; employment matters; probate; and cases involving sensitive business information.

David Hoffman says that the most robust predictor of success in negotiation is not the choice of process, but rather the intentions, skill, and chemistry of parties and counsel. This book describes ways you can improve your chance of success by focusing on each of these elements.

Escaping the Prison of Fear

Planned early negotiation processes include safeguards that can help you escape from the prison of fear. The following descriptions sketch out key features in the processes, which are described at greater length in the rest of the book.

Careful Case Assessment. In every case where you consider negotiating— whether using a planned or unplanned negotiation process—you should help your clients decide whether the investment in negotiation is worth the risk of trying to settle and failing. When you first consult with clients, you should help them carefully assess their situation, including all of the clients' interests as well as possible methods for dealing with the matter. You should routinely discuss the range of plausible dispute resolution options, including negotiation.

You can explain to prospective clients that you routinely do this assessment in *every* case, regardless of the strength of the case. You can tell them that although most cases eventually settle, you are prepared to litigate vigorously if necessary. Some lawyers negotiate very aggressively, so the mere fact that you may negotiate doesn't mean that you are necessarily going to "give away the store." Kathy Bryan says that she doesn't have any trouble in suggesting negotiation. She says that just talking and listening doesn't indicate that you are necessarily going to give anything away.

Presented in this way, you can avoid the perception that you are afraid to strongly advocate for clients, including in litigation. Indeed, even if you use a PEN process and work hard to reach a reasonable settlement, you should be prepared to advise clients to litigate if negotiation does not seem likely to satisfy their interests. During a PEN process, you and your clients can periodically consider whether it makes sense to continue the negotiation if you have doubts that it would be productive.

A critical part of the initial assessment is an analysis of the other side's interests (as they perceive them) and whether they might be interested in a reasonable negotiation process and outcome. To some extent, this is a function of the parties' relationship, although sometimes it is possible to conduct a productive negotiation even when the relationship is strained. Indeed, lawyers often function as "agents of cooperation" precisely when parties would benefit from negotiation but would have a hard time negotiating directly.[5] Thus, lawyers can promote productive negotiations even when the parties aren't getting along very well. Of course, sometimes lawyers bring counterproductive attitudes of their own, which can make negotiation more difficult. So it is essential to assess the *lawyers'* perspectives as well those of the parties.

In general, people should use a PEN process only if they think that everyone is willing to listen to others, consider their views, and take reasonable positions in negotiation—or can be effectively coached to do so. In making this assessment, you should carefully look beneath the surface of the parties' statements and consider whether, if approached properly, they might be good candidates for a PEN process. If you float the idea of using a PEN process with the other side and get a skeptical response, you might ask why they are responding that way, what might make negotiation attractive to them, and how they suggest handling the issues.

Appendix B provides the Early Case Assessment guidelines developed by the International Institute for Conflict Prevention and Resolution (CPR), which can help you analyze your cases.

Planned Exchange of Information. PEN processes provide for mutual exchange of information. Eric Galton, of Lakeside Mediation Center, says that the process should be designed so that everyone can fairly evaluate the case. Voluntarily sharing information signals that the parties have a high level of confidence and an interest in negotiating a fair agreement. In some cases, such as divorce cases, the parties may agree to provide each other all relevant information. In large, complex civil cases, parties may start with an agreement to exchange basic information initially and, if additional information is needed, agree to exchange the specific information needed to make good decisions and resolve the matter.

In unplanned negotiations, parties and lawyers often rely on information provided through formal discovery processes, which includes declarations under penalty of perjury. These declarations give some assurance that they can rely on the information and provide legal remedies in case of deception. In PEN processes, parties can also provide information under penalty of perjury, if desired. In a Settlement Counsel or Cooperative negotiation process, parties can use formal discovery to obtain information from people who are not parties in the dispute. If the parties settle a dispute, lawyers can include language in settlement agreements making representations about material facts that could be the basis for remedies for fraud.

Thus PEN processes can provide you with confidence in the accuracy of the information you use in negotiation. No procedure, including litigation, can provide total assurance that the parties will get all the relevant and accurate information they want, but unless they suspect that the other parties are willing to deceive them, a PEN process can provide reasonable assurance at a reasonable cost. Even when parties mistrust each other, you can assure them by obtaining information directly from third-party sources or conducting third-party audits.

Protection from Exploitation. A PEN process offers several ways to counter fears of being taken advantage of. First, much (and perhaps all) of the information exchanged would be legally discoverable, so parties presumably would have to provide the information even if they litigate the case. Some information needed for the most productive negotiation, such as identification of the parties' key interests and settlement priorities, is not discoverable. But even when discussing these matters, there are ways you can protect your clients. You may fear that you would expose yourself to risk by disclosing your clients' interests or priorities, as the other side can use this knowledge to demand greater concessions. For example, in a divorce negotiation, if a wife indicates that she really wants certain provisions in a parenting plan for the couple's young children, the husband could offer to accept her parenting plan only if she agrees to accept less child support or alimony than she might otherwise receive. Other examples of information that may not be discoverable include business trade secrets, potential commercial opportunities, plans, insurance coverage, etc.[6]

You can protect your clients from exploitation by limiting your disclosure—at least at first—to legally discoverable information that the other side would eventually get anyway. You can agree in writing that the information provided in the process is to be used only for settlement and can stamp documents "For settlement purposes only" to protect against use in litigation.

You can exchange information at the same time so that neither side gets an advantage over the other. You can hold off disclosing sensitive information about clients' interests until the middle of a process, after each side has had a chance to assess the other side's motives and trustworthiness, based in part on whether the other side has made appropriate disclosures. Such a process would enable you to build trust with each other by making a series of such exchanges, withholding the most sensitive or detailed information until later in the process. If you believe that the other side is trying to take advantage of such disclosures, you can decline to provide sensitive information in the future unless and until you receive adequate assurances from the other side.

You can take advantage of rules protecting the confidentiality of settlement negotiations, such as Federal Rule of Evidence 408 and state counterparts. You can also use a mediator and share sensitive information privately in "caucus," so that the mediator manages the exchange of certain information while protecting the confidentiality of other information. If you use mediation, communications in the process may be protected from use in litigation by privilege or other statutory provisions in your jurisdiction. Some states and courts have adopted rules protecting parties from use in litigation of certain communications in Collaborative negotiations. The recent adoption of the Uniform Collaborative Law Act may prompt additional jurisdictions to adopt such rules.

Doug Reynolds, of The New Law Center, says that people ask him whether the other side takes advantage of his clients' disclosure of their interests. He says, "The answer is no. If they did, I would know, and I would say that this isn't going to work. I would say that to the other side and to my client." He said, "Being transparent about my clients' interests is easy, because it is usually obvious. If their interests are not obvious, it is helpful to tell the other side because it signals to them what is important. I can't think of a case where the other side didn't know what my client's interests were. In my practice, being clear about my settlement role and my clients' real interests has not been used against my clients or me."

On the other hand, Anne Preston doesn't buy the argument that there are no surprises in litigation anymore because of liberal discovery. She notes that some lawyers don't do their "homework" very well, and the other side could sacrifice strategic advantages by using early negotiation. If the parties try a PEN process, don't settle, and then go to trial, the lawyers can better assess which arguments are likely to be "winners" or "losers" and thus present their best cases. From a societal perspective, this should improve the quality of trials and court decisions. From an individual litigant's perspective, however, it may not be such a great result if the other side would be in a stronger position at trial.

Many lawyers, however, probably overestimate the frequency of gaining significant strategic advantages in discovery or at trial from pivotal "Perry Mason" moments, where they dramatically present some "smoking gun" evidence that completely turns the case around. An experienced lawyer described finding a "smoking gun" in one case, which he said was "addictive" and he got "hooked" into looking for them in other cases. He never found any others—and even in the case where he found one, he would have won without it.

Spending long periods and large sums chasing such a remote possibility is usually not the best way to serve clients. Instead, you can help your clients thoughtfully weigh the relative advantages and risks of early negotiation and extensive litigation. This should help clients decide the likely benefits and risks of each approach and which one best serves their key interests and values.

Escape Hatches. PEN processes include "escape hatches" so that you can leave the process at any time. In a Cooperative negotiation, you can stop negotiating and proceed in litigation. In a Settlement Counsel or Collaborative process, parties can end the negotiation process, and the Settlement or Collaborative Counsel's services, and shift the focus to litigation. In a Settlement Counsel process, the parties may have previously retained litigation counsel to begin litigation or be available if needed. In a Collaborative case, parties may have contacted litigation counsel who may be available on "stand-by," or they may need to start looking for counsel if and when a Collaborative negotiation ends without agreement. The shift from negotiation to litigation may require additional time and expense, which may vary depending on the circumstances. Of course, this routinely occurs in "litigation as usual" (LAU), when parties negotiate but do not settle. The fact that parties' failure to settle would add to the time and cost required in a Settlement Counsel or Collaborative process creates incentives to settle to avoid the additional time and expense.

Protection against Legal Malpractice. While most of the preceding fears are relevant to both lawyers and parties, lawyers may have some special concerns about using a PEN process. Some lawyers might fear increasing their exposure to malpractice liability by engaging in early negotiation and settlement. Although such fear is understandable, there should be no additional risk if you handle the case properly. You might worry about settling cases before completing all discovery for fear of missing some critical information that might give the other side a litigation—and thus bargaining—advantage. As described above, however, a good planned negotiation will involve appropriate exchanges of information and assurances about the accuracy of information provided. If you need to use litigation procedures to obtain certain information from third parties, this could be arranged within the context of a planned negotiation.

Parties may wish to settle without obtaining all the information that they would otherwise collect in an adversarial litigation process. This may be a very prudent decision, balancing the time, expense, and other costs of obtaining additional discovery against the possibility of a more favorable outcome of the dispute due to the additional discovery. Parties and lawyers regularly make these decisions in litigation, and there is no reason why lawyers are at greater risk in helping clients make such decisions in a PEN process. In any case where parties decline to pursue potential discovery, it is good practice to help clients weigh the advantages and disadvantages of the options and to document their decision-making process.

Appropriate Compensation for Legal Services. PEN processes can save parties a lot of legal fees while producing results that may be as good as or better than what they might have received in LAU. The widespread system of lawyers billing for their services by the hour in LAU creates incentives for lawyers to act inefficiently. As a matter of fairness and practicality, it is appropriate for lawyers to receive a portion of the savings achieved through a PEN process. If you use your negotiation skills to produce good, efficient results for clients, it is fair that you receive appropriate compensation for your good work. And as a practical matter, you may not be willing to offer a PEN process if you would receive a lot less compensation than you would have received in a LAU process. Of course, clients should not be expected to pay the full amount they would have paid in a LAU process.

When the potential litigation costs would be substantial in a LAU process, there is a lot of room for you and your clients to negotiate alternative compensation arrangements that would benefit you both. Clients would benefit by paying less in total than the LAU fees and presumably obtaining a result at least as good as in LAU in a shorter time, even though the effective hourly rate may be higher than in a LAU approach. They would also probably incur less wear and tear on themselves and their relationship with the other party. They are especially likely to be satisfied with your services if you agree on a fee structure providing incentives for you to achieve their goals, not simply pay for as much time as you spend on a case.

In addition, the collection rate is generally much higher for skilled negotiators than for LAU lawyers. Satisfied clients usually pay their bills promptly. In a PEN process, the legal fees are paced somewhat uniformly throughout the process, which allows clients to plan how they will pay their fees. By contrast, litigation clients are less likely to pay suddenly increased legal fees at the end of a LAU case as you gear up for and go to trial. You may have a particularly hard time collecting bills when your clients experience a loss, a less-than-hoped-for "win," or a last-minute settlement to avoid trial. Such clients often demand large write-offs or simply refuse to pay.

If your practice includes PEN, you should be able to receive a higher effective hourly rate for a smaller number of hours in a case by working on other matters during the time you would have spent in a LAU process. In this situation, you should receive greater (or at least equal) total compensation over a period of time. In addition to receiving greater income, you are likely to accrue greater goodwill, which can lead to repeat business and increased referrals from satisfied clients. Providing your clients with the best possible attorney fee options will probably increase your professional satisfaction and business success.

This model may not work well for law firms that rely on maximizing the number of billable hours, especially of a large team of associates. Although some firms can continue with this business model, it is becoming increasingly difficult as clients demand greater value and efficiency in the face of economic pressures and competition. Paradoxically, firms using PEN processes may achieve greater success as the market for civil legal services evolves to meet changing conditions. Offering PEN, in addition to LAU, can position law firms to take the lead in these market conditions instead of lagging behind. This may require law firms to shrink somewhat to be successful, but the market is pressing law firms in that direction anyway.

There are many possible compensation arrangements that lawyers and clients can agree on. These include setting ranges for total billing and premiums for achieving specified goals within specified time periods. Chapter 3 describes these options in more detail.

Endnotes

1. ROGER FISHER & WILLIAM URY WITH BRUCE PATTON, GETTING TO YES: NEGOTIATING AGREEMENT WITHOUT GIVING IN (2d ed. 1991).

2. For more information about Settlement Counsel, see William F. Coyne, Jr., *The Case for Settlement Counsel*, 14 OHIO ST. J. ON DISP. RESOL. 367 (1999); John Lande, *The Movement Toward Early Case Handling in Courts and Private Dispute Resolution*, 24 OHIO ST. J. ON DISP. RESOL. 81, 112–17 (2008).

3. For more information about Cooperative Practice, see John Lande, *Practical Insights from an Empirical Study of Cooperative Lawyers in Wisconsin*, 2008 J. DISP. RESOL. 203. My website includes numerous other articles about Cooperative Practice. *See* http://www.law.missouri.edu/lande/publications.htm#ccl.

4. There is an extensive literature on Collaborative Practice. See the bibliography.

5. Ronald J. Gilson & Robert H. Mnookin, *Disputing Through Agents: Cooperation and Conflict Between Lawyers in Litigation*, 94 COLUM. L. REV. 509 (1994).

6. Carrie Menkel-Meadow, *Ethics in Alternative Dispute Resolution: New Issues, No Answers from the Adversary Conception of Lawyers' Responsibilities*, 38 S. TEX. L. REV. 407, 423 (1997).

Establishing Good Lawyer-Client Relationships | 2

Addressing Clients' Interests and Fears
Helping Clients Develop Realistic
   Expectations
Limiting the Scope of Representation to
   Negotiation
Developing Your Own Practice Philosophy

Lawyers and clients need good working relationships to work together profitably. I use the word "profitably" broadly, to include benefits beyond direct financial advantage. This reflects the fact that lawyers and clients each have economic and non-economic interests in their lawyer-client relationships.

Lawyers certainly have a financial interest in receiving fees for their legal services, and clients are more likely to pay their bills if they have a good relationship with their lawyers. Lawyers generally want to maintain good personal and professional relationships with clients for many additional reasons. Most lawyers are sincerely interested in protecting clients' interests and helping them achieve their goals. Having a good working relationship with clients helps lawyers do their work more effectively. Clients who are satisfied with their lawyers' work are more likely to use those lawyers to handle other matters in the future and refer potential clients to them. Lawyers can gain reputational value by being publicly identified as counsel for prestigious clients.

Similarly, clients have numerous interests in the relationships with their lawyers. Clients have an economic interest in obtaining the best possible results, and they rely on their lawyers to try to achieve them. Lawyers can provide particular value in getting good results because of their experience and relationships with lawyers and courts. Legal fees can be very expensive and hard for clients to evaluate, so they want to feel confident that the lawyers will be efficient in their use of time and charge fairly for their services. Clients often have an interest in having their perspectives validated by their lawyers, reassuring them that they are right and the other side is wrong. Clients often need to make difficult decisions, and they want to believe that their lawyers understand their interests, are really concerned about their welfare, and can give good advice for achieving their goals— even if it is not what they always want to hear. Sometimes clients benefit from their association with particular lawyers or law firms, as this can send important signals about their posture in dealing with disputes and in their status generally. For example, by hiring particular firms, clients can signal that they are important, will take tough positions, will be agreeable, etc. In some cases, lawyers serve as "matchmakers," connecting clients with financial or mental health professionals, financiers, other professionals, and social acquaintances. Clients often have multiple interests in a given situation, and it is important for lawyers to learn all their interests and which are given the highest priority.

Thus, lawyers and clients have complex relationships with different perspectives and interests. In effect, they conduct negotiations with each other "behind the negotiation table" before they negotiate with the other side "across the table."[1]

Addressing Clients' Interests and Fears

To develop the best relationships with clients and provide them with the best service, you must understand their real interests in a matter. Unfortunately, many lawyers learn from law school and legal practice that their job is primarily to win cases by making better legal arguments than the other side. They also learn to focus on "just the facts"—meaning only those facts relevant to a legal cause of action—and to disregard emotional considerations.

In most cases, clients care about a legal argument only to the extent that it affects their ability to achieve their goals. Clients generally want to feel that the law is on their side, providing justification for their positions. And they want to use the law as a "stick" to make the other side more willing to satisfy their demands without going to trial. Certainly, some parties want to win and get public vindication, but many simply want to resolve a problem in an acceptable way and move on to other things. If you focus only on the legally relevant facts and do not consider the parties' emotions to be significant factors, you can miss what is most important in a case and overlook possibilities for achieving satisfying results.

At the beginning of a legal representation, you and your client should have a thorough discussion of the client's interests and what you might realistically help him or her accomplish. (For a list of common client interests, see Chapter 5.) Assessing clients' interests—and determining which are the clients' highest priority—is easier said than done. Lawyers generally are not well trained to find out what is most important to clients beyond their stated or superficial goals. Sometimes clients themselves don't have a clear idea about what their interests are, especially if they are not thinking clearly because they are angry or upset. Indeed, at the outset, they may have unrealistic fantasies about easily winning a great legal victory that solves all their problems (often without thinking very much about the risk of losing or the cost). In the midst of a conflict, parties may not consider options other than either winning or capitulation to the other side. Thus they may initially present themselves as wanting you to litigate vigorously out of fear that they will not achieve their goals unless they take a tough position in litigation.

Organizational clients present additional challenges. In some cases, executives for organizational clients may have various personal interests that affect their decision making. Kathy Bryan, president and CEO of the CPR Institute, says that the interest and enthusiasm of inside counsel in negotiating complex business-to-business cases is the single most important factor in whether a business will try it. She says that if the inside counsel is interested, it will happen; if not, it won't. One lawyer interviewed for this book describes inside counsel as often being "former pit bull litigators," and Tom Woodrow, of Holland and Knight, says that some inside (and all outside) counsel have an interest in continuing with litigation as usual because it provides a steady flow of work that they do well and enjoy. Another lawyer reported hearing clients' representatives say things like, "My wife will think I'm a wuss if I settle this case"; "I'm only going to be in this company for another year. This case won't settle on my watch"; "If I settle this year, I'll get a bad performance review and won't get a bonus"; "If we get a bad result at trial, I can blame it on the judge."

Clearly, there may be many reasons why individual and organizational parties may not want to negotiate at the outset of a matter. Over time, however, parties' willingness to litigate often dissipates as they experience the hassles and risks of litigation and receive bills from their lawyers.

This common evolution of clients' expectations can present serious challenges for lawyers. In your first interview with a client, you have incomplete information—and usually no information from the other side that would provide a more complete and accurate picture. Your clients may not provide full or accurate information because their perceptions are distorted due to normal cognitive errors, such as self-serving bias. Or they may be reluctant to tell you the whole story if they are embarrassed, want your validation that they are "right," or are afraid that you won't take their case if you know all the facts.

This situation can present difficult dilemmas for lawyers. You have an interest in demonstrating that you will vigorously fight for clients and obtain a good result. You might worry that if you do not demonstrate sufficient confidence in an initial interview, prospective clients may not hire you. On the other hand, if you express too much confidence, clients may later be disappointed if the results are not as good as you led them to expect, especially since you can't be confident that you know all the relevant information. Moreover, your clients may be in a heightened emotional state, leading them to selectively hear or remember things.

Managing clients' anxiety, ambivalence, and confused expectations is a difficult but critically important part of building your relationship with them. You can deal with these challenges by acknowledging that clients are usually worried about their situation at the outset and that you will do everything you can to achieve their goals. Many clients recognize that lawyers may need to gather some information before making a confident prediction about the likely outcome of a matter. Thus you can help clients reduce their initial anxieties by summarizing the issues and your preliminary tentative analysis, describing what you will need to do before you can provide a reasonably confident assessment, and giving a time frame for doing so.

David Hoffman, of the Boston Law Collaborative, emphasizes that lawyers should consider that educating clients about the procedural and substantive options should be an ongoing process and not a "one-shot deal." Lawyers sometimes give clients only basic information and perhaps a notebook. Hoffman says that it is very hard for professionals to fully understand how little clients know about how courts look at issues and standard ways of resolving issues. Neither lawyers nor clients fully understand what clients don't know about the process and the substantive issues. So you should plan to *periodically* assess your clients' understanding of the issues and fill in important gaps in their understanding. You might think of this as a mutual process in which you and your clients continue to educate each other throughout a case.

It can be tempting to simply ask clients if they understand what you have told them, but many will not admit that they don't understand. To make sure that they comprehend the situation as well as possible, you can ask them to summarize their understanding of the issue and what they are deciding, and their expectations of the likely results. This should give a good reading of what they understand and expect. Even after a careful consultation, some clients may not fully grasp the situation, possibly because of complexity or emotional stress, so a follow-up letter can help.

Documenting key decisions can also help avoid later problems concerning their understandings and expectations.

Helping Clients Develop Realistic Expectations

It is hard for lawyers to give clients realistic expectations in many cases because legal matters generally involve a great deal of uncertainty. Although you can never completely eliminate the uncertainty, you can make increasingly well-educated analyses to help clients make decisions. The classic choice is whether to accept a specific offer or go to trial, although there are many other decisions, such as whether to file certain motions or use negotiation or other dispute resolution procedures.

Decision analysis (sometimes called "risk analysis" or "decision-tree" analysis) can be a useful tool to help clients develop realistic expectations, even at the outset of a matter. It involves identifying the key factors that might affect an outcome and estimating probabilities and consequences related to each factor to identify a range of possible outcomes and estimated probabilities. Even if you don't use formal decision analysis, you can use the logic of this approach to help clients understand what to expect.

Decision analysis is often done with "decision trees" estimating the probability of various outcomes. Figure 2 shows a very simple decision tree using assumptions that the plaintiff has a 70 percent chance of winning at trial, with varying probabilities of different verdicts. To calculate the expected value, the best single estimate, you multiply the estimated outcomes by the estimated probabilities of each outcome. In this example, you multiply the probabilities of each verdict by the amount of the verdict, and then multiply each of them by 70 percent to reflect the 30 percent probability of losing. Based on these estimates, the expected value is $77,000. Accepting these assumptions as accurate, there is still a wide range of possible outcomes, ranging from $0 to $200,000. Of course, these are only estimates based on assumptions that may or may not be accurate. So it is possible that the outcome could be more than $200,000, for example.

Figure 2. Simple Decision Tree Diagram

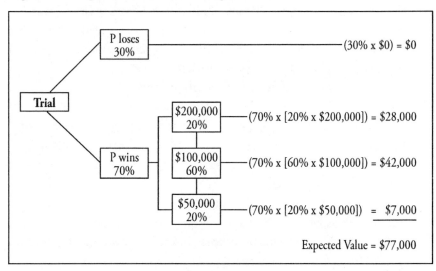

If you want to do a more rigorous decision-tree analysis, you can include numerous other contingencies, such as outcomes of summary judgment or other pretrial motions, effectiveness of particular witnesses, admissibility of particular pieces of evidence, ability to establish various elements of a cause of action or defense, whether attorney's fees or punitive damages would be awarded, and outcome of an appeal.

At the outset of a matter, it is particularly difficult to estimate the likely outcome because lawyers generally don't have much information. Even so, a decision analysis can help clients by demonstrating the effects of different "what if" assumptions. For example, one could recalculate the decision tree by assuming that the plaintiff has only a 50 percent chance of winning or by changing the amounts of the possible verdicts.

Jim McGuire has used decision analysis as both a Settlement Counsel and mediator and has found it useful in some cases to consider multiple scenarios based on the "true heart-to-heart analysis that can come when people are generally on the same page." If you use decision analyses with your clients, you may want to use ranges rather than single estimates for critical probabilities or outcome values. As a case progresses, you can gain increased confidence in a decision analysis by adjusting the values based on information developed in the litigation.

Decision analysis can become a discussion guide between client and lawyer by identifying key issues in the case from the outset. In describing a case to clients, it replaces adjectives such as "strong" with realistic numeric ranges of possible outcomes. Bruce Whitney, the former chief litigation counsel of Air Products and Chemicals, would retain several competing firms to provide, within 45 days, their best opening statement as well as a written legal analysis of all the ways in which the case could be lost. Although it may seem paradoxical to ask law firms about how they could *lose* a case, Whitney believed it was essential for them to identify the risks as a necessary analytical step in developing a strategy for reaching an "optimal resolution." He didn't use the word "win" because he says that everyone loses in civil litigation, and the objective is managing the risk to resolve the matter in the most cost-effective way possible.

Thomas Aldrich, former chief litigation counsel at Baxter Healthcare Corporation, described a "litigation advisory board" process that Baxter used to improve its assessments of complex cases. Baxter would get objective assessments from business managers, inside counsel, outside counsel, and litigators from firms that Baxter used but that were not involved in the case. Lawyers presented opening statements, trial summaries, and closing arguments for both sides and particularly focused on the risks in their case. Aldrich said, "Often management saw for the first time the vagaries of what they had previously believed to be a slam-dunk for our side. More than once, a manager confided that he or she had not looked at the problem from the opponent's perspective, or said, 'I never thought about the possibility that we could lose.'"[2] Insights from the process have affected Baxter's strategies in negotiation, mediation, and litigation.

The first stage of decision analysis does not reflect different litigation costs. Assume that you represent the plaintiff and you have confidence in the estimates shown in Figure 2. If the defendant offered to settle for $77,000, what would you advise your client to do? In most situations, you would probably recommend that your client accept the offer because the legal fees and other costs required to try the case (in addition to those already incurred) would yield a lower net recovery for your client. If the fees and costs if the client settled would be $30,000, and this would increase by $10,000 if you tried the case, the client would receive a net recovery of $47,000 from the settlement, compared with an expected net recovery of $37,000 from trial.

Of course, the trial outcome would be uncertain, and the net recovery after trial could be more or less than $37,000. Some clients are "risk-averse" and might be willing to accept an offer of substantially less than $77,000 to avoid the risk of a worse net result. On the other hand, some clients may be "risk-positive" and would be willing to take their chances at trial in the hope of getting a larger recovery, or out of a desire to have a court vindicate their complaints.

Decision trees generally focus only on the out-of-pocket monetary results, and you should discuss other factors with your clients. For example, continued litigation is likely to divert clients' attention from their business or other activities, and may harm their reputation and relationships, jeopardize other opportunities, or stimulate conflict within an organization. The general counsel of a *Fortune* 500 conglomerate described the importance of relationships in many of the firm's disputes this way: "[M]any of our businesses, for example, are with an industry in which it's primarily a customer-dominated market. In other words, if I have a dispute with a car company, or if I have a dispute with [names of companies], . . . the overriding consideration is the long-term relationship. Whether we win, lose, or draw, the economics, how strong our case is—none of that matters."[3]

There are many ways to use decision trees in advising clients, and you should decide which ways, if any, to use. Jim McGuire, of JAMS, says that there are several software programs for decision analysis. He has used the Treeage Pro program for many years and has found that it provides excellent technical support. Some people would be more comfortable with sketches on a yellow pad. Many lawyers use the logic of decision trees in orally explaining possible outcomes without computer software or even written graphics. Of course, if you use a decision analysis with clients, you should carefully explain that your projections are your best estimates, and that the actual results can be quite different from these projections. Providing a range of estimates can help avoid misunderstandings or claims that you "promised" particular results. You might summarize your analysis in appropriate documents for clients to avoid confusion.

Decision trees can be very useful in helping clients decide whether to negotiate and in conducting a negotiation. In negotiation, you can use a decision tree analysis to help develop settlement offers and anticipate how the other side might analyze the case and respond to your offers.

Regardless of whether you use a decision tree, you should advise clients about the plausible alternative procedural options, such as the early negotiation processes, mediation, arbitration, and litigation, and the advantages and disadvantages of each. Of course, clients can start with litigation and use another procedure later in the litigation process, and you can discuss the advantages and disadvantages of that approach.

You can relieve some of your own anxieties by helping clients relieve theirs. Cleveland lawyer James Skirbunt feels "freed" by helping clients make their own thoroughly informed decisions about how to handle their cases. He says, "If they choose a settlement process, I focus on that. If they choose litigation, I am comfortable in doing what is necessary in that process. The tension disappears when I give my clients a choice." Thus lawyers can do their best work when clients make decisions based on careful analysis instead of emotions or distorted perceptions.

Limiting the Scope of Representation to Negotiation

Although you can conduct a planned early negotiation by keeping the option of negotiating and litigating in the same case, i.e., a Cooperative process, some clients might want you to work only on negotiation and not litigation. These clients may be especially worried that litigation would aggravate and prolong the conflict, increase costs, and add risk to the process. Negotiation offers the opportunity to avoid these problems. Although most lawyers who litigate disputes also negotiate, some clients benefit from hiring lawyers to focus only on negotiation in a particular case. Litigation requires some documents and procedures that can easily require more time and money than needed when focusing solely on negotiation. In addition, the adversarial structure of litigation and the traditional culture of legal advocacy create risks of escalating and prolonging the conflict.

When clients engage lawyers to represent them solely in negotiation, it sends a signal that they are seriously interested in negotiation. If lawyers will not litigate a matter, this can significantly reduce the other side's fears about the lawyers' (and their clients') intentions. It is, in effect, declaring a cease-fire where the parties demonstrate a commitment to have their lawyers forswear battle in litigation. It demonstrates an investment in negotiation that would be sacrificed to some extent if the parties do not settle the matter and then proceed in litigation. Thus the clients would be "putting their money where their mouths are" in expressing a sincere desire to negotiate.

Limiting lawyers' representation to negotiation can enhance the relationship between lawyers and clients by clarifying the goals and strategies that they will use. When lawyers may both negotiate and litigate in a matter, it can send mixed and changing messages about whether the parties seriously intend to be cooperative. When clients authorize lawyers only to negotiate, there is an increased chance that both will be on the same wavelength.

There are two general ways that lawyers can limit their representation to negotiation: Settlement Counsel and Collaborative Practice. A Settlement Counsel process involves a unilateral decision by a party to use a limited-scope representation. Clients can hire Settlement Counsel with or without retaining separate Litigation Counsel. In some cases, a party may not want to hire Litigation Counsel while the negotiation process is under way. This may especially make sense in cases where there are smaller amounts at stake, and/or the client believes that there is a good chance to resolve the matter though negotiation. In some cases, a party may want to engage Litigation Counsel for advice during the negotiation (without undertaking litigation) or on "standby" to be available to proceed promptly if the parties litigate.

In some cases, Settlement Counsel may operate simultaneously with Litigation Counsel by coordinating their activities with each other and their shared client. Having Settlement Counsel and Litigation Counsel operate simultaneously makes sense when there is a substantial amount at stake and/or there is a substantial risk that litigation would be needed. It may also provide greater incentive for the other side to settle, as Settlement Counsel can point to litigation with tough Litigation Counsel as the "hard" option as opposed to the "easy" option of negotiation. Settlement and Litigation Counsel may be from the same or different law firms. If they are in the same firm, there is a better chance that they will work well together. On the other hand, if they are in separate firms, they are more likely to provide independent advice. For discussion of the relationship between Settlement Counsel and Litigation Counsel who are working simultaneously, see Chapter 3.

Clients may hire Settlement Counsel for a limited period, such as 90 or 180 days, especially if they are working simultaneously with Litigation Counsel. In his prior work as a Settlement Counsel, Jim McGuire (who now works as a neutral with JAMS) would describe himself to the other side as a "mayfly" with a limited lifespan, so they had a limited time to negotiate with him. If they didn't settle (or get close to settling) within his term, the parties would proceed solely in litigation (and McGuire noted that they would usually eventually settle, although much later). Although Settlement Counsel are often engaged only for a limited time early in a matter, Kathy Bryan suggests that in bigger cases, it would help to keep them involved periodically throughout the process to look for settlement opportunities.

Collaborative Practice involves an agreement between both parties to use Collaborative lawyers exclusively for negotiation. The agreement works through use of an enforceable "disqualification" provision that bars Collaborative lawyers from representing parties in litigation. The disqualification agreement and the practice culture developed by a community of Collaborative practitioners encourage the use of interest-based negotiation. Although the process can be used in many types of cases, virtually all of the cases so far have been in family law matters. The Collaborative movement has grown dramatically since its founding in 1990 and has developed an impressive infrastructure of local practice groups, trainings, ethical codes and protocols, websites, and publications.

David Hoffman says that the disqualification agreement enables lawyers to credibly reassure the parties that the lawyers will never be their adversary in litigation and that their only role is to negotiate. Fort Myers, Florida, lawyer Shelly Finman says that the disqualification agreement has a very significant effect, promoting a serious, "no-nonsense" attitude that demands commitment from the parties. Los Angeles mediator and Collaborative lawyer Forrest Mosten agrees, saying that the disqualification provision is helpful in setting a constructive and positive tone and getting people to be respectful and transparent faster than they otherwise would. Hoffman says that the disqualification provision is particularly helpful when lawyers don't have a lot of negotiation experience and skills, as this helps keep people focused on negotiation. On the other hand, Finman recommends a Cooperative process if you expect that the other side will be difficult to work with (or you aren't sure about them) and the client wants to be sure to be able to retain your services.

Obviously, there are advantages and disadvantages to limited-scope representation. By offering your clients different options, you can help them choose the one that best fits their needs. In doing so, you are more likely to develop a good working relationship with them.

Limiting the scope of representation raises special ethical issues, which are described in Chapter 10.

Developing Your Own Practice Philosophy

Although lawyers perform some generally similar tasks, such as analyzing problems and helping clients make decisions, there is no single cookbook recipe to follow in doing these tasks. Rather, you have great discretion and thus need to exercise professional judgment to help solve your clients' problems. Although there may be precedents for resolving their issues, there is usually enough variation in circumstances that you can't simply apply a standard solution. Precisely because there is so much discretion, a general philosophy of practice can serve as a lodestar to help you deal with difficult problems. For example, some lawyers see their role as protecting clients' interests and believe that the best way to do so is to vigorously assert their legal rights and press opponents to settle on the most favorable terms possible.

Lawyers interested in planned early negotiation are likely to have different philosophies. For example, one lawyer said that she would get drawn into the "drama triangle," where clients came into her office as "victims" and expected her to be the "rescuer" in dealing with the "villains" on the other side. She was uncomfortable in this role and wanted to work "sitting beside the clients instead of standing in front of them." She wanted them to be active participants in the negotiation, facing the issues giving rise to the conflict and taking responsibility for making decisions about the future.

Sevilla Claydon, of Garvey Schubert Barer, believes in acting with "integrity and grace" at all times, including in litigation. She explains this to clients at the outset and goes through a process of helping them understand how it benefits them not to objectify people. She encourages them to humanize the other side and empathize with them rather than demonizing them as evil or wrong.

Forrest Mosten sees his work as "peacemaking"—that is, reconciling parties in conflict. Clients' informed consent is central to his approach. This includes the formal duties required under ethical rules (described in Chapter 10) and goes well beyond it. He makes his office a "classroom of client education," with a website, information sheets, a library, and computers available to clients. He is considered the father of "unbundling" (sometimes called "discrete task representation" or, under ethics rules, "limited scope representation"), in which lawyers and clients agree, a *la carte*, on specific tasks that the lawyer will perform. From the outset of a matter, Mosten helps clients understand the available options and how they relate to each other. He explains that no one option is the end of the case, any option may be refined, and court is the very, very last of the options. He believes that there is always another way to solve a problem and that lawyers should approach their work with some humility, recognizing that both lawyers and clients can learn from each other.

Shelly Finman's philosophy is to be the same person all the time in whatever he is doing. He believes that if you respect others, you are going to be respected in return and receive your rewards, including information that you would not otherwise get. His goal, in both negotiation and litigation, is to have a process in which everyone respects the others' role and the legitimacy of their interests. He believes that lawyers should be honest with their clients and each other. In a problem-solving process, he believes that clients should determine the outcomes and lawyers should determine the process.

University of Wyoming Dean Stephen Easton wrote a wonderful article expressing his philosophy of practice based on his experience as a lawyer, which is required reading for all new law students at the University of Missouri. I think that all lawyers would benefit from reading it as well. Easton recommends that lawyers "determine what is worth fighting about and concede everything else." If something is worth fighting about, he says, "fight hard, fight smart, fight with conviction, passion, and perseverance, and fight to win." If it is not worth fighting about, he suggests finding a compromise that is acceptable to your client and the other side. If the other side asks for something that wouldn't sacrifice a significant interest of your client, he suggests that you grant the request. Noting that lawyers often engage in unproductive fights over discovery, he offers two simple suggestions: "(1) For parties seeking discovery: Be reasonable in what you request, [and] (2) For parties responding to discovery requests: Give it to them." This advice is based on his observation that lawyers' "quixotic searches for the holy grail of a 'smoking gun' document that would instantly win their case" almost always fail. He recognizes that this approach requires trust between lawyers that they will comply with their discovery obligations, which is too often lacking. He says that lawyers can earn trust through honesty and hard work.[4] Chapter 4 suggests some additional ways to build trust with the other lawyer.

You may want to write a general letter to clients describing your philosophy of practice. Just writing such a letter can force you to consider what is most important to you in your practice. Providing such a letter to clients can set clear expectations at the outset and help avoid some misunderstandings and disagreements. For example, see Appendix K for a general letter that Shelly Finman provides to his family law clients.

Endnotes

1. For an excellent analysis of how lawyer-client relationships affect negotiations with the other side, see ROBERT H. MNOOKIN, SCOTT R. PEPPET, & ANDREW S. TULUMELLO, BEYOND WINNING: NEGOTIATION TO CREATE VALUE IN DEALS AND DISPUTES (2000).

2. Thomas L. Aldrich, *A 'Reformed' Litigator Describes a Creative Complex Litigation Management Approach*, 27 ALTERNATIVES TO HIGH COST LITIG. 65, 71 (2009).

3. John Lande, *How Will Lawyering and Mediation Practices Transform Each Other?*, 24 FLA. ST. U. L. REV. 839, 875 n.175 (1997).

4. Stephen D. Easton, *My Last Lecture: Unsolicited Advice for Future and Current Lawyers*, 56 S.C. L. REV. 229 (2004).

Billing Systems: Managing the Financial Relationship between Lawyers and Clients

3

Retainers
Credit Card Authorization
Straight Hourly Billing
Pure Contingency Fee
Contingency Fees with Triggers
Combined Hourly and Contingent Fees
Fixed Fees or Task Fees
Value Billing
Premiums for Early Settlement

Clients often worry about the cost of litigation, which can be unpredictable and often quite substantial. Lawyers are understandably wary about predicting legal fees because the situation is so uncertain and depends on the decisions of many people outside their control, especially the other side. And clients are understandably anxious when their lawyers cannot provide confident estimates of the total cost.

Clients have a hard time evaluating whether particular tasks are needed or whether the amount of time devoted to them is appropriate. The hourly billing system contributes to clients' anxieties because it gives lawyers incentives to pad their bills by performing unnecessary tasks and prolonging litigation. Obviously, clients' doubts can erode confidence that their lawyers are dedicated more to advancing the clients' interests than the lawyers' financial interests. This suspicion can weaken the strong relationship that lawyers and clients need to work together effectively.

Unfortunately, there is no perfect billing system that prevents all clients' doubts. You can, however, increase your clients' confidence by offering them a choice of billing options. Although each system has limitations, you can work with clients to choose one that is as mutually profitable as possible. Providing clients with different options to pay for legal services has the potential to increase clients' satisfaction in several ways. Simply providing a choice gives clients greater control over their situation. Presumably clients would choose options that they believe best serve their interests and would thus improve the relationship with you. The billing arrangements can also be designed to create incentives to satisfy both your clients' and your own goals.

There are many reasons to consider alternatives to hourly billing. CPR's Kathy Bryan says that the number of hours worked is a poor way to connect the compensation and value received. She recognizes that this requires changing a whole mind-set to tie payment to results instead of hours billed. She suggests that law firms consider fee structures with bonuses for success. She says, "The advantage of a bonus system for law firms is that you don't have to work extra hours and pay extra overhead costs—it's pure profit. Law firms should look for more situations where they don't have to work extra hours to earn additional income."

If structured properly, such alternative systems can be quite profitable for lawyers. Eric Galton, of Lakeside Mediation Center, says that he has earned substantial fees from his work as Settlement Counsel because of the premiums he earns. Jim McGuire said that when he worked as Settlement Counsel in his former firm, Brown Rudnick, some engagements generated more premium income than any other alternative billing arrangements, such as contingent fees and fixed fees. Although McGuire's firm received substantial fees in those cases, the clients were quite satisfied because they received the value they were seeking at a much lower cost than if they had proceeded with litigation as usual.

FMC Technologies, Inc. is quite happy with the billing system its outside firms use, which includes bonuses for firms meeting its specified goals, including a premium for speed of resolution. According to its assistant general counsel, Mark Wolf, "We are buying less of what the law firms continue to sell—e.g., billable hours— but we're simultaneously paying higher effective hourly rates. It is value on both sides of the equation."[1]

Kathy Bryan suggests that in a business setting, clients may need to get their financial officers "on board" to use a creative fee structure. Bruce Whitney, the former chief litigation counsel of Air Products and Chemicals, agrees that the financial officers generally don't like paying bonuses to law firms and that you have to "bring them on board from the outset" for this system to work. Although some may be uncomfortable using unconventional fee structures, savvy financial officers will jump at the chance to create incentive structures that align the client's interests with the law firm's interests. The Association of Corporate Counsel conducts a project called the "Value Challenge" that encourages lawyers and clients to work out mutually beneficial fee arrangements. Its website includes descriptions of success stories and tools for lawyers and clients.[2]

Whitney's goal in setting attorney's fee arrangements was to modify law firm behavior so that lawyers would focus on legal services that are useful in disposing of cases. He says, "If you modify the firms' behavior to deliver the value that the client is buying, you will not only save money, but you will get better results and have more fun." The law firm and client first agree on which activities provide high, low, or no value. The client then monitors the amount of time and money spent on each category over time. High-value activities may include legal and factual analysis, jury research, or any activity that prepares the case for effective disposition. Low-value activities might include preparing pleadings or initiating written discovery. These are low value because they do not, by themselves, lead to disposal of the case. No-value activities never get used in disposing of the case, such as discovery motions, responding to opponents' discovery requests, and managing electronic vendors handling e-discovery issues. He says that lawyers generally have to do low- and no-value tasks, but they should concentrate on activities that provide the most value and minimize those that don't.

Whitney would keep track of the amount of work in each category separately for each lawyer and, if multiple law firms were involved, for each law firm. He found that many firms spent a surprising amount of time on low-value tasks and that it is hard to get lawyers to change their behaviors. However, tracking their work in this way was often quite effective. Although it wouldn't make sense to use such a formal system in many cases, especially relatively small cases, in a big multiyear case, this can provide a useful monthly reminder to pay attention to value-added activities. Even in small cases without such a system, you should keep in mind how much particular tasks contribute to achieving your clients' interests.

In a given matter, you may need to invest some time and effort to create an appropriate fee structure, and you should do so only when it seems worth the effort. Jim McGuire, of JAMS, says that in some business cases the inside counsel may have already done an evaluation of the case or, if the business is considering hiring you as a Settlement Counsel, the Litigation Counsel may have done an evaluation. In some cases, the client may hire you on an hourly basis to do a case evaluation and then work out a fee arrangement based on that evaluation. You may need to do some case evaluation as uncompensated overhead in the hope of getting a case. If a sophisticated client hires you for a fixed monthly retainer, the client may suggest that the retainer start from the date of your evaluation (as opposed to the date of retention). McGuire says, "For relatively short dollars, the client buys a ton of credibility and a really deep commitment from the Settlement Counsel to do the very best."

Using planned early negotiation techniques in appropriate cases can help you address these concerns. If the parties can negotiate relatively early and easily, your fees will be lower than if the matter is prolonged by forceful litigation of many issues in the case. Considering that early settlement can save substantial amounts of legal fees that would be incurred if cases would otherwise be heavily litigated, you and your client could share a great deal of "savings." Indeed, you can agree on billing arrangements that create incentives to reach satisfactory settlements in an efficient process, as described below. Such arrangements can be mutually profitable, as your clients can achieve specified goals faster and cheaper than through traditional litigation, and you can earn more than your normal hourly rate for helping them do so.

Cleveland lawyer James Skirbunt has some family law clients who were very open to alternative fees, especially in complex, higher-end Collaborative and Cooperative cases. They had heard horror stories of cases that went into litigation, so providing different options put them in control of the process. He has had clients who liked that their cases would be based on their interests; the resolution would address estate-planning and tax consequences that courts wouldn't consider; it would be a confidential process completed in 6–8 months; and it would cost a fraction of what litigation would cost. They also appreciated having alternative fee options to choose from.

The following are some billing arrangements that you might suggest to clients when appropriate. Of course, you don't have to use the same arrangement with all clients, and you can combine elements of the arrangements described below.

Retainers

Many lawyers charge a substantial initial retainer as security for payment and an indication of a client's commitment to the case. A variation is a replenishable—or "evergreen"—retainer. After a client pays your initial retainer, as you bill for your work, the client pays your fees for the preceding month, so that you maintain the same amount of the retainer. When you send your last bill, you deduct your fees from the retainer and refund any balance to the client.

Some lawyers charge a monthly retainer to be available "on call," handle routine matters, or do specified tasks at a fixed monthly rate. You can agree to additional fees for work that is not covered by the retainer.

Credit Card Authorization

By arranging for clients to sign a blanket authorization for credit card charges for your fees, you can get security for payment without requiring clients to pay a substantial amount at the outset. Los Angeles mediator and Collaborative lawyer Forrest Mosten loves this arrangement and says his clients do too. He doesn't like to charge a retainer, which he finds is an entrance barrier that compounds resistance to using a consensual process. He also thinks that professionals shouldn't take clients' money until they earn it. With a credit card system, clients authorize the charges before they get the bills. If there is a dispute, you can negotiate, but you will have the security of already having received payment.

Straight Hourly Billing

Traditionally, legal fees have been based on the amount of time that lawyers work on a case (except for plaintiffs in personal injury cases). This hourly billing system makes some sense for clients and lawyers, although it also causes some problems. On its face, it seems fair for a client to pay a lawyer based on the amount of time the lawyer devotes to the client's case. On the other hand, hourly billing creates incentives for lawyers to take longer than needed or perform unnecessary services. Although most lawyers are probably ethical in avoiding overbilling, the system undoubtedly prompts some lawyers to overbill. The potential for increasing the amount of work on a matter presumably lurks in the back of the mind of many ethical lawyers as they consider how to handle the matter.

Despite a lot of criticism of the hourly billing system, some clients are unwilling to consider alternatives because they feel that the "devil that they know" is better than the devil that they don't know. They may worry about being charged excessive fees using an hourly fee but also worry that they would pay too much with other systems as well.

Pure Contingency Fee

Plaintiffs' personal injury lawyers have long used contingency fee arrangements where the lawyers receive fees only if the plaintiffs get a recovery, and the fees are calculated as a percentage of the recovery. This system protects clients from paying legal fees if they do not recover from the defendants, and it creates an incentive for the lawyers to maximize the recovery.

In some cases, however, a contingency fee is problematic because it unreasonably overcompensates lawyers and creates tensions between lawyers and clients. A contingency fee arrangement particularly makes sense when there is real doubt about whether the plaintiff will recover. When it seems clear that there will be some substantial recovery, if lawyers use their standard contingency rates, it overcompensates for the amount of risk that the lawyers undertake.

Perhaps more significant, a contingency arrangement can create tensions between lawyers and clients if they disagree about whether to accept a settlement offer or proceed in litigation. If plaintiffs receive an offer above a certain point, lawyers may have a strong incentive to accept it because they may consider that the additional legal fees from a trial verdict may not be worth the time required to prepare for and conduct a trial. In addition, if they go to trial, they risk losing their entire investment of time as well as any out-of-pocket costs that they may not be able to recover from their clients. Although many plaintiffs may decide to accept offers recommended by their lawyers, some clients may be more willing to take the risk of trial than their lawyers. Since clients will pay no legal fees if they lose at trial, some may be more willing to take their chances at trial than their lawyers. Moreover, lawyers are likely to calculate the benefits and risks of trial based on their experience, whereas clients normally don't have extensive litigation experience and may have strong non-economic interests in going to trial, such as a desire for vindication. Conversely, some lawyers may have an interest in going to trial to get favorable publicity while their clients would prefer to cut off their risk by accepting a settlement.

Contingency Fees with Triggers

One way to avoid some of these problems is for lawyer and client to agree at the outset on the parameters for settlement. For example, when working as a Settlement Counsel for plaintiffs, Eric Galton sets a "strike number" with his clients, which is the minimum settlement required for him to get paid. If they receive an offer of at least the strike number, they would receive a percentage of the settlement (such as 35–40 percent), unless the client has retained Litigation Counsel, in which case he would get a percentage of the Litigation Counsel's fee. If there is no settlement or the settlement is less than the strike number, the client pays for out-of-pocket expenses but no legal fees.

Obviously, it is critical to set a reasonable strike number, which takes careful evaluation of the matter at the outset. Using decision analysis, described in Chapter 2, can be very helpful in structuring this arrangement. When done well, it assures the client that the lawyer has an incentive to obtain what the client agrees is at least a minimally adequate settlement, and that the lawyer earns the premium contingency fee that is appropriate. If a lawyer is concerned that a client might hold out for what the lawyer believes is an unreasonable settlement, they could agree that the client would be liable for the contingent fee if the defendant offers at least a specified amount, regardless of whether the client accepts the offer.

Although contingency fees are generally associated with the plaintiffs' side, defendants can use them too. For example, if a defendant and its counsel believe that the expected value of a trial judgment is $1 million, the fees might be set as a percentage of the difference between that amount and the payout. For example, if the defendant settles for $300,000, the lawyer would receive a percentage of $700,000.

Combined Hourly and Contingent Fees

One way to reduce the disadvantages of the hourly and contingency fee systems is to use a combination of both systems. For example, if a lawyer's normal hourly fee is $200 per hour and the normal percentage for contingency fees is 33 percent for pretrial settlement, the lawyer and client could agree that the client would pay $100 per hour plus 16.5 percent of any pretrial settlement. For the client, it provides a greater share of any recovery but commits to paying the hourly fees regardless of whether there is any settlement. Conversely, the lawyer is guaranteed to receive the hourly fees but receives a smaller percentage of a settlement. If the lawyer defers collection of the hourly fees until receipt of an award, the lawyer might set a higher hourly rate and/or obtain a lien on the recovery or other client assets.

Fixed Fees or Task Fees

A fixed total fee or a monthly fee may be appropriate in cases that seem to fit into a more-or-less standard pattern, such as some insurance cases. These fee structures may be especially appropriate in negotiation because lawyers may be able to estimate negotiation costs with greater confidence than litigation costs. Lawyers may charge for particular tasks, such as factual investigation, preparation of a decision tree, or conducting a settlement meeting. Eric Galton described a case for which he needed to do an unusual amount of factual analysis and was paid a fixed fee for that work in addition to the contingency fee he normally charges in such cases.

Value Billing

Another way to share the risk and rewards and increase client satisfaction is to set the fees at the end of the matter based on the client's perception of the value of the legal services. This approach has the potential to provide more predictability and client satisfaction. The system also requires the lawyer and client to set parameters for the fees at the outset. You can set the range in terms of total fees or multiples of the lawyer's hourly rates. For example, when Stradley Ronon's Ben Picker worked as a Settlement Counsel, he had a case in which he agreed to receive a minimum of 70 percent of his normal rate, with the potential of 150 percent of the rate if the client was satisfied. The client had complete discretion which of the two rates to choose. After the case ended, the client was, indeed, satisfied, and Picker received the premium rate.

James Skirbunt has also used value billing in which the client agrees to pay a fee within an agreed-upon range. Every time he has done so, the client has selected the highest number in the range. The clients wanted value for their money, and they valued the lawyers' advice more because they were "putting their fees on the line." Skirbunt cautions that this fee arrangement will work well only if lawyers have the experience and skills to produce value for the clients.

Premiums for Early Settlement

In early negotiation cases, clients may be willing to pay a premium if they can receive a satisfactory result within a certain period, such as 90 or 180 days. For example, a defendant might be willing to pay 150 percent or 200 percent of the lawyer's normal rate if the plaintiff settles for less than a specified amount within a certain time period. Some agreements establish declining premiums over a number of steps. For example, the percentage might drop by a certain amount every month. With this arrangement, some defendants would come out ahead if they would face substantial legal fees and liability exposure from protracted litigation. Obviously, in this situation, the lawyer would have a strong incentive to settle and could receive a substantial premium if successful. Depending on the circumstances, the lawyer and the client might agree to a reduced hourly rate if the case did not settle within the specified period.

Bruce Whitney used a version of this system when he was the chief litigation counsel of Air Products and Chemicals. He negotiated with law firms to create what he called a "bonus bank." As an indication of the law firm's confidence in being able to dispose of the case prior to trial, its bonus would be based on multiple of a fee discount. If a law firm was confident that it could promptly reach a good resolution, it would be willing to put a large discount at risk. The client and law firm would agree to a percentage reduction of the legal fees that would be set aside in the bonus bank. If they could quickly obtain a settlement offer, the firm would receive a very large multiple of what was in the bank. As the case progressed without settlement, the multiplier decreased. If they didn't dispose of the case before trial, the firm would get no premium—only the discounted fees. For example, the firm might agree to a 20 percent reduction of the legal fees, and if it could get an acceptable settlement offer (as defined in the fee agreement) within 90 days, the firm would receive a premium of five times the amount in the bonus bank (plus the 80 percent of their normal hourly fees). If it secured the offer within 91–120 days, it would receive a premium of four times the bonus bank, etc.

Appendix J provides sample attorney compensation clauses. These alternative billing arrangements are not appropriate for every case, lawyer, or client. If they depend on setting parameters for settlement, they may require more confidence in the accuracy of an early assessment of the outcome than is feasible in many cases, especially if the lawyer and client do not have critical information needed to make the assessment. If the decision about the amount of compensation is based on a subjective judgment of the client, or simply the client's willingness to settle without any predetermined parameters, the lawyer needs to have confidence in the client's integrity and presumably an expectation of additional representation in the future if the client is satisfied. You should also make sure that your compensation arrangements comply with any applicable ethical rules in your jurisdiction.

Endnotes

1. Mark D. Wolf, *Update: How Value Billing Helps Both the Client and the Law Firm*, 28 ALTERNATIVES TO THE HIGH COST OF LITIGATION 1, 1 (2010).

2. Association of Corporate Counsel, Value Challenge, http://www.acc.com/valuechallenge/index.cfm?utm_source=Homepage&utm_medium=Web&utm_campaign=ACCValueTip.

Establishing Good Working Relationships with Other Lawyers in a Case

4

Building Collegial Relationships
Special Issues for Settlement Counsel and
  Litigation Counsel

Your relationship with "opposing" counsel makes a big difference in how well a matter will be handled. If you have a good relationship, you are more likely to be able to exchange information informally, readily agree on procedural matters, take reasonable negotiation positions that recognize both parties' legitimate expectations, resolve matters efficiently, satisfy your clients, and enjoy your work.

On the other hand, if you have a bad relationship with opposing counsel, a case can become your own private hell. Your counterpart may decline to grant routine professional courtesies (such as extensions of deadlines to file court papers), bombard you with excessive and unjustified discovery requests, file frivolous motions, make outrageous negotiation demands, yell and scream at you, and generally behave badly.

The sad fact is that you might find yourself engaging in similar behaviors—or be sorely tempted to do so. When the other side acts like a bully, you may understandably believe that failing to respond forcefully sends the wrong signal to the other side and to your clients. You are likely to be concerned that the other side would feel rewarded for bad behavior and encouraged to continue it. In addition, your clients might feel discouraged and want you to act as their champion and fight back. If you retaliate—even if you are justified and you do so in a professional manner—the other side is likely to feel justified in making a counter-response, and the conflict is likely to continue escalating. This is likely to seriously damage the interests of both parties, prolong the dispute, and substantially increase the costs.

Once this spiral of conflict starts, it is very hard to stop. Even if you eventually reach a cease-fire, much damage will have been done. The parties can't recover the wasted time and money and it is very hard to restore the trust that is needed to work well together in litigation or negotiation.

A major root of the problem is that lawyers have been programmed like sophisticated GPS devices with what Professor Leonard Riskin calls the "lawyer's standard philosophical map." This map is based on two assumptions: "(1) that disputants are adversaries—i.e., if one wins, the others must lose, and (2) that disputes may be resolved through application, by a third party, of some general rule of law."[1] Given these assumptions, it is rational for lawyers to use legal rules and procedures to try to gain advantage over adversaries. Although there are many virtues of this perspective, strict and unconscious adherence to it can cause serious and unnecessary problems for clients, lawyers, courts, and society.

A problem-solving approach, embodied in interest-based negotiation (described in Chapter 5), relies on the opposite assumptions. Lawyers using this approach assume that legal matters are not purely zero-sum, and so it is possible to find solutions that make *both* parties better off. This approach assumes that the law isn't the only, or even necessarily the most important, standard for making decisions. This approach also assumes that the parties' interests should be the starting point in decision making and refers to the law as needed within the framework of the parties' interests.

Thus the adversarial-legal and problem-solving approaches reflect two different mind-sets or paradigms for dealing with legal problems. Many Collaborative practitioners use the term "paradigm shift," referring to a shift from an adversarial-legal to a problem-solving perspective. Fort Myers, Florida, lawyer Shelly Finman, who does Collaborative and Cooperative Practice as well as traditional representation, has seen a lot of "converts" to problem-solving in recent decades but still finds great resistance. Some lawyers are concerned that using a problem-solving approach would harm their clients. Some are uncomfortable with it because it feels too therapeutic, which is outside of their comfort zone in the adversarial-legal paradigm.

Fortunately, you don't have to make an either/or choice of one paradigm or the other for all times. Instead, you can consciously choose one or the other or some hybrid, depending on the circumstances. There are a lot of advantages to starting from a problem-solving approach and shifting to an adversarial-legal approach only when necessary. Finman believes that lawyers who use a problem-solving approach generally enjoy their work and feel that they are making a constructive difference for their clients and communities. Your clients are likely to be happier too.

Building Collegial Relationships

Obviously, it would be best to avoid getting into bad relationships with counsel for the other side in the first place. Good lawyers make a practice of reaching out to their counterparts at the outset of a case to establish good relationships. This makes the work easier and more enjoyable for you, and, more important, it is in the clients' interest to avoid picking up the tab for the lawyers' conflicts. Clients hire lawyers to resolve *the clients'* conflicts, not ones that the lawyers create between themselves.

Finman uses the term "colleagues" to refer to the lawyers representing the other party, and he often works to "mentor" his colleagues in a case. This reflects his view that lawyers representing adverse parties can and should work together in a professional manner. Indeed, opposing counsel often work together quite respectfully and professionally. It is not surprising that people pay particular attention when lawyers act out a conflict in a flamboyant fashion, but in workaday practice most lawyers act appropriately. Lawyers regularly cooperate because they believe that it is consistent with their professional identities, it is unpleasant to fight all the time, and, most important, it is in their clients' interests. Even so, it is easy to inadvertently get into an adversarial spat in response to a misunderstanding or even the tone of a letter, e-mail, or phone call.

If you don't know the lawyer on the other side, you can start your relationship on the right track by noting the benefits of cooperation for both sides. Say that you make a practice of being polite and respectful to the other side and you would prefer that everyone act that way in this matter. If appropriate, you can tell your colleague not to mistake your being nice for being afraid to protect your client's interests. If your colleague clearly threatens to take an adversarial approach, you can say that you can do the case together the "easy way or the hard way," and that you and your client would prefer the easy way, but you are prepared to do it the hard way if needed. The norm of reciprocity is very powerful, and the best way to encourage cooperation generally is to take the lead in initiating cooperative behavior.

Lakeside Mediation Center's Eric Galton, who sometimes works as a Settlement Counsel, says that he tries to represent his clients' interests while helping the lawyers on the other side look good to their clients. According to Galton, this is a slow, methodical educational process in which he tries to identify interests of the other side and help them satisfy their constituencies who have to sign off on (or at least acquiesce in) a settlement. He always starts by asking the other lawyer, "How can we help you? What do you need to fully evaluate this matter?" He offers to provide information and anything else he reasonably can. For example, if they ask to talk with his consulting expert, he is happy to make the expert available. Once he starts providing information, the other side usually reciprocates.

Some lawyers make it a regular practice to develop personal relationships with their colleagues on the other side of their cases. Ideally, at the outset of a case with a colleague you don't know, you would go out to lunch together. Over lunch you might spend most of the time talking about yourselves, your legal practices, hobbies, etc. Though you might talk about the case, this need not be the major part of the conversation. Of course, it may not be possible to have a lunch in every case with a lawyer you don't know, but you should be able to at least have a phone call to get to know each other personally.

Seattle-area lawyer Holly Hohlbein says that you are, in effect, forming a partnership with the other lawyer in service of your two clients, and you can't do that by e-mail. If you haven't met before, you should meet face to face if possible. She says you don't need to spend hours together, but you do need to talk. Eric Galton concurs about the importance of meeting face to face. He says that there is no substitute for meeting face to face for developing rapport with the other lawyer. "I can't tell you how much we value that personal relationship to build an atmosphere of trust."

The New Law Center's Doug Reynolds described one case where he represented two sisters against two other sisters in a fierce conflict. He wanted to meet face to face with other lawyer, and they talked for an hour about their lives and legal practices and generally got to know each other. In this conversation, they barely talked about the case. At the end of the conversation, they agreed that each would make an outline of the issues and then they would talk again. He consciously tried to establish a relationship so that the first time they had an issue, the other lawyer didn't just assume he was a jerk and take an adversarial position. Reynolds credited building this good relationship as a factor in successfully negotiating the case.

Another lawyer (who we'll call Sanchez) described a case where her persistent efforts to develop a relationship with the other side really paid off. She represented the plaintiff in a sexual harassment case as a Settlement Counsel and suggested to the other lawyer that they meet for coffee. It took about two weeks for Sanchez to convince her counterpart that this meeting would be a good use of time. She started by asking the other lawyer to tell her about her practice. They talked about their respective legal practices, how they handled cases, their approaches to negotiation, etc. Then Sanchez described Collaborative Practice, invited her colleague to take a handout sheet to her client, and offered to develop a negotiation process for that case. It took another three weeks of cajoling before they agreed to negotiate, and they ended up settling the case after an usually candid discussion.

In this case, the harasser was the CEO of the company, who had harassed other women in the past. The plaintiff, a 22-year-old woman, wanted to make sure that he wouldn't do it again. Sanchez was amazed to hear the other side say that they had been warning the CEO (who was not at the negotiation) about his legal obligations until they were "blue in the face." This led to some brainstorming about what might be effective to get him to stop. The other side was particularly intrigued by the idea of arranging for the CEO to meet a psychologist who works with sexual harassment victims to talk about the real emotional impact that a boss's sexual overtures typically have on subordinate female employees. This was a remarkable turn of events considering that the other side was initially reluctant to negotiate at all. It shows what can happen when lawyers develop a good working relationship. Doing so can require initiative, good listening, openness, patience, and persistence.

David Hoffman, of the Boston Law Collaborative, described a case where he got off to a bad start with the other lawyer. At one point they spent some time chatting, and he mentioned how much he enjoyed working with the other lawyer's brother. She was in practice with her brother and was very proud of him. The fact that Hoffman had hit it off so well with her brother meant a lot to her and "melted a lot of ice" in their relationship.

Hoffman described another lawyer with whom he works very well. The lawyer loves golf, which he plays everyday. Whenever the two of them talk, they always talk about golf. This is one of the things that has fostered rapport between them, which has contributed to the fact they have settled every case they have had together.

If you do develop a personal relationship, when problems arise, it is harder for either of you to react hostilely, such as by immediately firing off angry e-mails, which can quickly lead to a counterproductive escalation of conflict. Indeed, it can be helpful to agree that if a problem arises in the case, you will call each other before taking adverse action, such as sending a nasty letter or filing a motion. If you know of problems that are going to come up in a case, you should normally inform the other lawyer, who may be upset but is likely to appreciate hearing the news directly and promptly from you. This can be an important element of building a relationship of trust with the other lawyer. Lawyers who have good relationships with each other can take this for granted. When you start a case with a lawyer you don't know very well, it can be worthwhile to develop this understanding, possibly even in writing.

Part of the initial conversations with colleagues can involve candid assessments of the dispute and the key issues. If you can identify the key legal and factual issues in dispute, you can cooperate to efficiently do the research needed to resolve the issues. You can work together to develop "the third story"—how an outside observer might look at it—which can help both parties develop a realistic understanding of their case.

Conversations with your colleagues may also address your respective clients' interests and can help avoid unnecessary conflicts. For example, Sevilla Claydon, of Garvey Schubert Barer, tells her colleagues about things that will trigger her client to react badly. She tells the other lawyers, "If you do this, it will send things backward instead of forward." Even if you initially proceed in litigation, coaching your counterpart about possible "land mines" can lay the groundwork for eventual negotiation. Appendix M provides a checklist of things you might discuss in your initial conversations with your counterparts.

Generally, you should bolster your counterparts in front of their clients whenever it would be appropriate, as this is likely to stimulate their cooperation. So when you have face-to-face meetings with the other lawyer and party, you might praise your counterparts for their sincerity, competence, cooperation, diligence, etc., as appropriate. If you believe that they have made a mistake, it is better to discuss this with them privately and avoid embarrassing them in front of their clients, as a public admonishment can prompt a defensive reaction. This is also a good idea because it is possible that you are in error, which would not only irritate the other lawyers but also possibly embarrass you in front of *your* clients.

You should be aware of—and carefully manage—the risks in developing good relationships with your counterparts. Obviously, you must diligently advocate your clients' interests, which should not be sacrificed because of friendship with the lawyers on the other side of the case. Although lawyers probably do not sacrifice important client interests in this way very often, clients may worry about this when "opposing" lawyers seem too chummy. Thus you should avoid too much or too friendly conversation with opposing counsel in the clients' presence, as this could signal that your relationship with the other lawyer is more important than your relationship with your client. It is important to explain to your client, in advance, the advantages *to him or her* of your building a good negotiating relationship with the other lawyer. You should also encourage your client to share any concerns he or she might have about this with you so that you can address them directly.

Special Issues for Settlement Counsel and Litigation Counsel

When a client has retained Settlement Counsel and Litigation Counsel to work simultaneously on the same case, there is a potential for conflict that could undermine the client's interests. In effect, Settlement Counsel plays the "good cop" to the Litigation Counsel's "bad cop" in dealing with the other side. A Settlement Counsel can offer to work with the other side to try to develop an agreement that satisfies the interests of both parties, but if not, the Litigation Counsel is confident of winning in litigation and would like nothing more than to take the case to trial.

Although the two counsel are ostensibly on the same side in trying to achieve the client's best interests, they can easily find themselves in competition and even conflict. Litigation Counsel may feel threatened by having another lawyer involved who gives independent advice and effectively reduces his or her control over the matter. Traditionally, Litigation Counsel believe that parties shouldn't begin negotiation without first having a complete understanding of the case and building leverage over the other side. They may be skeptical that a Settlement Counsel could do a good job of negotiation because he or she doesn't know the case as well as the Litigation Counsel does.

Many Litigation Counsel have never heard of or worked with a Settlement Counsel, so if you take a case as Settlement Counsel, one of the first tasks may be to explain to the Litigation Counsel how the process works generally and how you might work together productively in the present case. This arrangement works well when you both respect each other and don't try to upstage each other with the client or the other side. Indeed, both counsel should make an explicit agreement that you will not embarrass each other with the client or the other side.

If both counsel trust each other, Settlement Counsel can provide great relief for Litigation Counsel. Litigation Counsel often prefer not to negotiate, so the engagement of Settlement Counsel can avoid the need for Litigation Counsel to negotiate. If Settlement Counsel negotiates and there is no settlement, this frees Litigation Counsel to focus vigorously on litigation, since it would be unlikely that the parties would settle, at least in the immediate future. This also provides justification for Litigation Counsel's fees, since the client had tried to settle but was unable to do so.

Working well on a case requires coordination between the two counsel as well as with the client. Internal conflict can be avoided by developing a clear, three-way agreement between the client, Settlement Counsel, and Litigation Counsel. Of course, the client controls both negotiation and litigation, and presumably Settlement Counsel and Litigation Counsel do not operate in each other's area. For example, Settlement Counsel normally would not offer "stand-still" agreements to hold off litigation during negotiation, and litigation counsel normally would not get involved in the negotiation, except as agreed between the client and both counsel. If the other side raises a litigation issue, such as discovery, with the Settlement Counsel, this should be referred to Litigation Counsel. By the same token, if the other side makes a settlement overture to Litigation Counsel, this should be referred to Settlement Counsel.

If the case proceeds to mediation, the Settlement Counsel presumably would manage the mediation process for the client. This includes managing the submission of materials to the mediator, planning who will attend and who will play what role, analyzing client interests and settlement options, developing offers, and responding to the other side's offers. Litigation Counsel may attend the mediation and, at an early stage in the process, may make a presentation demonstrating how the client has a strong case in litigation. After this presentation and discussion of the litigation potential, Litigation Counsel would take a passive role or may even leave the mediation. Jim McGuire, now of JAMS, liked to have the Litigation Counsel give an initial presentation showing why they were confident that they would win if they went to court. On the other hand, Bruce Whitney, the former chief litigation counsel of Air Products and Chemicals, preferred that the Settlement Counsel conduct all the negotiation, and that if Litigation Counsel attended the mediation at all, they spoke only in caucus.

Since exchange of information is critical for the success of litigation, there should be a clear understanding about what information will or will not be provided to the other side and a procedure for making decisions about sharing information. Often, Settlement Counsel want to volunteer information to the other side as a way of inducing trust and the reciprocal exchange of information, but there may be information that the client does not want the Settlement Counsel to provide, at least at the outset. Holland and Knight's Tom Woodrow says that this can happen when the other side has overlooked information that would be very damaging to their case. Litigation Counsel may be tempted to hold off sharing that information in order to get a tactical advantage at trial. Settlement Counsel may be anxious to share the information to increase leverage for a favorable settlement or even an outright dismissal. In this situation, the lawyers may need to consult the client about whether to provide the information in negotiation.

There should be a clear agreement between all parties and lawyers on both sides about whether information provided to the Settlement Counsel will be provided to the Litigation Counsel. Jim McGuire says there should be only a one-way flow of information between Settlement Counsel and Litigation Counsel on each side so that Litigation Counsel may provide information to Settlement Counsel on its side but Settlement Counsel will not provide any information from the other side to Litigation Counsel. Although Settlement Counsel would not disclose confidential information to Litigation Counsel, it is important that the both keep each other generally informed about what they are doing in the case.

Obviously, Settlement Counsel and Litigation Counsel can be most effective when they develop a good working relationship. So it can be useful to spend time together or at least talk by phone to get to know each other personally, as described above for colleagues on opposite sides of a case.

Endnotes

1. Leonard L. Riskin, *Mediators and Lawyers*, 43 OHIO ST. L.J. 29, 43–44 (1982).

Overview of 5
Negotiation
Techniques Generally

There are two general approaches to negotiation: positional and interest-based.[1] Although they are quite distinct in theory, in practice, many negotiations involve some combination or variations of these approaches. This chapter describes both approaches, including their respective advantages and disadvantages. Interest-based negotiation (IBN) has the potential to produce great benefit for clients and lawyers. Planned early negotiation (PEN) processes provide the opportunity to realize these benefits, which is a major reason to consider using PEN whenever it might be appropriate.

Positional Negotiation

In General. For simplicity, we will focus on negotiation of a civil case in litigation where the only issue is the amount of money that a defendant would pay the plaintiff. The same principles apply in other types of cases, including those with issues other than allocation of money, and where the negotiation involves a transaction instead of a litigated dispute.

In positional negotiation, each side tries to get as much (or pay as little) as possible for itself, based on an assumption that there is a fixed amount of resources to divide. This is called a "zero-sum" situation, as the sum of one side's gain in a change in bargaining position exactly equals the amount of the other side's loss. So if a plaintiff initially demands $100,000 and offers to accept $70,000, the plaintiff's "loss" of $30,000 (compared with the initial demand) represents a "gain" of $30,000 by the defendant.

"Positional" negotiation refers to the fact that parties take a series of positions in exchanging offers and counteroffers. Consider the following scenario. A plaintiff makes an initial demand (or "position") of $100,000; the defendant offers $30,000, which prompts a series of counteroffers of $70,000 (plaintiff), $50,000 (defendant), $60,000 (plaintiff). Finally the defendant offers $55,000 by the defendant, which the plaintiff accepts, settling the case. This hypothetical negotiation illustrates the common features of positional negotiation, where the parties start with extreme positions and then make a series of changes in positions ("concessions") intended to result in a resolution as close as possible to each side's initial position. Typically, each side makes the smallest concessions it reasonably can to maximize its gain (or minimize its loss).

For lawyers in the United States, positional negotiation is the default approach. Lawyers can protect their clients by demanding a lot (or offering a little) at the outset, since they expect to make a series of concessions during the negotiation. They can manage the negotiation by controlling the timing and amount of concessions depending on various factors. If one side believes that it is in a strong bargaining position, it may make small concessions and drag out the process. If it feels it is in a weak position and is anxious to settle, it is likely to make large concessions and proceed more quickly.

Relationship between Alternatives to a Negotiated Agreement and Bargaining Power. The strength of one's bargaining position is affected by many factors, including the assessment of the outcome if the parties do not reach agreement.[2] Analysis of alternatives to a negotiated agreement is important because it provides the basis of implicit or explicit threats to walk away from negotiation if the other side does not give in to one's demands. For example, if both parties are certain that a plaintiff would get a $100,000 verdict at trial, one would theoretically expect that they would settle for about $100,000 (ignoring, for the moment, legal fees and other factors). If the most that the defendant would offer would be a lot less—say, $50,000— the plaintiff would presumably decide that he would get a more favorable result if he went to trial. Similarly, if the lowest demand that the plaintiff would accept would be $150,000, the defendant would presumably decide to try the case to reduce the liability.

Of course, people are almost never certain of the results of a contested litigation, as there are so many variables that are impossible to predict and control. Lawyers often try to predict the probable court outcome, which is called the Most Likely Alternative to a Negotiated Agreement (MLATNA) in negotiation theory. In the preceding example, the MLATNA would be $100,000. Of course, it is possible for the plaintiff to lose at trial, and the plaintiff's *Worst* Alternative to a Negotiated Agreement (WATNA) would be $0 (assuming that there was no counterclaim). On the other hand, the plaintiff's lawyer could estimate her *Best* Alternative to a Negotiated Agreement (BATNA) if she wins big. Lawyers estimate these values based on their understanding of the applicable substantive and procedural legal rules, the strength of the evidence, and expected reactions of the trier of fact, among other factors. A major part of positional negotiation is trying to persuade the other side that their probable alternative to a negotiated agreement is less favorable than they previously thought.

If the plaintiff thought that there was a 80 percent chance of getting a $100,000 verdict and a 20 percent chance of a complete defense verdict, she might accept $80,000. This is the logic of decision analysis, described in Chapter 2. The plaintiff might adjust her "bottom line"—the least she would be willing to accept in settlement—based on a number of factors. If she would incur an additional $10,000 in litigation costs (above her costs to obtain the settlement), she might be willing to accept $70,000. Although this calculation already includes a risk assessment, the plaintiff might be risk-averse—uncomfortable taking risks—and might be willing to accept even less than $70,000 to gain the certainty of getting some recovery. Similarly, the plaintiff's determination of her bottom line might be adjusted to reflect her valuation of the extra time that would be required to try the case, the costs of her time to attend to the litigation, the effect of trial publicity on her reputation, the effect of continued litigation on her relationship with the defendant, and various other factors. Although these factors might lead her to reduce the amount she would be willing to accept in settlement, some factors have the opposite effect. For example, she might increase her bottom line if she was willing to take a greater risk to obtain a larger award, gain publicity, publicize the defendant's wrongdoing, establish a precedent, demonstrate that she can't be pushed around, and so on.

Defendants generally have the opposite considerations in deciding the most that they would be willing to pay in settlement. Some defendants worry—sometimes with good reason—that if they settle too easily or too generously, others would be encouraged to file weak or frivolous claims in the hope of an easy settlement. So defendants may not be willing to pay as much as might seem warranted in a given case to establish a reputation for not settling too easily if they get (or anticipate getting) an ongoing series of similar complaints. On the other hand, some defendants may increase the "top dollar" they are willing to pay in order to minimize bad publicity, reduce litigation expenses, or develop a reputation for reasonableness.

There is often a "zone of possible agreement" (ZOPA), which is the difference between the least that a plaintiff would accept and the most that a defendant would pay. The ZOPA is not a fixed range, however, because the parties' bottom lines often change during negotiation. Parties' decisions about where to draw their (bottom) line in the sand is affected by their perception of what the other side is or is not willing to accept. So if one side credibly threatens to walk away from the negotiation if its demand isn't met, the other side may accept the demand even though it is less favorable than what it had previously set as its bottom line.

Of course, neither side generally will disclose its true bottom line (except, perhaps, at the very end of a negotiation) because the other side would take advantage of this by offering only that amount. Since both sides have some uncertainty about what would happen in litigation and would incur transaction costs if they proceed with litigation, there is often room for compromise. Positional negotiations break down without agreement, however, when the parties' respective assessments of the alternatives to negotiated agreement differ substantially, at least one side would prefer an alternative to settlement, and/or at least one side is willing to take substantial risks.

The ZOPA represents the surplus generated from settlement. Even when there is a substantial ZOPA—and thus room for settlement—the parties may deadlock. This happens when they cannot agree where to settle within the ZOPA because each side wants to gain more of the surplus than the other side is willing to concede. Thus a major risk of positional negotiation is that parties do not reach an agreement that would be in both of their interests because they can't agree how to share the surplus.

Other factors affect parties' relative bargaining power in addition to expectations about alternatives to a negotiated agreement. These include experience and expertise, resources to engage in the conflict, access to critical information, weight of expert opinion, affiliation with important actors, perceived legitimacy of the individuals and entities involved, greater risk tolerance, ability to unilaterally help or harm the other side, and personal characteristics such as status, integrity, strength, charisma, and patience. Parties also may exercise more bargaining power if they use "hardball" tactics such as threats, intimidation, personal attacks, demands for items that can be throw-away concessions, contrived deadlines, claims of limited settlement authority, take-it-or-leave-it offers, allying with others, stubbornness, and apparent irrationality. Such tactics can backfire, however, if they prompt the other side to resist instead of capitulate.

Typical Tactics in Positional Negotiation. In positional negotiation, each side believes that it would get a bad deal if it started the bidding by offering an amount that it believes is reasonable. Since each side typically expects the other to play the positional game, negotiators assume that each party will make concessions and interpret the offers accordingly. For example, if a plaintiff believes that $60,000 is a reasonable settlement and starts the bargaining at that number, the defendant would presumably start with a much lower number—say, $10,000—and the final settlement might be around $30,000. Similarly, if the defendant's first offer was $60,000, the final settlement would presumably be higher than that, perhaps $80,000. Because everyone expects that both sides will make a series of concessions, there is an incentive to start with extreme positions to leave room to make concessions and still (hopefully) end up with a favorable agreement.

In the culture of positional negotiation, it is considered bad faith to go back on an offer unless, in the interim, there is significant new information or the circumstances change substantially. In other words, if a plaintiff demands $100,000, defendants would be insulted if the plaintiff later demanded $150,000. Similarly, if a defendant offers $30,000, it is considered bad form to later offer only $20,000.

Another convention is that parties alternate making offers so that, for example, a plaintiff would not demand $100,000 and then $90,000 without the defendant making an intervening offer. This is called "bidding against oneself" and is considered a sign of great weakness, which is why negotiators are extremely reluctant to do it.

A major challenge in positional negotiation is deciding when to begin. Lawyers worry that even suggesting negotiation may make them appear weak, which would put them at a disadvantage in the negotiation. This is based on the assumption that lawyers suggest negotiation only if they don't have confidence that they would win at trial. Although this logic is seriously flawed—as parties with strong positions usually have an interest in settling for an appropriate amount—it is deeply ingrained in our legal culture. Since lawyers and parties on both sides can have the same fears, this often leads to delay in starting negotiation. Indeed, this dynamic, coupled with a desire to complete most or all discovery before starting to negotiate, and the deadline-oriented nature of most law practices often results in delaying negotiation until late in a litigation.

Another problem is deciding where to start the bidding. Each side has an incentive to make an extreme offer in the hope of ending up with what it considers a favorable result, or at least a result that is as good as possible under the circumstances. Although experienced lawyers expect the other side to start with an extreme position, they are (or act as if they are) offended when the other side takes what they consider to be an *excessively* extreme position. Starting with an opening position that the other side considers "out of the ballpark" risks ending the negotiation right from the start, as the insulted side "packs up its briefcase" and leaves. Even if the offended party does not leave, it may not be willing to make a counteroffer, putting the first party in the awkward position of bidding against itself. And even if the other side makes a counteroffer, an extreme initial position risks straining the relationship in negotiation, making the negotiation unnecessarily difficult, and possibly ending without reaching what would have been an achievable settlement.

Each side also generally wants to avoid starting with an offer that is too generous given the norms of positional negotiation. If one side starts with what the other side (privately) considers an overly generous offer, the recipient may interpret it as a sign of weakness, desperation, and/or lack of negotiation skill. This puts the offeror in a difficult position because there may be little room to make concessions and reach an acceptable outcome. It is particularly problematic if the other side "smells blood," prompting them to use a tough bargaining strategy.

Considering all this, parties often want the other side to make the first offer, as this reduces the risk of making an initial offer that is too high or low under the circumstances. Some parties who are particularly confident, however, may prefer to make the first offer to assert control in the bargaining and set expectations. In any case, parties who are interested in settling are likely to start with the most extreme offer that they think would not prompt the other side to quit the negotiation. Parties control the timing and amount of concessions to communicate with the other side and try to direct the process in their favor. Parties often try to make the smallest concessions needed to keep the other side "in the game" and motivated to make a reasonable counteroffer and keep the negotiation going. Negotiators often hold off making concessions as long as possible to avoid appearing overeager to settle (and thus weak). They also hope that this will pressure the other side into making more generous concessions. These dynamics can contribute to what one mediator calls the "positional negotiation death spiral," where there is a substantial gap between offers, and each side makes such small concessions that they get discouraged and give up negotiation even though there may be a zone of possible agreement.

Given that positional negotiation is premised on each side's goal of maximizing its outcome and an assumption that all the options have a zero sum, negotiators have incentives to use various tactics to get the other side to make favorable concessions. Because bargaining power and negotiation outcomes are closely related to perceptions of alternatives to a negotiated agreement, parties portray the MLATNA as being favorable to themselves. Reliance on arguments about the likely court results creates an incentive to provide self-serving representations of the law and the facts and withhold unfavorable information. Negotiators thus exaggerate the strength of their legal case and belittle the other side's prospects in court.

The law permits a form of misrepresentation in negotiation called "puffing." Negotiators are prohibited from making false statements of "material facts," but that term is defined to exclude some types of statements, such as characterization of the merit or value of an item or a party's beliefs about an acceptable settlement. For example, if a party falsely says, "We believe that we have a strong case," or "I won't accept anything less than $50,000," these are generally not considered actionable for fraud, and lawyers do not violate their ethical duties if they make such statements. Given the competitive structure of positional negotiation, there is an incentive to make such statements.

Positional negotiation also creates incentives to use various tactics to change the other side's risk assessments and preferences. Threats can prompt parties to reduce their expectations and decide that the risk and cost of continued negotiation is not worth holding out for their preferred bottom line. Threats can include such things as dragging out the process, making it unpleasant and expensive, creating unfavorable publicity, and damaging valued relationships with third parties. Sometimes these threats are communicated by taking action rather than making explicit threatening statements. Parties may threaten not to make any further concessions, which, if believed, forces the other side to accept the last offer or have the negotiation break down. Misleading the other side about one's real interests is a related tactic, intended to convince them that one is not willing to make substantial concessions to settle on particular terms.

This brief summary shows that positional negotiation can be based on reasoned arguments as well as pressure tactics.

Advantages and Disadvantages. Lawyers in the United States generally feel comfortable with positional negotiation because it is familiar, expected, and taken for granted by lawyers and parties as the normal way to negotiate. It's pretty easy to learn the "rules of the game." If you think you have a strong legal case (and thus a strong negotiation position), you can use this approach to obtain a favorable settlement. Even if you have a weak position, it provides a conservative approach to the risk of giving up too much in negotiation by enabling negotiators to make one concession at a time.

On the other hand, positional negotiation creates the risk of failing to reach an agreement that both sides would find to be in their interests. Even if the parties reach an agreement, it may be lower quality than necessary.

The process invites deception and brinksmanship, which some people find troubling. Negotiating can feel like a game, where everyone is expected to make offers that they don't really believe are fair or accurate estimates of the likely court results. However, you may feel trapped into playing this game because being honest puts you at risk of being a "sucker" and sacrificing your clients' interests. Unfortunately, the way this "game" is played can hurt relationships, especially for parties who are not repeat negotiators. Although sophisticated repeat-player negotiators may not be upset by the ritual deceptions, even some of them are troubled by the often disingenuous and disrespectful nature of negotiations.

Positional negotiation creates particular problems for lawyers, who are negotiating as their clients' agents with a duty to protect the clients' interests. Even if lawyers might find some negotiation tactics distasteful for handling their own affairs, some may feel obliged to use them, believing that this is part of their professional duty to their clients.

Interest-Based Negotiation

In General. The theory of interest-based negotiation (IBN) is the opposite of positional negotiation in many ways. IBN theory assumes that negotiation is not necessarily a zero-sum game, and thus is it possible to develop agreements that make both parties better off (or at least one party better off without harming the other). Given this assumption, negotiators look for settlement options that satisfy both parties' interests. Instead of simply competing to split up a "fixed pie," IBN negotiators try to first "enlarge the pie" by identifying a range of options that would improve both parties' situations and then look for fair ways to divide it. IBN relies primarily on reason and cooperation rather than threat and competition. This approach can be summarized as "us working together against the problem" instead of "me fighting you."

This approach is called "interest-based" because the heart of the process is identifying parties' interests and developing an agreement that satisfies the most important interests of both parties. You can think of "interests" as parties' goals and "positions" as ways of achieving those goals. A basic insight of IBN is that there are usually multiple ways to satisfy an interest. Parties often get stuck by having too narrow a view of possible solutions and thinking that their preferred position is the only or best way to satisfy their interests. Thus the IBN process helps people think more systematically and creatively about solutions that would satisfy their interests.

IBN is especially appropriate when there are multiple issues, some shared interests, and/or the potential for an ongoing relationship in the future, especially if the relationship involves interests beyond an immediate payment of money. For example, it may be helpful in family, employment, probate, guardianship, commercial, or landlord-tenant cases. Whereas the classic case for positional negotiation is a personal injury case involving a plaintiff and insurance company to agree on a monetary settlement and have no further relationship, the classic case for IBN is a divorce in which the spouses have a shared interest in the welfare of their minor children, requiring ongoing cooperation about many issues. Nonetheless, some parties use IBN in personal injury cases and some use positional negotiation in divorce cases.

In virtually any kind of case, the parties may have an interest in being treated respectfully and fairly, minimizing the cost and length of the process, freeing time to focus on matters other than the dispute, reducing the emotional wear and tear caused by continued disputing, and protecting privacy and reputations.

Even when the parties do not expect to have continuing relationships, they may have interrelated interests other than negotiating the immediate payment of money. For example, plaintiffs may have interests beyond maximizing direct recoveries, such as obtaining favorable tax consequences, getting non-monetary opportunities (such as employment, business, or insurance opportunities), receiving explanations or apologies from defendants, changing an employee's title or working conditions, receiving favorable references for future employment, preventing future harms, and arranging contributions to charities, among others. Defendants may have interests such as receiving vindication or other acknowledgments, making payments in kind instead of money, stretching payments over a period of time, sharing liability with other defendants, preventing ancillary harm (such as loss of credit rating or business or professional opportunities), receiving favorable tax consequences, obtaining non-disclosure agreements, and avoiding future lawsuits.

To illustrate an IBN approach, consider a case where a couple with young children is divorcing. One spouse may have an interest in remaining in the family home with the children, receiving adequate financial support, taking the lead in managing the children's lives, getting some relief from child care, and receiving a fair division of the property. The other spouse may have an interest in finding a suitable new house near the family home, having sufficient resources to maintain a suitable lifestyle after providing child support and alimony, maintaining an important role in the children's lives, and receiving a fair division of the property. Although the spouses may focus on differences in their positions, they may both share a strong interest in having their children have happy and healthy childhoods, minimizing harmful disruption in the children's lives because of the divorce, and providing financial security to both parties. Framed in this way the parties can consider a range of options for meeting the needs of the parents and the children.

IBN negotiation can also be helpful for managing the process and negotiating procedural matters, such as arrangement for exchange of information or obtaining expert input, as well as working out the terms of an agreement, including payment schedules.

Bruce Whitney, the former chief litigation counsel of Air Products and Chemicals, has used an IBN approach even when the negotiation has been primarily positional. He would prepare in advance by anticipating the need for "gap-fillers" that would bridge the gap between the parties' apparently firm bottom lines. This could be anything that has value to one side but costs the other side little or nothing. For example, in one case, the gap-filler was a commercial opportunity not directly related to the lawsuit. Air Products sought an opportunity for a transaction with the defendant that didn't cost anything from the defendant but that had great value to Air Products. The defendant wasn't willing to pay a monetary settlement and wouldn't have offered the transaction if it weren't for the leverage from the lawsuit. Although Air Products didn't receive a monetary settlement, it was satisfied because it received a business opportunity that it valued. Another example is that, as part of a settlement, an insurance company can provide free or discounted insurance for a future period. Whitney recommends developing gap-filler proposals in advance and, if appropriate, bringing a written proposal.

Since IBN sounds so good in theory, why don't lawyers use this approach more often? In part, this is due to self-fulfilling expectations. Because it is not the norm, some lawyers are not familiar with it and may be uncomfortable using it. Some fear that the other side will interpret the mere suggestion of negotiation (particularly IBN) or consideration of the other side's needs as a sign of a weak legal position and thus an invitation to try to take advantage. Some may be particularly wary of IBN because they fear exposing their clients to risks that the other side might take advantage of open disclosure of their clients' interests and possible options for resolution. Open discussion of various options may be scary because the other side might infer that a particular option is acceptable, even if brainstorming rules indicate that parties should make no such inferences.

Despite these sources of resistance, lawyers do use IBN in some cases because of their general preference in negotiation approach and/or because they believe it is particularly appropriate for some cases. Indeed, studies have found that lawyers assess that they (or their counterparts) are more effective when they use interest-based approaches.[3]

Typical Tactics in Interest-Based Negotiation. In a classic IBN negotiation, the parties list their interests and develop an explicit agenda to deal with the issues involved. Because the goal is to produce an agreement satisfying the key interests of all parties through cooperation, negotiators focus on learning about both sides' interests. They may begin by noting areas of agreement and disagreement and acknowledging the legitimacy of the other side's interests. They may dig deeper by asking each other why their stated interests are important to them, seeking to understand hidden interests that might lead to fruitful avenues for resolution. Before considering possible resolutions of issues, parties share information that would help the other side evaluate the situation and look for options that would satisfy them.

For each issue, the parties would consider a number of options and then hopefully agree on one option that would satisfy the interests of both parties. For example, in a divorce where the spouses need to decide what to do about a family home, they might consider options such as having one spouse buy the other spouse's interest during the divorce, buying it at some later time, taking a mortgage on the house to finance the sale, or selling it to a third party.

Sometimes parties use an explicit brainstorming process in which they generate a list of every option they can think of—including some options that may seem crazy—to stimulate a creative approach to the negotiation. Under the "rules" for brainstorming, parties must resist the normal temptation to evaluate particular options until after generating the entire list, because evaluating options can dampen creativity and prevent identification of options that might be optimal. After generating a list of options, the couple would evaluate all the plausible options to see how each would affect them and their kids, consider possible modifications to make them acceptable to both parties, and ideally reach an agreement that works for everyone.

When there are differences of opinion, negotiators may look for mutually acceptable standards for decision making, such as industry standards, expert opinions, legal rules, or moral values. Discussion of legal rules and alternatives to negotiated agreement is intended to provide parameters for negotiation rather than pressure the other side to make concessions.

In some cases, negotiators may start by negotiating principles for agreement and then use those principles to work out a detailed agreement. For example, businesses may start by developing a framework for a joint venture and then develop specific plans to implement the elements of the framework. In some cases, negotiators may agree on procedures for resolving issues. For example, if negotiators want to get an appraisal of an asset, they may agree on the criteria or procedures for selecting the appraiser, the information that would be provided, and whether the appraisal would be binding.

Sometimes problems arise in negotiation because of interpersonal factors, such as a history of a troubled relationship, feelings of being treated disrespectfully or unfairly, and misunderstandings. The landmark book *Getting to Yes* recommends "separating the people from the problem" by identifying the interpersonal issues and addressing them directly.[4] If one party feels offended by something that the other side did or said, the parties may discuss the incident, and there may be an exchange of explanations or apologies. Conversations like these can "clear the air" effective in removing barriers to negotiation. In some cases, the people *are* the problem in that the fundamental conflict is about the parties' relationship, and the dispute is a symptom of the underlying conflict. In that situation, the parties may focus on the history of the relationship and aspects of the relationship that continue to cause problems. A successful negotiation would not only resolve the immediate dispute but also help parties work better together in the future (or perhaps arrange for a respectful parting of the ways).

Advantages and Disadvantages. When successful, IBN produces much better results than positional negotiation. Because of differences in the parties' interests, negotiators may discover exchanges that make both sides better off. For example, if the parties agree that the defendant will pay the plaintiff a sum of money and if the plaintiff can afford to receive the money over a period of time, the defendant may be quite willing to pay a larger amount. In an intellectual property dispute, the parties may agree to a licensing agreement that may be worth much more to both parties than payment of a fixed amount of damages. If a couple reaches a satisfactory agreement to resolve the issues in their divorce, they may establish a good working relationship that can enable them to successfully work through issues as they arise in the future. Indeed, the IBN process itself is less likely to damage relationships.

Negotiators who are comfortable using this approach are likely to find the process more satisfying and less harmful than positional negotiation. It encourages negotiators to be more candid and respectful. This encourages a pattern of reciprocal positive gestures, and so negotiators are likely to feel that they have been treated well by the other side. Both sides are more likely to experience the outcome as consistent with their values and goals.

An IBN process can be a very efficient use of time, money, and effort in resolving disputes. If negotiators get to the heart of the dispute and focus on the critical issues, they can avoid activities in litigation that do not lead to resolution and that can actually prolong and aggravate the dispute. If an IBN process removes major barriers to successful negotiation, it can save a tremendous amount of time and money in litigation.

On the downside, some negotiators prefer a more competitive approach, either generally or in particular disputes. To be successful, IBN requires negotiators to become skilled at a new set of techniques and to demonstrate more openness than they may be comfortable with. This caution may be quite appropriate if the other side seems untrustworthy and likely to try to take advantage of the process, particularly when you are just getting up to speed on IBN skills. To perform the process well, the parties must invest a certain amount time and effort in training and practice, which some may not be willing to do. Although the process can be useful even when the parties do not reach agreement, parties can spend more time and money in IBN than they otherwise would.

Positional and interest-based negotiation are important theoretical concepts reflecting important aspects of negotiation in real life. In practice, negotiation is much more complex than is suggested by either of these conceptions, and many negotiations blend elements of both approaches. Getting trained in and becoming comfortable with these concepts can be very helpful for parties and lawyers in planning and conducting negotiation so that they can consciously adopt elements of either or both approaches.

Endnotes

1. Various writers have used different terms referring to similar concepts. For example, positional negotiation is sometimes called zero-sum, distributive, competitive, adversarial, or hard negotiation. Interest-based negotiation is sometimes called win-win, integrative, cooperative, problem-solving, or principled negotiation. *See* Leonard L. Riskin, *Understanding Mediators' Orientations, Strategies, and Techniques: A Grid for the Perplexed*, 1 Harv. Negotiation L. Rev. 7, 13–14 n. 21 (1996).

2. Transactional negotiations may differ from negotiation of litigated disputes as in litigation, there is likely to be a single alternative to a negotiated agreement—the court's judgment—whereas there may be multiple alternatives for one or both sides. For example, in a negotiation for the sale of a business from S to B, if B does not buy the business from S, B might buy a business from other sellers. Similarly, if S does not sell the business to B, it could sell it to other buyers. Even so, the general theory of positional negotiation applies to both transactions and disputes.

3. See Andrea Kupfer Schneider, *Shattering Negotiation Myths: Empirical Evidence on the Effectiveness of Negotiation Style*, 7 Harv. Negot. L. Rev. 143 (2002); Gerald R. Williams, Legal Negotiation and Settlement (1983).

4. Roger Fisher & William Ury with Bruce Patton, Getting to Yes: Negotiating Agreement Without Giving in 17-39 (2d ed. 1991).

Planning and Conducting Planned Early Negotiation

6

Suppose that you think that a planned early negotiation (PEN) process might be appropriate for a client. How would you set one up? The following are suggestions to apply in your cases as appropriate. There are many variations, and you should tailor the process to fit the clients' needs and goals in each case.

Assessing Whether the Case Is Appropriate for a PEN Process

The first thing you should do is to consider whether a PEN process is likely to be worth trying. You should do an "early case assessment" to answer this question. (See Appendix B for an early case assessment checklist.) In a relatively small proportion of cases, negotiation cannot provide what a party wants, such as a court's public determination of right and wrong or a published court decision. Sometimes at the outset of a case, parties *think* that they want such things, but after extensive litigation (and substantial legal bills) they decide that settlement is acceptable after all. If you have potential clients who say that trial is the only procedure that will satisfy their interests, you can help them by probing their interests and whether this assumption makes sense. In the vast majority of cases, clients will be satisfied with an acceptable settlement. In such cases, you should consider whether your clients would benefit from planned early negotiation.

Given that parties often are angry and don't trust each other at the outset, the main question is whether the parties and their lawyers will want to cooperate to reach a reasonable resolution. Lawyers have their own motivations and emotions, so it is important to consider the chemistry of all the individuals who might be involved. If negotiators want to work things out, they are likely to find a way to do so, especially when they use a process designed to promote constructive agreement.

Many lawyers say that the attitude of the other lawyer is an especially important factor in assessing the appropriateness of a PEN process. For example, Wharton Aldhizer & Weaver's Marshall Yoder says, "If the right attorney is on the other side, it doesn't matter which negotiation model you use. If the other lawyer is not inclined to cooperate, trying to use an interest-based negotiation model probably won't help, although I generally start from the assumption that there is at least some openness to a cooperative, interest-based framework." Similarly, Anne Preston, of Garvey Schubert

Barer, says that it's important to get "buy-in" from the other side. When the process has failed, in her experience, it was because of lack of buy-in. Some lawyers think that offering Collaborative or Cooperative Practice and other forms of ADR may be a way to get additional business, but they may not be very willing or able to act cooperatively in dealing with clients' matters. Obviously, you should go beyond the label to assess the approach of the particular lawyers you will be working with.

It is also critical to assess whether the parties are good candidates for a PEN process, which can be more difficult than it might seem at first. People often have complex combinations of motivations. Sometimes people want to be simultaneously cooperative and yet uncompromising on some issues. And if a party is an organization, various individuals in the organization may have different perspectives about negotiation. This can get even more complicated when there are multiple parties in a dispute. So this assessment is more complicated than checking off a box for whether parties want to cooperate or not.

Fort Myers, Florida, lawyer Shelly Finman says that he is a "real bear" about explaining all the process options to clients. When people first see him, many are like "deer in the headlights" and don't fully understand what he is saying. Often they are overwrought, depressed, or stressed out, and so they are poor candidates for being able to listen, comprehend, and digest what he says. He guesses that they may understand 40–50 percent of what he tells them. So he is very careful to check what they understand. He wants to know both how they see the situation and how the other party sees the situation. He concentrates on giving the person his full attention and respect, regardless of what they say. Even when they may seem bizarre, he works hard to respectfully listen and acknowledge what they are saying to understand their perspectives and interests accurately. Finman believes that too many lawyers think they know what is best for their clients. When they interview clients, they listen poorly, interrupt them, reject their desires by telling them that "the law doesn't provide" what they want, and tell them what to do and what not to do. This approach is not normally appropriate for good assessment and counseling, particularly for PEN processes.

There are some warning flags suggesting that a negotiation process may not be appropriate. For example, if you have doubts about whether negotiators would be honest and trustworthy, you should think twice before potentially wasting time and money on a negotiation that is likely to be unproductive or, perhaps even worse, result in an agreement that the other side doesn't live up to. These processes require parties to share relevant and accurate information, so PEN is not appropriate if any party appears unlikely to do so.

Sometimes it is hard to assess people's motivations, especially at an early stage of a dispute when people are often distrustful. Some warning signs involve impairments of a person's ability to negotiate, such as mental health problems, substance abuse, or domestic abuse. In situations like these, people may not be able to reliably control their actions, so it may not make sense to try to negotiate with them. This should not be a hard-and-fast rule, however. For example, if a party in a divorce is working well with a mental health professional (sometimes called a "coach"), the party may be able to manage well enough to negotiate constructively. You should consider whether parties need referrals to mental health or other professionals as appropriate, regardless of whether they retain you. Chapter 8 discusses how you might engage such professionals in your cases.

Even when you aren't sure that you can trust the other side, negotiating may be better than the alternative, such as litigating or walking away from the situation. Mistrust and uncooperative behavior may diminish over time in a well-structured process. Parties often feel relief with even small successes in reaching agreements, which can lead to increased trust and openness and a reversal of a downward spiral of conflict. If you negotiate in a case where the parties initially mistrust each other, you should build in protections, such as obtaining verified information during the negotiation process, negotiating warranties, and being cautious about sharing sensitive information until you see how the other side behaves. Doubts about the other side's trustworthiness may lead you to decide not to negotiate, but consider whether negotiation may be your client's best option even if you have some doubts.

In addition to assessing the personalities and motivations of all the potential negotiators, you should consider the parties' preferences for different procedural variations. For example, some parties prefer having lawyers who focus exclusively on negotiation instead of both negotiation and litigation. These parties would presumably prefer a Collaborative or Settlement Counsel process, and they should be willing and able to incur additional expense for Litigation Counsel if needed (or be highly confident that they will settle in the process). Parties choosing a Collaborative process should believe that the other side would not try to take advantage of the disqualification provision to gain a bargaining advantage by threatening to end the negotiation at a strategic time (or be willing to take the risk that the other side would try to do so).

On the other hand, some parties would prefer a Cooperative process so that the lawyers who negotiate for them are also available to litigate if needed. These parties are presumably willing to take the risk that the potential for increased adversarial tension in negotiation would be outweighed by the efficiency of maintaining the relationships with the same lawyers if litigation is needed or by increased seriousness about negotiation because of easier access to litigation.

Cleveland lawyer James Skirbunt emphasizes the importance of educating clients about all the procedural options, including litigation. He tries to clearly explain the processes and how they relate to the clients' interests. He then helps clients make their own choices without trying to steer them toward any particular process.

Appendix C is a chart summarizing key factors affecting the appropriateness of mediation, Collaborative Law, and Cooperative Law procedures in divorce cases, and can be adapted for other types of cases. Appendixes D, E, and F provide more specific information about Collaborative Law, Cooperative Law, and Settlement Counsel processes, respectively, including benefits and risks. Appendix G provides information for clients about privacy in a Collaborative Law process.

If, after consulting with your client, you think that the other side might be interested in using a PEN process, you should contact them. If the other side has a lawyer, you might discuss this by phone. Appendix L is a sample letter to an unrepresented party in a divorce case inviting him to consider using a Collaborative or Cooperative process.

When clients hire you to represent them in a PEN process, it is a good idea to address this in your retainer agreement. Appendixes H and I provide sample provisions you might use or adapt.

Designing a Flexible Process to Meet Clients' Needs

There is no one right or best way to negotiate. It is tempting for some practitioners who have become enthusiastic about their preferred approach to advocate that others follow it without deviation. Some processes, such as Collaborative Practice, are subject to more protocols than others. Having a uniform protocol can give everyone a sense of security and confidence. On the other hand, some practitioners can become so dependent on their comfortable routines that they are not open to adapting the procedures to fit the circumstances of particular cases. Shelly Finman, who does both Collaborative and Cooperative Practice, argues that there is no one right way to do a negotiation, and lawyers should respect different practices. Los Angeles mediator and Collaborative lawyer Forrest Mosten believes that the process should focus on meeting client needs instead of simply following a professional protocol. He believes that professionals should seriously consider clients' procedural needs and desires, even if they differ from the local protocols and norms.

Too much flexibility, on the other hand, can also be problematic. Some lawyers want to "cut to the chase," skipping important parts of the process without considering what value might be lost in doing so. Jumping into bargaining without doing proper preparation may not only be ineffective, it can actually aggravate a conflict. So you and your client should consider the amount of structure and flexibility you prefer.

Setting Up the Process

In General. If your client and the other side are interested in using PEN, the next step is to plan the process, typically in a conversation between the lawyers. Anne Preston says that it's important to have a thorough discussion with the other lawyer on the front end, preferably in a face-to-face meeting. This should cover the substantive concerns of each party, procedural plans, potential problems in the negotiation, ideas for making the negotiation work successfully, and an agenda for a meeting with the parties. If you will use a written agreement to negotiate (often called a "participation agreement"), you should agree on the basic provisions of the agreement, subject to revision based on the parties' preferences.

Lawyers can be especially effective in orchestrating productive negotiations because they generally have had some negotiation experience and have a professional detachment. This can be extremely helpful in preventing parties' emotional reactions from interfering with effective negotiation. Of course, sometimes lawyers' own emotions get in the way. Part of your responsibility as a professional is to be aware of how your own "stuff" affects the process and make sure that it doesn't harm your clients' interests.

Normally, the lawyers and parties will get together in one or more meetings to negotiate. Sometimes these are called "four-way" meetings, indicating that both lawyers and clients attend, but sometimes other professionals attend as well, so these aren't strictly limited to four people. Many lawyers interviewed for this book emphasized the importance of arranging for a face-to-face settlement event. This is important because it gets everyone focused solely on negotiation and provides much better opportunities for direct communication and problem solving. In complex civil cases involving organizational parties, you should carefully plan who will and will not attend from each side. If at all possible, the decision makers for each side—the people who can authorize payment and accept offers—should attend in person. Being able to look each other in the eye and talk in the hall can be critical factors in making progress. Sometimes videoconferences or continuous participation by phone is the best that can be arranged. Having the decision makers "on call" at another location is clearly the least desirable option, because the people on the phone miss the context of the discussion and the impact of the interactions.

In some cases, however, you may want to plan to avoid or minimize direct interaction between the parties. For example, you should separate parties if they would have a hard time even sitting in the same room with each other. Obviously, this procedure can be appropriate in cases involving domestic abuse or sexual harassment, but you should consider it in any kind of case when it might be appropriate. Sometimes two corporate CEOs may hate each others' guts, for example, but recognize that their businesses have an interest in a negotiated resolution. In that case, it might be wise to keep them apart for much of the time. When the parties are separated, you should be alert for a possible "sea change" in their attitudes suggesting that it might be productive to bring them together.

In general, you should discuss with your counterpart what professionals might be needed for the negotiation, if any, and how they might be retained and used in the process. Some professionals may assist with the negotiation process itself. These might include mediators, case managers, coaches, or communication specialists. Some might help with negotiation and/or provide substantive expertise, which might include financial or family relations professionals. Some Collaborative practitioners normally use a team of professionals and build the team before the first negotiation session. In other cases, the negotiators do not engage additional professionals until later in the process when they decide which, if any, professionals to hire. You should discuss this issue with both your client and the other side. For discussion about engaging various professionals in negotiation, see Chapter 8.

Holland and Knight's Tom Woodrow suggests that you anticipate and understand third-party claims and liens before a negotiation session where you might resolve the case, as these issues may interfere with an otherwise seemingly easy settlement. For example, he says that if a plaintiff claiming medical expenses is a Medicare beneficiary, you will need a conditional payment summary from the Center for Medicaid and Medicare Services because the parties will be responsible for protecting Medicare's interests regarding future health-care costs.

Logistics of the Negotiation. James Skirbunt believes that it is important to establish a general time line at the outset or else the process may languish for a long time. Even though the time line may need to be adjusted, it can be helpful to plan for a specific time period such as three or six months. Anne Preston agrees on the importance of setting a schedule, saying that it is important to frame the process as something different from the "same-old, same-old." This helps people diligently focus on the case from the outset. She says that if you let it linger too long, lawyers may go back to their "old tricks." It's important to maintain a sense of momentum and not be too "loosey-goosey" about deadlines.

Planning for a negotiation session involves agreeing on a suitable place, time, and duration for the meeting. Make sure that there will be at least one extra room for lawyers and clients to meet privately if needed. Consider whether to use a flip chart, blackboard, and/or laptop computer to make notes of the discussion. Arranging for drinks or snacks can put people at ease and make them more comfortable during the meeting. You and your colleague should be very clear about the planned start and end times of the meeting and confirm this with all participants at the outset. If, during a meeting, a critical participant abruptly says that he or she needs to leave sooner than expected, this can seriously undermine people's confidence in the negotiation process.

Plan an agenda for the negotiation with your colleague to make sure that all of the issues are on the table and to avoid surprising anyone by raising issues they weren't expecting. You should normally plan and circulate an agenda an appropriate time before the negotiation. Sometimes you will arrive at a negotiation and find that issues have come up after everyone has agreed on the agenda. New issues may particulary arise in divorce cases, where people expect the process to unfold during a number of meetings over a period of time. In these situations, the negotiators should decide whether to address the new issue at that meeting or at a later meeting. Generally, you should be open to modifying the agenda if appropriate.

If you do not expect to complete the negotiation in a single meeting, you should consider if there are any issues that need to be resolved at a given meeting. For example, in a divorce, the parties may need to work out immediate arrangements for transporting children on a regular schedule or dealing with finances while the divorce is pending. So, at the beginning of a meeting, you might ask if there is anything that the parties need to resolve by the end of the meeting. This can help them focus on the things that are on their minds and relieve their anxiety about a specific issue.

The lawyers should make sure that the agenda reflects the clients' needs and priorities. If there are important court deadlines, legal considerations, or critical-path sequencing issues affecting the timing, you should inform the clients about them and set the agenda accordingly. It is also important to "share" the agenda by making sure that both sides' important priorities are being addressed. In some cases, you might divide the available time in half and let each side choose what issues to spend "their" time on.

Sometimes the order of the agenda is significant, because parties may fear being exploited if they make concessions early in a negotiation and the other side does not reciprocate on later issues. You can ease the negotiation if you know about these concerns in advance and plan to address them. For example, the parties can agree that agreements on specific issues are tentative and subject to agreement on some or all other issues. Another option would be to plan to negotiate several issues at the same time to try to reach a "package" deal.

In some situations, you may want to start with issues that should be relatively easy for the parties to agree about, giving them a sense of accomplishment and increasing their confidence that they can negotiate successfully. Other times, you might want to put the most critical—and perhaps hardest—issue first if you think that the parties won't be able to focus constructively on anything else until that issue has been addressed.

In any case, the agenda can make a big difference in people's reactions. So consult your client and the other side about the agenda, and plan it carefully.

Exchanging Information. The parties and lawyers should have a clear and common understanding about sharing information in the process. Parties often make mutual commitments to exchange information as part of the agreement setting up the process. Before the first negotiation session, lawyers and parties should consider various issues about exchanging information. For example, you should discuss, at least generally, what types of information that each party would be expected to exchange and under what schedule. You should also consider whether the parties have specific concerns about maintaining the privacy of certain information or documents and how they can provide adequate assurances about this.

In some cases you might want to unilaterally provide information to the other side, an approach that Settlement Counsel sometimes uses. For example, when Jim McGuire, now of JAMS, worked as Settlement Counsel at Brown Rudnick, he would send a package of information to the other side with a cover letter saying that they would need the information to evaluate the case in the negotiation process. The letter would offer to provide additional information upon request. He would usually provide this information with "no strings attached"—that is, without asking for information that he needed. He says that under the norm of reciprocity, the other side "owes you big-time." Sometimes this would prompt the other lawyer to make a "nice guy macho" response by trying to outdo McGuire in making even more generous unilateral disclosures. If the other side doesn't volunteer to provide information, obviously you should request it so that you can competently evaluate the case. If you are engaged for a limited time as Settlement Counsel, there is a premium on exchanging information as quickly as possible.

Collaborative and Cooperative family law cases typically involve participation agreements where parties promise to exchange "all relevant information." Some lawyers interpret relevance to mean information that is legally relevant—that is, admissible in court. The scope of discovery is substantially broader than what would be admissible, and the parties might commit to that standard. The lawyers and parties may have an even broader standard requiring disclosure of information that might reasonably affect parties' decisions.

The level of disclosure should reflect the parties' goals for the process. David Hoffman, of the Boston Law Collaborative, notes that in some cases the parties really want a process to make deeper and meaningful exchanges. In other cases, the process is simply a container to manage a potentially destructive dispute.

Hoffman described a divorce case in which his client, who was ending a 33-year marriage, became romantically involved with his childhood sweetheart. That relationship started after the marital separation and didn't affect the wife's legal rights. The wife would have been very upset to learn about the new relationship and would have considered it to be relevant to the negotiation. Hoffman's client didn't disclose the relationship because they expected that it would have caused "things to come off the rails" if he did. Hoffman believes, however, that most Collaborative lawyers would conclude that this disclosure would be required even if the other party's legal rights were not affected by the post-separation relationship.

Another example of ambiguity about what is "relevant" is if a party is expecting a new opportunity or other change in circumstances that might affect the parties' feelings and expectations about the negotiations. Should the party be expected to disclose that? If the changed circumstance would affect the parties' rights (such as a new business opportunity or change in income in a divorce case affecting the amount of child support), how certain must one be that the change would occur? Must it be absolutely certain? Probable? Possible?[1] The point is that as lawyers, you should discuss these issues in advance so that you are operating from the same "ground rules" and can advise your respective clients consistently.

Although a standard of "full disclosure" can make sense in divorce cases, it may be counterproductive in many civil cases where the scope of potentially admissible or discoverable information is very large, and you want to limit the amount of information exchanged to what is actually useful. In these situations, you should work with the other side to identify the critical information that each side needs to evaluate the case and make well-informed decisions. You can negotiate using this information, and if someone needs additional information, you can exchange the particular additional information needed.

An agreement to negotiate should accurately address these issues of exchange of information, though the key thing is for parties and their lawyers to have candid conversations about this at the outset. You should have in-depth conversations with your clients about what information they would or would not provide to the other side and what information they would expect from the other side. You should inform them that communications from negotiation generally would not be admissible in court if the matter is eventually litigated. Even so, information provided in negotiation could be used against them, as it could lead the other side to identify independently discoverable evidence.

You should have also have a conversation with the other side about the scope of information exchange, including what would *not* be disclosed, at least in general principles. This can be tricky, because simply having the conversation may tip them off about information you believe is not necessary to disclose. Hopefully, both sides could agree on what information would not be required, although that may be difficult in situations like Hoffman's client's romantic relationship.

Holly Hohlbein, a Seattle-area Collaborative lawyer, suggests helping clients who are reluctant to disclose information by discussing "what if" scenarios with them. You can ask clients, "If you were on the other side, would you want the other person to disclose that? What if the other side finds out about this on their own, without hearing it from you? Would their independently learning that information hurt your ability to get what you want from them?" This discussion can help the client decide how to disclose important information in a way that feels safe.

Although much of the focus of preparation is on exchange of factual information, you may also want to exchange memos that sketch out the legal issues and governing law. This may not be necessary if the law is fairly straightforward and clear, but it can be helpful if it is not.

Drafting an Agreement to Negotiate. A PEN process involves an agreement to negotiate, which you should discuss with the other lawyer before the first negotiation session. Preferably, the agreement should be in writing to set expectations clearly and have a document to refer to in case of disagreement. Some lawyers use an oral agreement, especially if they have worked together on other cases and are familiar with the procedural expectations. Even when you have worked with the other lawyer, however, it is generally a good idea to use a written agreement for the parties' benefit, as this may be their first experience with this kind of negotiation. Although some parts of the agreement aren't intended to be legally enforceable, it would be especially important to have a written agreement for some provisions, such as provisions about preclusion or use of information in litigation, and choice of dispute resolution process if needed. And a written agreement is likely to provide more legitimacy and detailed guidance for the negotiation process, so lawyers should plan to use one unless there is a good reason not to do so.

Anne Preston thinks that a written agreement is important because it symbolizes the fact that the process is really different from litigation as usual. James Skirbunt agrees, saying that it reflects a commitment to use a problem-solving process. He finds that signing a participation agreement is a helpful part of the ritual that significantly increases the likelihood of reaching an agreement. Without a written agreement, he says, there is a greater risk that your clients will just give lip service and won't be sincere. A written agreement can stimulate parties' commitment to follow the process and can be used later to help recalcitrant parties get back on track if needed.

Skirbunt's participation agreements include both a negotiation model and a mechanism for resolving disputes if the parties don't reach agreement. Negotiation models vary on such things as how much of the negotiation is done in face-to-face meetings, whether a mediator is used, and whether lawyers attend mediation sessions. The dispute resolution models might be arbitration, private judging, or litigation, for example. He finds that designating a dispute resolution mechanism up front "takes the mystery out of the process" and sometimes helps to avoid disputes. In one case involving a substantial amount of property, the parties set aside two days for negotiation and agreed to arbitrate if they didn't settle. Skirbunt thinks the fact that they designated arbitration was helpful in getting an agreement. They were having a hard time in negotiation, and if litigation was the dispute resolution option, they might not have settled because they would have wanted to be able to appeal the decision, which would not be possible in arbitration.

You should tailor the language and tone of the agreement to negotiate to fit the clients. David Hoffman says that his participation agreements in family law cases include a lot of language about the parties' intentions that is not intended to be legally enforceable. These include provisions in which the parties agree to listen carefully, treat each other respectfully, and promote the welfare of the children. Such language can be very helpful in family cases, but parties in business cases can be turned off by language that seems too "touchy-feely" to them—even though the "nuts and bolts" of the agreement are the same. So he suggests that lawyers use language that the clients would feel comfortable with. Similarly, in some cases people may feel more comfortable using an agreement in the form of letters at the outset of the process rather than a document signed at the first negotiation meeting.

Some local Collaborative and Cooperative Practice groups have developed standard form agreements to negotiate, which reflect local practice norms and make it easier to develop a negotiation process without "reinventing the wheel" in every case. Appendixes P and Q provide sample agreements to negotiate that you can use or adapt. Lawyers and parties should review the agreement in advance to make any adjustments appropriate for their particular situation. If there are significant procedural concerns, the lawyers should discuss them before a negotiation session.

You may want to include provisions for planned early negotiation as a dispute resolution process in transactional agreements, such as commercial contracts, leases, etc. Appendix T provides a sample contract provision for early negotiation of future disputes.

Preparing Clients to Negotiate Effectively. Before attending the first negotiation session, each pair of lawyers and clients should discuss what they want to happen in the negotiation as well as potential problems. The lawyers should explain that their job is to help the clients achieve their goals. Doing so requires being cooperative with the other side at times as well as firmly asserting their interests in response to unacceptable approaches from the other side.

Garvey Schubert Barer's Sevilla Claydon, who often represents businesses in employment matters, highlights the importance of preparing clients before negotiation. She says that it's not uncommon for her to meet with a client for half a day, take a break, and then meet for another half a day on a different date. She especially focuses on the client's attitude. Starting with where they are "coming from" emotionally, she helps them get to the point where they can manage their emotions during the negotiation. She says, "Regardless of whether they claim to have an emotion or not, it's always there." Claydon says that it's very hard for everyone, including her, to really move away from thinking about right and wrong because we usually feel, "We're right." She coaches clients to go into negotiations with the attitude that "we're here to listen and solve a problem, not to prove who is right and wrong."

Marshall Yoder meets with clients in advance to set realistic expectations about what they will each do. He says, "Some people still have the notion that the attorneys are going to figure out the problem and solve it with little effort on the client's part. I'm not going to go in there waving a sword. My clients have to realize going in that this is hard work, and they are going to have to work in ways that they haven't done before. They have to commit to make full disclosure of relevant information. The upside is that they are more likely to end up with resolution that satisfies more of their underlying interests."

Like virtually all of the lawyers interviewed for this book, Doug Reynolds, of The New Law Center, is a "big believer" in client preparation for negotiation. This is also important in helping him get prepared, as he needs clients to tell him what he needs to know so that he can get "up to speed." He finds that this helps make his clients more comfortable and confident so that they don't have to take tough positions out of ignorance or fear.

Perhaps surprisingly, many lawyers are afraid of direct expressions of conflict in negotiation and prefer to avoid them by keeping the parties separate as much as possible and minimizing how much they talk. Although sometimes this is appropriate, it can often result in the loss of important opportunities to deal with the conflict and solve the problems. Lawyers often assume—sometimes correctly—that all the clients really want is for lawyers to get rid of the dispute with as little client involvement as possible. Lawyers also sometimes assume that clients would not be able to negotiate constructively if there was direct expression of emotions.

If you make these assumptions and you are wrong, you do your clients a disservice, and they may feel very frustrated with you. Sometimes clients very much want to participate actively in the process. You should discuss with your clients the nature of their participation and try to find a way to satisfy their wishes. In some situations, you may believe that clients' participation would harm their case. If so, you need to find a tactful way to deal with this.

If you generally feel uncomfortable with parties' direct expression of conflict, you may find it hard to effectively handle difficult cases. If you find this to be a challenge, you can develop skill and confidence with training and practice, as described in Chapter 9.

Before a negotiation session, you and your counterpart can signal to each other what your respective clients' main interests would be—as well as any "hot buttons" that could derail a negotiation. For example, if a party is particularly concerned about a certain issue, you can make sure that the issue is on the agenda. If the parties have strong feelings about who is to blame for the problem, you can prepare them before they meet to try to avoid inflaming tensions by engaging in a series of unproductive recriminations. This is not to suggest that you should always try to prevent expression of any criticisms. Rather, you should anticipate the other side's sensitive points and coach your clients to express their own concerns constructively and in ways that the other side will be able to "hear" without going crazy. Indeed, based on lawyers' conversations, you can encourage your respective clients to give appropriate acknowledgments or assurances to the other party that would address sensitive fears or concerns and thus make the negotiation go more smoothly.

Although the focus of negotiation is generally on how to resolve things in the future, sometimes it is very important for parties to talk about what happened in the past and their feelings about those events. I generally avoid using the word "vent" to describe this because it seems disrespectful and suggests that these concerns have no value and just need to be disposed of. In some situations, parties won't be able to move forward until they have had a chance to talk about the past. If they want to spend some time airing these issues and you think that it might be productive, you should be prepared to spend some time on this during the negotiation. Instead or in addition, parties might address these concerns, individually or jointly, with communication coaches or other professionals. So while you should sometimes steer the conversation in negotiation from the past to the future, this isn't always the best approach, and you and your client should carefully consider what would be most productive.

Lawyers and parties should recognize that it is *completely normal* to encounter problems in negotiation. You should advise your clients that when problems do arise, no one should be surprised or unduly upset. This, in itself, can provide reassurance that you regularly deal with such problems and, your clients usually come out all right. Instead of getting upset, you need to figure out how to solve the problems. You should counsel your clients that if they get upset, they should continue to treat everyone respectfully and give everyone time to speak. When problems do arise, if you have developed a good collegial relationship with the other lawyer, as described in Chapter 4, you will be better able to manage the problems successfully together and avoid engaging in counterproductive adversarial exchanges. Chapter 7 describes many specific things you can do to solve the problems.

You should privately alert your clients ahead of time that, during the negotiation, you will inform them if you think their approach is causing problems. This might occur, for example, if they take positions that don't advance their interests or if they are using a disrespectful tone that antagonizes the other side. During negotiation, you may want to have these conversations with clients in private so they don't feel that you are abandoning or embarrassing them. In your initial preparations, however, you should alert them that you might discuss this in front of the other side, depending on the situation. If your client is willing to have this conversation in a joint meeting, you may be able to build trust with the other side by showing that you are committed to a constructive process and that you may ask your clients to change their approach if you think it is not appropriate.

Appendix N is a checklist to prepare your clients for their first negotiation session.

Conducting Negotiation Sessions

At the first negotiation session, you should normally begin by reviewing the agreement to negotiate and the agenda for the meeting. (For a checklist for conducting a negotiation session, see Appendix O.) It can be tempting to avoid discussion of the process and jump right into the substantive issues. In particular, the parties may feel that they have discussed this enough before the meeting, they may want to save time and money, or they may just be anxious to deal with the issues that they are most concerned about. Although reviewing the process agreement may seem unnecessary or tedious, completely skipping this discussion can lead to problems later. This discussion can be important to make sure that everyone has the same expectations, and it can contribute to a cooperative attitude that will help in resolving difficult issues.

Seattle-area lawyer Holly Hohlbein, who specializes in Collaborative family practice using a full-team model, reports that the norm in her area is for people to take turns reading the complete agreement aloud at the first meeting. She says that when people are "going sideways," you can bring them back to the agreement, reminding them of what it says and asking if they still want to follow it. Practitioners in her area have found that reading the agreement aloud has a ritual quality and is effective in getting to know each other, bonding as a group, and making a commitment in front of witnesses. She says that this is important because the Collaborative process involves promises that people don't normally associate with a divorce, and it brings up different kinds of questions. If the first meeting will involve an extensive discussion of the process like this, she says that it's important to prepare the clients ahead of time to expect this.

With experience, lawyers who do not want to read the full agreement aloud may find a good balance of discussing key process issues without going into unnecessary detail. If you have done a good job discussing the process with your client in advance, you should have a good idea about the concerns that are most important to discuss at the first face-to-face meeting.

After reviewing the agreement, the parties should decide whether to sign it. If any parties are concerned about the process, these concerns should be discussed. If, after a thorough discussion, parties are reluctant to sign the agreement, you have a few options. One is to "sleep on it" and see if they change their preferences. For example, if parties fear losing their attorney if they litigate, they might be better off in a Cooperative process rather than a Collaborative process. In Collaborative cases, it is particularly important that parties are committed to using this Collaborative process before signing the participation agreement because of the implications of disqualification of their Collaborative lawyers.

Moving to discuss the agenda for the meeting can be a good segue from focusing on the process to the particular issues that the parties want to discuss. Presumably, the lawyers and parties will have agreed on an agenda for the meeting in advance. Even if so, it is a good idea to review it together to make sure everyone agrees and check if there is a need to change in the agenda. In some cases, it may make sense to end the first meeting at this point, planning to begin substantive discussions at the next meeting. This would give people time to reflect on the process and be prepared to "hit the ground running" at the next meeting. In other cases, the parties may be ready to move straight into the substantive discussion. If you expect that the process will take a number of meetings, you might suggest working on one or two small and easy issues for the first meeting to give the parties a sense of accomplishment and success from the outset.

One of the first issues people may want to discuss is planning to collect and exchange information they will need to resolve the issues. It is important to have discussed this with your client and the other side in advance, as described above. This is an important procedural issue that has obvious substantive implications, so making plans for this can give people the sense that they are making progress on the issues they really care about. It is also a necessary pre-condition for having the substantive conversations, so it will often make sense to address this early in the process.

In some situations, such as many divorce cases, the basic information needed is pretty standard and straightforward. In other cases, you may need to develop individualized plans, which might include such things as access to experts' reports, inspection of physical evidence, or visits to critical sites. In any case, it is important to specifically plan for the method and timing of exchange of particular documents or other information needed. Presumably the lawyers will have discussed this with their clients before the meeting, but, even if so, it is important to review this at the meeting to make sure that everyone understands and agrees to the plan for information exchange.

Sometimes at an early stage in a negotiation, it is helpful to have a discussion about parties' interests—the goals that they would like to achieve in the negotiation. For example, in a commercial dispute, you could ask if the parties might have a continuing business relationship if they can reach a satisfactory resolution. If so, what would make it attractive for each of them? In divorce cases where the couples have kids, you might ask the parents what they would like for their children in five years. In some cases, it may *not* be a good idea to ask parties about their interests at the outset if there is a real risk that it would prompt them to disclose sensitive information too early in the process or make statements that would aggravate a conflict. This will be less of a concern if you have prepared your client well and the attorneys are skilled in handling conflict.

In conducting the negotiation, you should follow the agenda and use interest-based negotiation techniques as much as possible. In some cases, the negotiation will be completed in a single day. In family cases, it is common to have a number of meetings for negotiation that usually last one to two hours. There may also be conversations between meetings, just between lawyers or just between parties or with other professionals. In Collaborative cases, there is a strong norm of conducting all the substantive negotiations in face-to-face meetings with the parties. Collaborative lawyers often talk with their counterpart lawyers and any members of the Collaborative team before meetings to prepare for the discussion and/or afterwards to plan any follow-up actions. Parties and lawyers should use their judgment about the scheduling of meetings or conversations that would be most productive at any given time.

If you don't finish a negotiation in one meeting and plan to continue it at a later time, one of the attorneys should write a memo summarizing the discussion at the meeting and, if applicable, specifying who will perform certain tasks before the next meeting. When negotiations involve multiple meetings, Marshall Yoder says that it's important to debrief with your client after each meeting to find out what your client thought about it. After that, he says you should discuss with your colleague what you each thought worked or didn't work in the meeting and what you might do differently in the future, if anything. Of course, if other professionals are members of the negotiation team, such as a mental health professional in a divorce case, you should include all the members of the team in the debriefing.

If you think that you might reach agreement at an upcoming negotiation session, it can be helpful to draft a settlement agreement ahead of time, leaving blanks for terms to be agreed upon during the negotiation. You might share the draft with the other side (and mediator, if you are using one) in advance, noting your standard provisions. Having agreed in advance on standard provisions can be especially helpful at the end of a long negotiation session to avoid last-minute disputes. People are often tired at the end of a negotiation. Either side can derail the agreement and destroy the feeling of accomplishment if one side is uncomfortable with what it sees as a new issue raised for the first time at the very end. Not only can you avoid some disputes by reviewing standard provisions in advance, but you can set a positive tone by demonstrating your serious interest in settlement and working constructively with your colleague on issues that are presumably not very controversial. If some issues you thought were innocuous turn out to be controversial, you can plan to discuss them in the negotiation.

Drafting the Settlement Agreement

If the parties reach agreement, you will need to draft or review the agreement. Obviously, it should clearly and accurately reflect the parties' intentions and be readily enforceable in court if needed. The parties may want to include a provision protecting the confidentiality of the settlement, and if so, you should draft it carefully. If any third parties, such as Medicare, may have an interest in the settlement, be sure to take that into account in reaching and documenting the settlement.

The characterization of payments or other provisions in a settlement agreement may have significant tax consequences. If a financial professional knowledgeable about tax matters has been engaged in the process by your client or the parties jointly, you should ask for advice about how to structure the agreement in the best way possible. If no such professional is involved in the case, you should be sure you understand the tax consequences and possibly engage a tax professional for advice.

David Hoffman notes that it is very important for settlement agreements to be especially clear about what happens if things go wrong. For example, some agreements say that in the event of a dispute, the parties will use mediation or Collaborative Law, without specifying which would be used first. Agreements should specify details about issues, such as the time frame for initiating the process, how professionals would be selected, and who will pay for the dispute resolution professionals. Since the provisions would be invoked only when the parties would be in a dispute, you should draft them so that they can be implemented without further agreement by the parties at that point. If they have a dispute and can agree to modify the terms of the dispute resolution provision, that's fine, but you shouldn't count on it.

In Collaborative cases, Seattle-area attorney Holly Hohlbein likes to have the attorneys jointly draft the settlement documents and send them to the clients, rather than have one attorney-client pair send them to the other. This allows the lawyers to work out the technical and legal issues themselves if possible. If the lawyers or clients identify substantive differences as the documents are being drafted, the lawyers and clients can discuss them at a later negotiating session.

After you draft the agreement and the parties sign it, be sure to draft any related documents needed to implement the agreement (such as deeds) and arrange for the parties to take the actions needed for implementation (such as disbursement of funds).

A Success Story

One lawyer described a Cooperative case that she mediated. At the outset of an employment lawsuit, the employee didn't even want to be in the same room as the employer's representative. The two lawyers knew each other, which helped them to work together in planning the mediation. They designed a process that encouraged their clients to engage in face-to-face discussions as part of the mediation process. During the mediation, the employee needed some time to figure out what she wanted to do. Everyone was patient and helped her work through this. She eventually decided to resign. At the end of the session, she sat next to the same manager she initially didn't want to be in the same room with. They worked together at a laptop computer, jointly writing his letter of recommendation to help her in looking for another job. While they were writing the recommendation, the lawyers worked together at another laptop writing up the settlement agreement.

As this chapter indicates, doing a good job of negotiation requires careful assessment, planning, and implementation; well-developed knowledge and skills; a constructive attitude; and a lot of patience and persistence. Sometimes you have to go slow to go fast.

Endnotes

1. A study of Cooperative family lawyers found that they had very different expectations about what information would be required to be disclosed. *See* John Lande, *Practical Insights from an Empirical Study of Cooperative Lawyers in Wisconsin*, 2008 J. Disp. Resol. 203, 243–47.

Handling Problems in Negotiation 7

When lawyers negotiate, they may face a dilemma of simultaneously doing two things that may seem contradictory: advocating diligently and being cooperative. Law school and legal practice prepare lawyers to internalize the goal of protecting their clients, which is a mind-set that becomes second nature for most lawyers. Even so, lawyers recognize that in most cases, it is in their clients' interests to cooperate with the other side sufficiently to settle a dispute.

The tension between the deeply ingrained duty to protect clients and the desire to promote their interests through negotiation leads some lawyers to take strong positions about negotiation as a way to protect their clients. As described in Chapter 1, lawyers often worry that if they negotiate, they will give up too much in a positional negotiation (or their clients will think that). During a negotiation, lawyers naturally think about what will happen if they don't reach an agreement and, at least in the back of their minds, anticipate how they will protect their clients if they end up in litigation. Indeed, even *Getting to Yes*, the "bible" of interest-based negotiation, recommends that negotiators carefully analyze the alternatives to negotiated agreement. Lawyers regularly find that the other side is willing to become more "reasonable" (by which they generally mean "make significant concessions") in negotiations only in response to credible arguments that they are likely to receive less at trial than they previously thought. So in negotiation, it often feels quite natural for lawyers to forcefully advocate their clients' case and demonstrate a willingness to try the case if the other side doesn't take "reasonable" positions.

On the other hand, if you act too aggressively in negotiation, you risk scaring off the other side from being cooperative and reaching an agreement. So, although you may feel it is often helpful (and even necessary) to argue about the strengths of your legal arguments, this can also feel counterproductive. Clients often feel a similar dilemma about whether to take an adversarial or cooperative posture, which can reinforce their lawyers' ambivalence.

This dilemma can create a real—though sometimes unconscious—sense of confusion about how to act. Some lawyers might feel that it would be easier if they could focus solely on one task or the other—negotiation or trial preparation. But most lawyers, except perhaps trial specialists, cannot escape this dilemma. Even lawyers committed solely to negotiation in a case—Collaborative lawyers and Settlement Counsel—must consider whether their clients' interests would be better served by litigation, at least in contentious cases. Even though these lawyers would not be the ones representing the clients in litigation, they have an ethical duty to consider and discuss with clients whether continued negotiation would be in the clients' interests.[1]

In addition to these built-in structural conflicts that can cause difficulty in negotiation, some lawyers do not use good negotiation behaviors for other reasons. Many lawyers never were taught in law school about how to negotiate because the curriculum of most law schools focuses almost exclusively on litigation. Although some lawyers get negotiation training in continuing education programs after law school, many do not. Moreover, good negotiation requires interpersonal skills, such as self-awareness, listening, empathy, and problem solving, that derive from general personal qualities that some lawyers do not develop very much.

Even with the best skills, planning, and implementation, many— perhaps most—negotiations will run into problems. This is normal. As described in the preceding chapter, you should expect this and prepare your client to expect it as well. This chapter suggests techniques that can be used to deal with common problems in virtually any negotiation. They are particularly appropriate in *planned early* negotiations.

Dealing with Problems in Negotiation Generally

Although it would be ideal if all lawyers were well prepared to negotiate, many lawyers negotiate without much, if any, training and self-reflection about negotiation. Even lawyers who are generally well prepared encounter difficult cases. How can you effectively represent your clients and negotiate cooperatively in such cases?

In a given case, it is almost always best to start by developing good relationships between the lawyers and their clients, as described in Chapter 2, and between the lawyers, as described in Chapter 4. In general, developing good working relationships will prevent some problems from arising in the first place. The lawyers and parties should have a better understanding of each others' interests and "hot buttons" and should avoid unnecessarily antagonizing each other. Such preparation should also "humanize" everyone, making it harder to immediately respond in an adversarial way to people who know each other personally.

You can work with your clients to anticipate specific problems that might come up in their cases. Based on the clients' knowledge of themselves and the other party, you can ask what might "set off" either party and what might be effective in de-escalating an incident. Appendix A provides a list of questions that can help your clients do this kind of analysis.

You should also try to orient clients about what to expect from the lawyer on the other side. If you have worked with this lawyer before, you can describe your sense of whether he or she is likely to be cooperative. If you haven't worked with the other lawyer, you might check with other colleagues to learn about their experiences with him or her. Fort Myers, Florida, lawyer Shelly Finman describes "run-the-gauntlet lawyers" who make it hard to get through the process, though he finds that they are usually reasonable by the end of the case. When working with such lawyers, he cautions his clients that they should be patient and let the process happen. This doesn't mean that he is passive, as he may need to request a court order in some situations. But he counsels clients that they may need to let things to settle down for a while before they can make progress. If you do not know or necessarily trust your counterpart, it is generally a bad idea to disparage him or her to your client, as this could make it harder for you both to work with the lawyer. Instead, it is generally better to try to understand the other lawyer's perspective and interests and try to work constructively together as much as possible.

You can prepare your clients about possible ways to handle situations when people feel stuck in negotiation. Los Angeles mediator and Collaborative lawyer Forrest Mosten doesn't believe in the using the word "impasse," a term that people often use in negotiation and mediation. Instead, he thinks in terms of problems or challenges. In these situations, he says that there is a need for professionals to redesign or manage the process to encourage the parties to talk more, change the format, or try some different approach.

Table 2 is a handy checklist of ways that lawyers and clients can work through problems together when they get stuck. In initial conversations with your clients, you may want to highlight a few common techniques to prepare them to expect problems and assure them that you can deal with those problems effectively. After you have these conversations with your client, you can have similar conversations with the other lawyer so that the other side can be prepared as well. Simply going through this preparation may be effective in preventing some problems from arising at all. Of course, these discussions will not necessarily avoid all disputes, and you may need to use some of the techniques in Table 2. For a description of professional services described in the Table, see Chapter 8.

Table 2. Techniques for Dealing with Problems in Negotiation

Treat everyone with respect despite any frustrations and disagreements. Ask everyone else to do the same. Model good behavior.
Tell the other side that you would like to know if and when they are uncomfortable with the negotiation so that you can deal with any problems.
Use humor to defuse tension *if* you can do so without alienating others, such as by using self-deprecating humor.
Give people time to compose themselves. Have a box of tissues available.
Summarize the issues to highlight both parties' legitimate interests and perspectives without language that anyone might find insulting.
Ask questions to better understand the other side's feelings, perspectives, and interests. Summarize your understanding and check if it is accurate. Acknowledge that you believe that their perspective is legitimate, even though you may disagree in some ways. Ask if they would like to better understand your perspective.
Thank the other side for anything that you honestly appreciate, such as their hard work, commitment, sincerity, positive gestures, etc.
Highlight areas of agreement and note the losses that would result from continued disputing. Note that it does not make sense to justify continued disputing because of "sunk costs" that already have been incurred, as parties are unlikely to recover them in any case.
Ask parties who have had a prior relationship (such as spouses or business partners) what they appreciated about each other when the relationship was going well.

Reflect on and discuss with the other side what may have caused the negotiation problems (such as misunderstandings, mistaken assumptions, and cultural differences) and possible ways to get back on the right track.

Objectively describe behavior you find problematic and ask if it is helpful in resolving the problems (perhaps saying that the behavior differs from commitments in an agreement to negotiate).

Review the agreement to negotiate and ask if parties still want to continue with their commitments.

Try to agree about applicable principles of fairness, and then use the principles to guide the discussion.

Ask "what can we do differently?"

Make process agreements, such as having only one person speak at a time.

Take a break for each side to analyze what happened and "cool off," perhaps for a few minutes, a few days, or longer.

Temporarily change the subject to talk about matters of common personal interest such as hobbies, travel, or sports.

Walk around the block or share a meal.

Reschedule the meeting for another time of day, length of time, or location.

Identify any information you might exchange that could help resolve the problem.

Conduct factual investigation or legal research to clarify critical issues. Verify critical facts with reliable documents or third-party sources of information.

Negotiate representations and warranties to increase confidence and provide reasonable remedies.

Negotiate a dispute resolution agreement to resolve particular types of disputes when you cannot resolve the issues now because of uncertainty about the future.

Break a big issue into smaller issues that can be negotiated separately.

Consider several issues simultaneously to reach a "package deal."

Negotiate a partial agreement, an agreement for a trial period, or an agreement contingent on facts to be determined later.

Negotiate an agreement in principle and then "flesh out" the principles with specific commitments.

Reassess the full range of each party's interests related to the dispute. Highlight the parties' shared interests, including an interest in efficient and fair dispute resolution.

Look for options that would make one party better off with little or no cost to the other, taking advantage of differences in valuations, expectations, risk preferences, and time preferences.

Consider the interests of others who might affect each side's position (such as supervisors, boards of directors, creditors, customers, suppliers, or spouses) and how these people's interests might be satisfied. Consider inviting other individuals to participate by phone or in a later negotiation session. Consider whether certain individuals should be excluded from later negotiation sessions.

Brainstorm to identify options that haven't been considered, including adding new elements to the negotiation that could create mutual benefit (such as negotiation of a new transaction).

Candidly reanalyze the likelihood of possible alternatives to a negotiated agreement, possibly using decision analysis. Think about what the parties' "worlds will realistically look like" if they do settle and if they don't.

Ask parties to imagine how they might analyze the issues if they were lawyers advising clients or judges hearing the case.

Ask each party to summarize the other party's perspective and then ask the other party to confirm whether the summary was accurate or not.

Educate clients about the reality of trial by doing a mock cross-examination or suggesting that they take a "field trip" to see what really happens in court.

Change your position to provide something that the other side wants. Give the other side a sincere acknowledgment, apology, or other gesture that they would appreciate. State your interest in reaching a reasonable agreement. Invite the other side to take a reciprocal action.

"Bracket" the negotiation by agreeing to a narrower bargaining range so that the plaintiff reduces the current demand if the defendant simultaneously increases the current offer to specified amounts.

Choose to let go of anger and forgive the other side.

Have a conversation between the lawyers without the clients.

Have a conversation between the clients without the lawyers.

Suggest that one or more parties meet with a communications coach or consultant.

Hire a mediator to help resolve the problems.

Conduct a mock trial solely with the negotiators.

Conduct a mock trial with respected experts.

Hire a neutral expert to assess the issues and possibly give recommendations.

Hire an arbitrator or private judge to resolve the dispute.

Use the court as a tool of cooperation, jointly consulting informally with a judge, scheduling a case management conference, asking a judge to lecture uncooperative parties, or obtaining a ruling on a key disputed issue—and then resuming negotiation.

Don't give up too soon. Keep talking as long as there is any reasonable chance of making progress.

Discuss how you would proceed in litigation and consider if both sides can agree on pretrial and trial procedures.

Seattle-area lawyer Holly Hohlbein notes the importance of modeling good behavior for clients, who often take their lead from the professionals. She makes a conscious effort to demonstrate constructive approaches and encourages everyone else to follow suit.

Sevilla Claydon, of Garvey Schubert Barer, emphasizes the importance of flexibility in dealing with problems. "You don't use the same hammer for every nail. You have to understand the dispute, the people, and interests involved and then figure out what will work well in that situation." A colleague joked that the successful resolution of a difficult case was due to "pixie dust," but Claydon believes that it involved being open to the psychology of the parties and lawyers and figuring out what would satisfy them.

David Hoffman, of the Boston Law Collaborative, generally includes a 60-day cooling-off period in his participation agreements. He finds that is it not usually necessary to invoke the cooling-off period, but it keeps people at the table, which is the desired effect. His agreements also include a mediation provision to deal with difficult disputes. Using the two provisions together is a "belt and suspenders" approach to perseverance in negotiation. In one of his current cases, the other side invoked the cooling-off period as an adversarial tactic. The parties had agreed to use mediation, which helped cool things off, and the parties are on the verge of settlement. A cooling-off period can be especially helpful in Collaborative cases, as the parties might need time to hire Litigation Counsel.

Dealing with Uncooperative Behavior

Dealing with Your Clients. Sometimes you may find that your own clients behave uncooperatively, which can present a serious dilemma. On one hand, at least in planned early negotiation processes, the client has presumably agreed to negotiate sincerely and directed you to do the same. Acquiescing in uncooperative conduct can jeopardize your clients' interests in a successful negotiation. On the other hand, to operate effectively, you need to maintain your clients' confidence. When preparing clients for the negotiation, you should specifically discuss the possibility that you will have concerns about things that they may say or the way that they say it, as described in Chapter 6.

You should develop a clear understanding with your clients about how you will respond in such situations. In general, you should be very careful to treat everyone with respect. You might summarize your clients' concerns in a way that would not offend the other side. And you might remind your clients about their agreement to negotiate respectfully, identifying statements that were not helpful in advancing anyone's interests. Depending on the circumstances, you might say this to your client privately or in the presence of the other side. It is particularly important to demonstrate to the other side that you are still committed to cooperative negotiation. Without such a demonstration, the other side may lose confidence in the process, which can lead to a breakdown of the negotiation.

Most lawyers have had clients with unrealistic expectations. David Hoffman believes that it's important to win the trust of such clients by acknowledging their problems—which they may experience as a horrible ordeal. After giving this acknowledgment, he tries to engage them in a realistic analysis by asking what they think the other party is telling his or her lawyer. Although you may get only the "tip of the iceberg" this way, it can be helpful in eliciting useful information and giving the client a better sense of other perspectives. Some clients strongly believe that they are "right," the merits of their case would be obvious to the court, and therefore the court would rule in their favor. You can help your clients anticipate the consequences of taking various positions, including a "hard line." Obviously, this can be tricky, because it is normally impossible to know what would happen. Moreover, some clients interpret lawyers' predictions as reflections of the lawyers' confidence and ability rather than the merits of the case based on the law.

For some clients, reviewing a decision analysis, described in Chapter 2, may be helpful. If clients still have what Hoffman believes to be unrealistic expectations, he sometimes suggests getting confidential "case evaluation" opinions from up to three experts. If his clients want to pursue this approach, he writes a balanced summary of the facts so that the reader wouldn't be able to tell which side wrote the summary. To make sure that the memo isn't obviously biased, he sometimes asks colleagues in his office to see if they can tell which side wrote it. Then he gets the client to approve the memo before sending it to the experts. Hoffman finds that the case evaluation opinions produced by this procedure have a powerful impact on clients and relieve him of "taking the heat" for giving the client a disappointing evaluation. After discussing the risks with your clients (with or without a decision tree or outside opinion), you can assure them that you care about them and that if they want to continue taking a hard line, you will fight for them at trial.

If you think that your client is behaving unreasonably during a negotiation, you may want to have a private conversation with the client. Sevilla Claydon recommends that lawyers listen deeply to get to the root of why clients feel so strongly. She cautions that this is not easy. Sometimes the clients themselves sometimes don't even know why they feel so strongly, and it may take a while for them to say what's really going on. Sometimes they just don't want to admit they're wrong. After you identify the problem, you can try to figure out a more constructive way to satisfy their needs.

Holly Hohlbein says that one of her roles is to help coach clients to be most effective. She tells them that they can operate from their deepest fears or highest hopes. When she finds people taking hard positions, she says that they are usually operating from their deepest fears. She asks them, "Help me understand this. You are taking a hard line and the other side isn't going along. How do you think this is going to advance your goals?" They will tell her their story and she will work with it. She sees her job as figuring what is not working well, what is important, and what is likely to be effective. If the client is self-reflective and willing to "go a few layers down," she will go down with them or have a coach work with them.

Along the same lines, Forrest Mosten tries to "join with the clients" by demonstrating an empathy with their fears and concerns rather than engaging in a debate or power struggle. He tries to create an educational process that "turns clients into their own advisors" so that they can figure out what is likely to be effective in solving their problems. Mosten says that sometimes it's hard to avoid a conflict with clients. In these situations, he tries to get them to see that their plan is not likely to get what they really want and that there may be another way to "skin the cat."

Even when clients have agreed to make full disclosure of relevant information, such as in Collaborative and Cooperative cases, clients can nonetheless be reluctant to disclose sensitive information. In these situations, Marshall Yoder, of Wharton Aldhizer & Weaver, works with his clients to determine what needs to be disclosed and how to share the information with the other side. He asks how they expect the other side to react to the disclosures and how he can prepare them for that. Even with this preparation, he says that there still is usually tension, and he subtly coaches clients during the negotiations to help them provide the information in the most constructive way possible. How something is communicated is often as important as the substance of the message itself.

Sometimes it is helpful to confront the client directly and respectfully. Shelly Finman says that sometimes he asks his clients in Collaborative or Cooperative cases, "Do you understand that what you are doing is inconsistent with the participation agreement?" Or he might say, "I feel uncomfortable that what you are asking would require me to do something contrary to the process we agreed to." If he believes that his client may have done something inappropriate, he usually says, "Is that what you intended to say? Because that is not in the spirit of what we are trying to do." Cleveland lawyer James Skirbunt reflected on the lawyers he respects, and he believes that they all decline to simply do whatever the client wants them to do. Instead, if they believe that what a client wants to do is inconsistent with her interests, they tell her so. To be able to have this conversation with your clients, you must have previously talked with them to identify their interests.

Doug Reynolds, of The New Law Center, gauges his responses to clients based on what he knows about them. For example, he has one client who has a "great instinct" for when to be tough. When that client says "no," he simply accepts that. He has another client who often gets stuck on his emotions, so Reynolds may be more assertive and say something like, "You have risk, and I think we need to settle this." He has learned how to say this in a way that his clients can hear. They know that he has their best interest at heart and that he is generally right. He has worked with many clients over a long period of time, so they know each other pretty well. He cautions that counseling candidly is more difficult with clients with whom you haven't worked for very long.

Under most Collaborative and Cooperative negotiation agreements, lawyers are required to withdraw if their clients refuse to disclose relevant information. If clients are reluctant or unwilling to disclose certain information that you believe they are required to disclose, you should ask them why they don't want to do so. Sometimes lawyers can help clients make disclosures in a way that does not cause the problems they fear. If they are not willing to disclose information that you believe they are required to provide, you should inform them that you will be required to withdraw from the representation if they do not comply with their obligation.

When there is a tense incident with the other side or with your client, you should usually suggest taking a break to let things settle down. Although this may sound trivial, many people find that taking a break helps them get back on track. During the break, you should confer with your client and/ or the other lawyer to discuss what happened and what they can do to encourage productive discussion when the negotiation resumes. If there are recurring problems during a negotiation, you and your counterpart (and presumably any other professionals on the negotiation team) should have additional conversations to figure out the problems and potential solutions. These conversations may or may not occur during joint negotiation sessions with clients present. In some situations, it is helpful to have a full joint discussion of the problems, and in other situations, it is better to have these conversations more privately and without the pressure of a scheduled negotiation session.

Dealing with the Other Side. Negotiators sometimes complain, "You're not negotiating in good faith. You're not being collaborative [or cooperative]." They sometimes have these reactions even when the lawyers have been highly trained, prepared cases well, and tried to act constructively. These reactions may reflect the norms of positional negotiation in an adversarial environment that lawyers are generally used to. Under stress, the other lawyer may revert to adversarial form. Sometimes the problem isn't the *other* lawyer but may be *your* own behavior or (possibly unrealistic) expectations. Sometimes, the problem is just due to a misunderstanding.

Responding to such challenges with inquiry rather than accusation is more likely to produce a cooperative response. James Skirbunt strongly recommends against telling the other lawyer, "You are not behaving collaboratively," which he says "makes his skin crawl" and doesn't do anything helpful. If you express puzzlement and surprise, it invites the other side to respond positively, possibly including acknowledgment of some error. If you start with a cooperative tone, it is easy to become more confrontational if you think that would be appropriate. If you start by challenging the other side's intentions, they are likely to react defensively and deny the accusation, even if they are wrong. Rather than getting the negotiation back on a cooperative track, this risks making things worse.

In general, when you perceive that the other side is being uncooperative, you should stay calm and avoid responding adversarially. There are several reasons why you should start by exploring the possibility that the other side is operating with good intentions. First, the other side may have a valid point. In a tense negotiation, people—probably including you—often have heightened emotions, which can distort their perceptions. It is easy to jump to an erroneous conclusion about the other side's motivations. In this situation, you should respond by respectfully asking about the other side's reasoning, and be open to the possibility that they have legitimate reasons (at least from their perspective). This may present an opportunity to advance the negotiation by clarifying the problems and each side's strong interests.

Forrest Mosten suggests dealing with these problems through inquiry and collaboration with the other lawyer by asking, "How can we solve this together?" You can be humble and ask for your colleague's help in understanding the problem and solving your client's problems. James Skirbunt sometimes pulls out the participation agreement and reviews what the clients hired the lawyers to do. When the clients hire lawyers to be problem solvers, he asks, "How is what you are saying going to help us solve the problem?"

Sometimes Skirbunt will ask his counterpart, "What can I do to help you move this forward?" Although this may be a surprising reaction to a perception that the other side is being particularly difficult, he usually gets a response describing what the other party needs. In that situation, he tries to help them if it wouldn't harm his clients' interests. He says that the toughest part is dealing with his instinctive reaction to become more aggressive. It is very hard to "suck it up" and ask the other lawyer how he can help. But Skirbunt finds that it is one of the most effective things he can do.

When describing your perceptions of problems, it helps to do so as objectively, specifically, and respectfully as possible rather than making sweeping, unflattering characterizations. For example, you might say that the other lawyer presented certain information that is inconsistent with your understanding and you want to understand the difference. This is normally better than starting off by accusing other lawyer of trying to take advantage of your client by misrepresenting the facts. Similarly, if you believe that the other lawyer is taking an unreasonable position, you might ask why the lawyer's proposal is fair for both parties (instead of making an accusation of being unfair or negotiating in bad faith). This can lead to a discussion of other possible ways to solve the problem.

Shelly Finman says that occasionally the other lawyers will act or say something in a very disrespectful way, and they may or may not be aware of it. If they have a history of doing this, he warns his clients in advance. He tells them that if this happens, they can let him or the lawyer know how they feel or they can simply clam up. When this does happen, he generally makes a point of communicating about problems with his colleagues as they occur and before the problems get worse. Finman usually interjects by reframing the other side's comments in a more constructive fashion and then asks for a time-out to talk with his client and/or the colleague. Before he engages in the "time-out," he always asks for permission to do so as a matter of courtesy and respect. He notes that if he just says "time out," that in itself can be considered disrespectful. In the time-out, he tells the colleague what he thought he heard and that he (and/or his client) perceived it to be disrespectful, whether intended or not. He wants to get the colleague to take responsibility and be a part of the solution, so he asks him or her what would be the best way to remedy the situation. Sometimes the most he can do is to get them to acknowledge that it is his client's perception. Even that sometimes can be helpful.

Finman gave an example that included both the right way and wrong way to communicate problems to a colleague. He had a case where the other lawyer told Finman that his (Finman's) client wasn't paying child support as ordered but was giving money directly to the kids. Finman said that this was an objective description, but the other lawyer got off track by saying that Finman's client was "being a 'Disney World dad' and was making the mom into the 'bad guy.'" This lawyer had good intentions but didn't know how to communicate in a way that would avoid infuriating his client. Sometimes after an interaction like this, Finman talks with the colleague, saying that lawyers should be good role models and leaders and express as little judgment as possible.

Repeated Problems with Certain Lawyers. Some lawyers are generally difficult to work with for various reasons. Some sincerely intend to be cooperative, but they lack self-awareness and don't realize that their behavior often stimulates negative reactions. Other lawyers have only a superficial interest in being cooperative. They will do so only if it is in their partisan advantage. Although this is normal in positional negotiation, it is inconsistent with the spirit of Collaborative and Cooperative Practice, which are premised on using interest-based negotiation.

These situations are obviously harder to deal with than misunderstandings or one-time problems. You may find it especially difficult to deal with such generally uncooperative lawyers if you expect to work with them again. Although you may have an incentive to improve relationships with such lawyers and minimize future problems, it may also feel risky to try to address the issues directly because this could further aggravate your relationships.

If you want to try to change the approach of such generally uncooperative lawyers, there are several ways you might do so. First and foremost, consider what you might have contributed to the strained relationship. This can be hard when you think the other person is responsible for most of the problems. However, you might cause an important shift by that person if you take the initiative to acknowledge your contribution, even by simply saying, "I reacted (too) strongly when you did X." Under the norm of reciprocity, this may prompt the other lawyer to acknowledge some of his or her contributions and how you might work together to avoid problems in the future.

When working with difficult colleagues, you might want to invite them to go out to lunch and, in the course of a normal conversation, ask them about their perspectives about legal practice. If they seem open to hearing feedback, you might ask if they would like to hear your experience in working with them. If you don't have any cases pending with each other at that time, they may feel less need to be defensive. Obviously, your feedback should be framed so that they know you intend it to be helpful. You might find that they are sincerely surprised, as they might believe that their behavior is generally quite cooperative. If they are interested to hear more, you could describe specific behaviors of theirs, your reactions, and suggestions for other ways they might act in future cases. Don't forget to ask them for feedback about their experience in working with you.

In some extreme cases, lawyers might hire a mediator or coach to help them resolve their own conflicts. For example, Shelly Finman mediated a case in which two family lawyers had a long-standing relationship that interfered with their ability to represent their clients properly when they were on opposite sides. The mediation was quite successful in helping them get past their lingering conflict and work together productively in the future. This may be an unusual situation, as most lawyers would probably be unwilling to hire a mediator to resolve such conflicts. Lawyers are more likely to seek informal advice about how to deal with lawyers they have a hard time with, or to have a respected colleague mediate informally. Finman has performed these roles in a number of situations.

Local Collaborative or Cooperative Practice groups have the potential to deal constructively with lawyers whom others find to be generally uncooperative. As members of a group get to know one another, they can better understand each others' style of practice. Respected members of the group may function as informal coaches or mediators to help deal with these problems. Indeed, these groups might create an explicit procedure or expectation that one of the functions of the group would be to help work out such problems. Again, such efforts are likely to be most effective if lawyers perceived as problematic are approached respectfully and with a spirit of open and sincere inquiry.

None of the strategies described in this chapter will avoid or solve all problems in negotiation. In some cases, people are not ready to settle, sometimes for very good reasons. And some lawyers are not ready to shift their mind-set to be cooperative. However, these suggested strategies are likely to prevent and resolve many difficult negotiation problems in a principled and respectful way that protects clients' interests.

Endnotes

1. MODEL RULE OF PROF'L CONDUCT 2.1 states: "In representing a client, a lawyer shall exercise independent professional judgment and render candid advice." Comment 1 to the Rule states:

> A client is entitled to straightforward advice expressing the lawyer's honest assessment. Legal advice often involves unpleasant facts and alternatives that a client may be disinclined to confront. In presenting advice, a lawyer endeavors to sustain the client's morale and may put advice in as acceptable a form as honesty permits. However, a lawyer should not be deterred from giving candid advice by the prospect that the advice will be unpalatable to the client.

Engaging Additional Professionals | 8

Lawyers and clients need help from other professionals to resolve some issues in negotiation. Professionals can provide factual or legal analysis to help with decision-making and/or help the negotiation process work better. This chapter describes types of professionals that lawyers commonly engage and some issues related to using them.

When and How to Engage Professionals

Some preliminary questions are whether and when to engage professionals at all. Many parties use additional professionals as needed in what is sometimes called a "referral model." In these situations, the parties may believe that the lawyers can provide most of the professional assistance that they need or can afford. From this perspective, the clients hold off engaging additional professionals unless and until they determine that it would be worthwhile.

Some lawyers, particularly some offering Collaborative Practice, believe that parties benefit from assembling a team of professionals from the outset of the case. This approach normalizes the use of these professionals instead of signaling that there is a problem or that there is something wrong with the parties that requires the engagement of additional professionals. Some lawyers think that Collaborative Practice (especially when using a full team from the outset) is a specialized process that should be used primarily for high-conflict cases and may be "overkill" for less difficult cases. Others believe that even parties with moderate conflict can benefit greatly from a Collaborative team approach.

When using a full team, parties can—paradoxically—save both time and money if the professionals are involved early and prevent issues from escalating into major disputes. Parties can save money if they meet separately with some members of the professional team, especially if the other professionals have lower billing rates than the lawyers. To make this model work properly, members of the professional team need to keep each other informed of developments throughout the case. Obviously, this approach reduces costs for parties if the savings exceed the additional costs. Even if using a team from the outset costs more in a given case than a referral model, some parties may value the extra service and believe that it is worth the extra cost. To make the team model work properly, the professionals must manage the process well and avoid duplication of services. Especially in more difficult cases, it is important that the professionals are highly skilled in dealing with conflict and are competent in their specialties.

Marshall Yoder, of Wharton Aldhizer & Weaver, says that in his area, parties in Collaborative divorces normally use a referral model rather than a full team approach from the outset. Most parties have modest means, and it doesn't make financial sense to use a full team unless they have a lot of conflict, although his preference is to include other professionals if possible. Some clients are hesitant to use coaches because they associate them with mental health issues, even though he advises them otherwise. He finds that the mental health and financial professionals have done "fantastic work" with his clients, and he selectively refers clients to them when needed. In one case, Yoder and the other lawyer discounted their rates so that the clients could afford to hire a coach, which "made a huge difference," got them "unstuck," and eventually led to the resolution of the dispute. Unfortunately, clients in a referral model often do not hire coaches until after the attorneys have already spent a lot of time on non-legal issues.

Planned negotiation processes especially lend themselves to use of *jointly retained neutral* professionals, who can provide impartial services, avoid or reduce adversarial "battles of the experts," and save parties money. A virtue of a planned negotiation is that parties are more likely to use neutral experts when appropriate, and the parties can coordinate their decisions about such issues. In planned negotiations, parties may decide to use individually retained professionals instead of or in addition to jointly retained experts. Even when parties do use separate professionals, the parties can reduce the level of mutual fear by agreeing to inform each other that they will use separate professionals, even if they do not disclose the separate information or advice they receive.

In PEN processes, negotiators should carefully plan the services they hire experts to perform. For example, Los Angeles mediator and Collaborative lawyer Forrest Mosten suggests that negotiators should instruct experts to report a range of possible values or options, rather than a single one. The report should describe any variables that would affect the conclusion, possibly indicating which are likely to be most critical. This kind of report engages people in the negotiation and thus helps them to think more creatively. Cleveland lawyer James Skirbunt agrees, noting that there is a common illusion that there is a single right answer, but he says that, in fact, there is some discretion by the experts, which results in a range of legitimate results.

Unlike litigation, where dueling experts are advocates for their positions and don't solve problems, a joint neutral expert can be an important part of a problem-solving team. Skirbunt had a divorce case where a business owned by the couple had declined in value. The parties agreed that the wife would get a "tag-along" partnership interest, and that there would be certain triggering events when she could liquidate her interest. He said that it was very helpful to have a single expert help structure the deal, including by suggesting possible triggers for liquidation.

Types of Professionals

Mediators. Although collegial lawyers often can successfully manage a dispute resolution process without professional assistance, sometimes parties can benefit from using mediators. Mediators help parties reach agreement but do not have the authority to impose a decision if the parties do not settle. Thus it is possible that the parties will not resolve a matter through mediation, though parties in mediated cases generally settle at least half of their cases during mediation or soon afterward. Even when parties do not settle in mediation, the process can help clarify the issues and lead to later settlement.

Using mediation can be helpful because even when lawyers are working cooperatively, it can be hard to fully escape the adversarial dynamics when lawyers separately represent adverse parties. This can be especially difficult when the parties do not trust each other very much, they have an intense conflict, and/or the disputed issues are especially challenging. In these situations, parties may be suspicious of the other lawyer, even regarding apparently innocuous procedural issues.

Using mediators can avoid or reduce these problems because the mediators are neutral and can impartially manage the process and improve communication. Indeed, mediators typically meet separately with each side (in a procedure called "caucusing") to have confidential conversations so that the parties can openly discuss their concerns. Caucusing allows parties to avoid the risk of disclosing sensitive information that they fear the other side would try to exploit. Mediators can help the parties develop realistic assessments of the likely outcomes in negotiation and litigation and coach them to negotiate most effectively based on an understanding of each side's perspectives. In some cases, parties would completely lose opportunities to make mutually advantageous agreements if they didn't have mediators to help with the negotiation. Even when parties could settle without mediation, mediators can help them reach more satisfactory agreements.

Many states and courts have adopted statutes and rules providing broader protections for communications in mediation than in unmediated negotiation. If such protections would be important for your client or both parties, engaging a mediator would provide these protections in addition to the other benefits of mediation.

Social scientists have found that mediation helps solve difficult problems for lawyers, including "how to pursue both negotiation and trial preparation; how to encourage client participation in case preparation while retaining one's professional authority; how to provide clients with legal advice while addressing vitally important nonlegal issues; and how to structure and manage cases so that they can be moved predictably and expeditiously."[1]

Bruce Whitney, the former chief litigation counsel of Air Products and Chemicals, loved using mediation because the client can have a "day in court" with no rules of engagement, look the other side directly in the eye, and work out a solution. Stradley Ronon's Ben Picker says that as a mediator, his job is to make sure that the parties and lawyers do a good analysis and risk assessment. He wants to make sure that they avoid cognitive errors that cause overconfidence, such as selective perception and self-serving bias. Picker asks them to think about "what the world will look like" if they do settle and if they don't. He helps them get a more complete analysis, not only including the legal issues but also "looking behind the dispute" to analyze what is really going on and what the real differences are between the parties. Whitney valued mediators who recognized that the facts and the client's equity position were the most important factors in disputes. He says that the law is a useful framework for discussion in commercial disputes but not the most important factor in dispute resolution. He would get frustrated with mediators and outside lawyers who thought that the law was the "be-all and end-all" in resolving disputes.

Mediators differ in their goals and techniques. In particular, some mediators give their assessments of strengths and weaknesses of cases, predict likely court outcomes, suggest options and recommendations for resolution, and even press parties to change their positions. These techniques are sometimes called "evaluative" or "directive" (as opposed to "facilitative" or "elicitive"). Some professionals believe that some or all of the evaluative techniques may be counterproductive. For example, Sevilla Claydon, of Garvey Schubert Barer, has worked with mediators who have actually hindered communication because they said that "it's all about money" and focused only on settlement. One mediator told her, "I don't care about their feelings—I just want a number." On the other hand, sometimes the negotiators really *do* just want to focus on the money, and mediators who focus the discussion on the parties' communication and relationship can be just as frustrating.

Sometimes the parties may want validation from a mediator. James Skirbunt said that in several cases, he was asked by the court to help the lawyers resolve the case. The only thing he did was to say that the offer on the table was reasonable and within the range of fairness. All the negotiators needed to hear was that it was a good deal and it was okay to take it. Just that validation was enough to help them settle. In cases involving large organizations, sometimes negotiators may want the mediator's validation that a settlement is reasonable so that they can "sell" it to their superiors back in the office.

You should work with mediators, lawyers, and the parties to tailor the process for particular cases. You should begin these conversations before all the negotiators convene for the mediation, and you may continue them during a mediation session as appropriate.

It is especially important to prepare your clients for mediation sessions, as they may not be familiar with the process at all, or their experiences may be quite different from the approach that will be used in the present case. You should help them develop a clear understanding of the process, the issues, and their real interests. They are likely to hear things that they will disagree with, and the mediator or the other side may ask them challenging questions. They should be prepared to change their positions based on what they learn in mediation. The discussion of preparing clients for negotiation in Chapter 5 is also relevant to preparing them for mediation. The Task Force on Improving Mediation Quality of the ABA's Section of Dispute Resolution issued a report with helpful suggestions about preparing for and participating in mediation.[2]

Financial Professionals and Appraisers. Many cases involve complex financial issues that require technical analysis to help parties and lawyers understand the issues and make informed decisions. There is a wide range of financial issues and professionals, some of whom can provide several different types of services. Some professionals provide analysis and advice, including collecting and analyzing data, developing financial options, considering potential tax consequences, and making recommendations. For example, some financial professionals focus specifically on certain matters, such as advice in tax, estate planning, or divorce matters. Some professionals may appraise certain assets. Some professional appraisers specialize in certain types of assets, such as businesses and commercial or residential real estate. Financial professionals can be especially helpful in divorce cases to advise couples about dividing a single marital estate and income stream into two. Many financial professionals have a general mind-set as a neutral technical advisor, so they often work well as jointly retained neutral experts. Accountants who have been working for the parties are often very good in this role, although some parties may be suspicious of potential bias and so may want to retain a different accountant.

Technical Experts. Technical experts are used in many types of litigation, and their input can help parties and lawyers in negotiation as well. For example, scientists, engineers, realtors, doctors, statisticians, economists, vocational experts, and actuaries are used in various types of litigation to establish critical facts. Because expectations about possible outcomes of litigation can affect negotiation, as described in Chapter 5, these same facts are typically critical in negotiation. Obtaining credible input in negotiation can help parties resolve difficult factual disputes. Even if the parties retain separate experts, they may engage the experts in the negotiation to help understand and resolve differences of expert opinion. If the parties will (or might) have a continuing relationship in the future, the experts may recommend options to handle the technical issues optimally. For example, when parties in divorce cases use vocational experts to assess a party's earning capacity, the expert can also recommend strategies for the party to gain employment or develop his or her career.

Mental Health Professionals. Lawyers and parties in family cases use mental health professionals in various capacities to help parties deal with the sometimes traumatic disruptions of family life. In Collaborative and Cooperative cases, lawyers recommend that clients use "coaches"—sometimes called "communication consultants"—to help parties deal constructively with painful issues in negotiation. Typically, coaches focus on issues between the parties, but sometimes there are tensions between lawyers or other team members, and the coaches can help work through them too.

Coaches may meet separately with each party, jointly with both parties, jointly with the lawyers (possibly including other members of a professional team), or jointly with the parties and the entire team. Coaches sometimes work with the parties without the lawyers present. This can help parties bond with the coaches and establish their role as key members of the team. Meeting without the lawyers obviously reduces the parties' costs, especially where the work does not require the lawyers' expertise. Having parties meet separately with the coach also helps them develop a strong relationship with the parties, which can make the coaches more effective if the parties have difficulties later in the case.

James Skirbunt has used coaches with great success. He had a large Collaborative divorce case where one of the assets was an auto dealership. At the first meeting, which took place without a coach, the parties did some exercises where they set out their visions and hopes for the future. Skirbunt said that the parties couldn't communicate well and it was an awful meeting, despite the fact that the lawyers were highly skilled and did everything they could. The parties then hired a communication coach who helped them so much that the couple reconciled. Not only that, the husband was so impressed with the coach that he hired her to coach his sales staff.

Within the Collaborative community, there are different philosophies about whether it is generally better to use a single coach for both parties or separate coaches for each party. A single coach for both parties is a neutral professional helping both parties. Of course, a single coach costs less than two coaches. On the other hand, some parties prefer to have separate coaches who are both committed to constructive negotiation and whom the parties can confide in without the coach having the same commitment to the other party. Using two coaches may exacerbate adversarial dynamics, however.

When couples are in conflict about issues relating to their children, it can be helpful to engage child specialists to assess the situation and help the parents get a better understanding of what would—and would not—help children as they live through their parents' conflict and separation. Usually, the child specialists meet separately with the children and, if requested, talk with other key people in the children's lives, such as their teachers. The specialists are trained to elicit valid information in ways that do not aggravate the children's difficulties, as can happen when parents or lawyers talk with them about sensitive issues. The specialists can provide their information to the parents, lawyers, and other team members in a constructive way to help the parents resolve the conflicts.

Outside Evaluators. Some parties need to get expert opinions about their legal cases before they are ready to settle a dispute. Often, this is due to parties' or lawyers' conflicting expectations about a likely trial verdict in the event the parties do not agree. Negotiators may make sharply different predictions because the outcome is uncertain and/or they make faulty analyses. In these situations, negotiators may value getting a neutral evaluation from a respected expert. Some experienced lawyers, retired judges, and other experts regularly offer this service. Others are asked to give their opinions on an ad hoc basis. Negotiators may ask for such "second opinions" to be used privately by one side or shared between both sides, depending on the circumstances. Sometimes sitting judges provide this service for negotiators through informal consultations or more formal settlement conferences.

When people hire professionals to furnish evaluations, they agree about what information will be provided to the evaluators (e.g., documents and/or oral presentations) and the form of the evaluation. Evaluations may include an analysis of the strengths and weaknesses of each side's arguments about various issues.

Some parties may prefer to use evaluations from separately engaged experts, particularly if the parties have previously hired them and trust them. In this situation, you might invite the experts to the negotiation and ask them to discuss their analyses so that they can identify the reasons for the differences between them. The parties and lawyers might just watch this discussion and afterward consult privately with their experts to help the negotiators identify the real differences between them and make more realistic assessments.

When evaluators provide well-reasoned and persuasive opinions, one or more negotiators may revise their analysis to become more realistic. Even if the disputing parties do not accept the evaluators' specific conclusions, injection of the neutral evaluation can affect the dynamic of the negotiation and encourage negotiators to have more realistic expectations.

Forrest Mosten sometimes uses what he calls a "confidential mini-evaluation." The evaluator provides an oral report in a short time so that the parties can proceed promptly in negotiation. Appendix S is a sample form for a stipulation to use a mini-evaluation.

Some courts offer "early neutral evaluation" (or "ENE") programs, which are specifically designed to provide negotiators with realistic analyses early in a case. These programs have procedures for selecting evaluators and conducting the evaluations. In some programs, the neutrals not only provide evaluations but may also mediate to help negotiators reach agreement. Sometimes the neutrals may help the negotiators plan litigation by identifying key factual and legal issues and suggesting ways that they can efficiently clarify those issues (such as taking depositions of particular individuals or obtaining legal rulings focusing on specific issues) and then try to settle the matter.

Private Adjudicators. Most people, including many litigators, generally recommend going to trial only as a last resort because of the expense, risk, adversarial dynamics, adverse publicity, and other disadvantages of trial. Although parties and lawyers generally prefer to negotiate settlements with the other side (if only "on the courthouse steps" shortly before trial), sometimes they find that possible settlement would not be satisfactory. They may conclude that, even after diligent and skillful negotiation, there is no "zone of possible agreement" as described in Chapter 5. Even when such a zone theoretically exists, negotiators may not actually reach a settlement because of unreasonable demands, antagonism between the negotiators, miscalculation, poor handling of negotiation, and inability to agree on how to allocate any savings that might be generated by settlement. So some parties may prefer to take their chances with a binding decision from a neutral adjudicator.

Parties who want to resolve disputes through adjudication have various choices. Before or after a dispute arises, they can agree to have a private arbitrator (or panel of arbitrators) decide the case. Using arbitrators rather than going to court enables parties to choose arbitrators who have specific expertise and are acceptable to both sides. Using arbitration also gives parties more control over the procedure. Many experts have sharply criticized arbitration as having become too complex and expensive—resembling litigation too much—and efforts have been made to streamline arbitration procedures to make it more efficient.[3] Using arbitration increases the likelihood of getting prompt enforcement of decisions because of the limited grounds for vacating arbitration awards.

Of course, this can be a great benefit, but it can also be problematic if you believe that an arbitration award is seriously flawed in ways that could be corrected on appeal if a court made the same decision. To avoid this problem, parties can jointly ask courts to appoint special masters (sometimes called "private judges") who may use procedures similar to arbitration, but parties preserve the right to appeal. The master makes a recommendation that the court can adopt as its judgment and which can then be appealed.

Parties establish an arbitration by contract and thus have great control over the process. To limit the risk of extremely unfavorable awards, the parties can make a "high-low" agreement establishing upper and lower bounds of the eventual arbitration award. For example, the parties could agree that the award would be no less than $100,000 and no greater than $2 million. In that situation, for example, if the arbitrator made a $5 million award, the defendant would be liable for only $2 million.

"Final offer" arbitration is another variation that limits the risk of extreme decisions. In this procedure, at the end of the arbitration proceeding, each party privately submits a final offer to the arbitrator, who can make an award only by accepting one of the offers without modification. This creates an incentive for each side to moderate its offer to increase the chance that the arbitrator would pick its offer. This is sometimes called "baseball arbitration," because it is used to resolve disputes over baseball players' compensation.

A variation called "mediation-arbitration" ("med-arb") can be helpful in some cases. The med-arbitrator begins by mediating, and if the parties reach impasse, the med-arbitrator "switches hats" to become an arbitrator and make a binding arbitration award. This procedure has the advantage of ensuring that there will be a binding decision in case the parties do not reach a settlement. Although parties could hire a separate arbitrator if there is no agreement in mediation, med-arb is more efficient because it avoids the need to hire a second neutral (the arbitrator) and conduct a second proceeding. Med-arb can be risky because the med-arbitrator can impose a binding decision based on information that one side provided in caucus that the other side didn't hear and couldn't respond to. Thus parties should use med-arbitration only if they have great confidence in the professional who would serve in that role.

Arbitration-mediation (or "arb-med") is a process where arb-mediators conduct arbitration proceedings and write awards without immediately disclosing them to the parties. After that, the arb-mediators attempt to mediate so that the parties can reach an agreement and thus retain some control over the outcome. If the parties cannot reach agreement, they are assured of having a binding resolution, as the arb-mediators would issue the award. This procedure has the advantage over med-arbitration in that, before deciding on the award, the arb-mediators would not caucus with the parties and thus would not be influenced in making awards by having ex parte conversations. On the other hand, when mediating, arb-mediators may effectively steer the parties to agree to the decision that they have already made.

In family matters, parents who have great difficulty resolving parenting issues may use a specialized form of med-arb called "parenting coordination." Parenting coordinators are neutral experts on parenting issues who may interview the parents, children, and others as appropriate. They typically try to help improve communication, educate the parents about the children's needs, and mediate disputes about the children. They may be authorized to make recommendations to a court or make decisions within the scope of a court order or contract with the parents.

Public Adjudicators. A fully contested trial in court is the paradigmatic form of adjudication in U.S. society. Trial is a legitimate and important dispute resolution procedure, guaranteed as a constitutional right under federal and state constitutions. Parties use forms of court adjudication instead of or in addition to trial. Court rulings on pretrial motions can play a valuable role in leading to settlement. For example, rulings on motions for preliminary injunctions, discovery disputes, summary judgment, and evidence that may not be admitted at trial can clarify the likely trial outcome and help narrow the bargaining range. In addition, merely scheduling a hearing on a motion may motivate parties to settle as they anticipate the risk of an unfavorable ruling.

Though this may sound paradoxical, you can work together with your counterpart lawyer to use courts as tools for cooperation. Judges can provide influential opinions, much like private experts, except that the judges are more authoritative and don't charge fees. For example, David Hoffman, of the Boston Law Collaborative, has had cases where both sides agreed on some issues but not others, and they developed a joint pretrial memo outlining the issues. He finds that judges like this procedure because they can focus on serious legitimate disputes instead of the extreme and unrealistic advocacy positions they have to deal with too often.

In a divorce case, both lawyers may recognize that one party may need to get a temporary order setting out the child support and custody arrangements during litigation and, only after getting such a ruling, be ready to negotiate. One lawyer describes this as "reality therapy." In this situation, the adversarial hearing can be the precursor to productive negotiation rather than bitter and prolonged litigation. Fort Myers, Florida, lawyer Shelly Finman described a case where the lawyers had a hard time with both their clients. The parties had a parenting coordinator who told the lawyers that the parents were not willing to cooperate to do the right thing for the kids. The lawyers and parenting coordinator jointly asked the judge to set a hearing and give the parents a "scared straight" lecture, threatening to put the kids in foster care if the parents didn't change their behavior. This had a major impact on the parents, who did, indeed, improve their behavior.

Sometimes lawyers can cooperate in invoking a litigation procedure, such as a deposition or court hearing, with the goal of prompting lawyers and parties to negotiate and avoid the cost and hassle of the litigation procedure. For example, Shelly Finman might tell a colleague that his (Finman's) client isn't going to timely respond to a discovery request and may need some incentive to comply, and invite the colleague to send a respectful letter explaining the consequences, possibly including a motion to compel a response to the request. In this situation, Finman is disclosing something that the other side would soon learn anyway, but by disclosing it to his colleague in advance, they can try to develop a creative solution together that would satisfy both parties' interests. Lawyers frequently work together this way, though this isn't highly publicized. This strategy raises ethical issues relating to diligence and loyalty, which are discussed in Chapter 10, so you should be careful to comply with your ethical duties.

Even in a contested hearing or trial, you can cooperate with your counterpart by developing a coordinated plan. This can involve narrowing the issues to be argued, identifying expert witnesses to be called, sharing exhibits, and generally informing each other of their plans. Although this goes against a culture where lawyers try to gain advantage by surprising the other side, this is not required by legal ethical rules. Indeed, courts generally try to avoid "trial by ambush," often with rules requiring lawyers to jointly plan litigation and trial. To use litigation as a tool for cooperation, you would work with your counterpart by informing each other of your cooperative intentions and coordinating your actions to achieve their desired results.

Confidentiality and Use of Professionals' Work Product

Lawyers need to work out the details of the engagement of any professionals in a case, including whether the professionals' testimony and/or work product may be used in litigation. In general, prohibiting use of such evidence may promote greater candor by the professionals, as they would have less concern about having to defend statements in litigation. Similarly, parties and others providing information to professionals may feel more comfortable sharing information openly if the professionals' opinions and work product would not be available for litigation.

On the other hand, the potential use of professionals' testimony and work product in litigation could motivate them to be more careful and candid. If the professional is a jointly retained neutral, this arrangement creates incentives for parties to stay in negotiation, because a party dissatisfied with the neutral expert would need to hire partisan experts to fight an uphill battle to discredit the neutral's findings. In addition, if the professionals' opinions and work product would not be admissible, parties might need to hire additional professionals for litigation to duplicate the work of those engaged for negotiation—even if the parties were satisfied with the expert's work. This could obviously increase the cost of litigation, perhaps substantially. This can also create problems if there is a limited pool of qualified professionals.

In any case, the parties and professionals all benefit from having clear expectations and protections about this from the outset of the professionals' engagement. In general, these expectations should be reflected in written agreements signed by the parties. Since parties sometimes do not settle and do proceed to litigation, it is important to have predictable and enforceable arrangements in advance. Obviously, failing to make such arrangements invites disputes if and when parties engage in contested litigation. For a sample agreement for retention of experts, see Appendix R.

There are statutes, rules, and practice norms about use of particular professionals' opinions and work in litigation. For example, some statutes and rules prohibit mediators from testifying in court. On the other hand, if the parties have a court hearing, parenting coordinators who have relevant observations are often expected to testify in court. Obviously, before engaging professionals for negotiation or mediation, lawyers should research applicable authority on this issue.

Continued Engagement after Negotiation Ends

A related issue is whether professionals may continue working for one or both parties after a negotiation ends. In general, it is appropriate to limit professionals' engagement to the negotiation, as this discourages professionals from shading their work in negotiation in the hope of securing additional employment. Thus maintaining this "bright line" can provide more confidence in the professionals' work.

On the other hand, there are situations where it would be appropriate to permit such continued engagement. For example, if a couple hires a child specialist in a Collaborative case who really "clicks" with the family, a strict application of this principle would prevent the family from using the specialist after the Collaborative "case" is over. This would be an unfortunate result, considering that it can be very hard to find professionals who are such a good fit. An intermediate approach would allow for a transition period for the family (such as up to a year after the legal divorce is completed), which allows the professional to assist in the divorce transition and then make referrals for any ongoing therapy needs of the children.

It is important to inform your clients of the limited scope of the services of the various professionals they may be hiring and to consider alternative arrangements. You should make sure that the arrangement selected is accurately reflected in the agreement retaining the professional in question.

Endnotes

1.   Craig A. McEwen et al., *Lawyers, Mediation, and the Management of Divorce Practice*, 28 LAW & SOCIETY REVIEW 149, 150 (1994).

2.   ABA Section on Dispute Resolution, Task Force on Improving Mediation Quality, Final Report 12 (2006–2008), *available at* http://www.abanet.org/dispute/documents/FinalTaskForceMediation.pdf. For a short summary, *see* John Lande, Doing The Best Mediation You Can, 14 DISPUTE RESOLUTION MAGAZINE 43 (Spring/Summer 2008).

3.   COLLEGE OF COMMERCIAL ARBITRATORS, PROTOCOLS FOR EXPEDITIOUS, COST-EFFECTIVE COMMERCIAL ARBITRATION: KEY ACTION STEPS FOR BUSINESS USERS, COUNSEL, ARBITRATORS & ARBITRATION PROVIDER INSTITUTIONS (2010).

Improving the Quality of Your Negotiation 9

Getting Training and Education
Getting Systematic Feedback
  on Your Performance
Revising Your Practices

You presumably want to provide the best possible service to your clients, but this can be very challenging, as described in the preceding chapters. Clients normally engage lawyers when they consider matters to be important, face substantial uncertainty and conflict, must grapple with situations governed by legal rules that are often complex and confusing, and worry about litigation costs. They generally would prefer to settle than become embroiled in a long legal proceeding, but they worry about "losing" if they negotiate. Not surprisingly, you probably have clients who are very anxious, and you may "take on" some of their anxieties. Indeed, you and your clients may feel caught in a "prison of fear," described in Chapter 1.

Many lawyers' adversarial mind-sets have become so deeply ingrained that adversarial tactics become the default behavior, even sometimes when it is clearly counterproductive. A mediator described a case involving a lawyer who aspired to be collaborative but struggled with it. In this case, the lawyer had worked hard to get the other side to agree to mediate. The lawyer represented an employee who sued the employer, claiming race discrimination. In her opening statement in mediation, the lawyer talked about the employer's alleged historical connections to the Ku Klux Klan more than a hundred years earlier—and the mediation "went downhill from there." Although the lawyer's heart was in the right place, she "blew" the mediation without intending to do so. The mediator said, "As much as she talks the talk, she hadn't learned to walk the talk. Not surprisingly, she defaulted to what she knew, which was to enter the ring punching." Negotiation is hard work, even for experienced lawyers, and so Cleveland lawyer James Skirbunt, who has been in practice for 35 years, encourages lawyers to be gentle with themselves.

The suggestions in this book are designed to help you and your clients effectively deal with often-unconscious fears and habits to achieve your clients' goals as well as possible. As described in the preceding chapters, you are likely to provide high-quality service if you develop good relationships with your clients and counterpart lawyer, establish and use negotiation procedures designed to satisfy the parties' interests, and use additional professionals, as appropriate. To perform well, you need to develop good skills in a wide range of lawyering tasks through a combination of education, training, and experience. These skills include communication, interviewing, counseling, negotiating, problem solving, procedural planning, legal research and analysis, advocacy, and drafting. Of course, your actions should be informed by a good understanding of the applicable legal rules, procedures, and norms in your cases.

Getting Training and Education

Even if you have outstanding natural skills, you will improve your practice through continued learning. To negotiate at the highest skill levels, lawyers need substantial and repeated training, opportunities to practice their skills, and reflection on their experiences. Mediation and Collaborative Practice trainings can be especially helpful. You may find mediation training to be particularly helpful to step out of your perspective as an advocate so that you can better understand both sides of a dispute. Mediation trainings teach numerous procedures and techniques to structure negotiations and resolve difficult problems. You can benefit from taking multiple trainings because of the differences in mediation philosophies and techniques that various trainers and mediators use. Collaborative Law trainings offer similar benefits, though explicitly from the advocates' perspective. Attending continuing legal education programs and conferences can also be quite helpful.

As the director of an LL.M. program in dispute resolution, I would be remiss if I didn't suggest that you consider enrolling in an academic program. Obviously, they involve a greater investment of time and money than continuing education and training programs, but they offer greater benefit as well. Many of the students in my program come with 10–20 years or more of experience as advocates and neutrals, and I used to worry whether they got any benefit from it. I have been repeatedly reassured that even some of our brightest students said, in effect, that after completing our program, they now understand what they had been doing all those years. Gaining a deeper theoretical understanding of dispute resolution practice can provide you with a wider range of choices in how you practice.

One of the advantages of enrolling in an academic program is that it creates a structure and provides incentives for careful study. For many lawyers, it is not practical to enroll in another program after four years of college and three years of law school. If this wouldn't fit into your life, you might create your own self-study program, perhaps starting with materials listed in the bibliography of this book.

You can also improve your work by developing a philosophy of practice, such as those described in Chapter 2. Having such a philosophy can help you grapple with difficult judgment calls and develop self-confidence, which can make you more effective working with clients, lawyers, and courts.

Getting Systematic Feedback on Your Performance

Many lawyers don't take full advantage of their experience to improve their performance. If you don't consciously focus on how you perform, you are likely to miss important learning opportunities. Some say that the worst thing lawyers can do is to win their first trial because it makes them complacent about their skills. A spectacular failure at trial, negotiation, or other process can cause you to seriously reflect about your performance and how you might improve it in the future. Even if you are successful, there are probably things you might have done better. And when you are successful, it is important for you to understand what led to that success. You are likely to gain some valuable insights if you take a little time to write out what happened, what you did well, and what you might have done better. Appendixes U and V are self-assessment forms you can use or adapt. These forms are likely to be most helpful for lawyers doing a process that is new for them, although even experienced practitioners continue to learn throughout their careers.

After you complete cases, you can regularly seek client feedback about how you handled them. Although it may feel odd, and perhaps a bit scary, to solicit client feedback, this can be the source of important insights to help improve your service in future cases. Many clients will be flattered that you asked for their feedback, as it reflects your concern about their perspectives, and this may build loyalty and goodwill. If you identify previously unexpressed frustrations, you can adjust your practices, and this may encourage your clients to hire you again in the future rather switching to other lawyers.

You can get client feedback through surveys or interviews. Each method has advantages and disadvantages. Surveys can collect feedback from a larger number of clients, especially with convenient online survey programs. On the other hand, many clients may not want to take the time to respond, or will give only superficial responses. Some clients may feel uncomfortable disclosing their reactions, fearing that it could alienate you. If the survey is intended to be anonymous, clients may nonetheless worry that you will figure out which client provided which responses, especially if they are critical. One way to minimize this risk would be to inform clients that you are doing this every quarter for all clients who completed a case in the prior quarter.

Some clients would be more comfortable giving feedback through interviews, as they can gauge how their feedback is being received. Using interviews may encourage a more representative sample of clients to provide feedback, but it requires more time. You or others in your firm might conduct these interviews, or, if you want to invest more in the process, you might hire outside professionals who can provide more independence. Some clients may feel uncomfortable expressing criticisms directly to lawyers who handled their cases, so they might more honest in interviews conducted by others.

Survey or interview questions can include basic open questions asking what worked well in the representation and what might be improved. In addition to such general questions, you might ask about specific aspects of the handling of the case, such as satisfaction with the information provided, communications, legal advice, negotiation, litigation proceedings, interactions with the other side, results achieved, attorney's fees, and interaction with office staff, among other things. If the questions are asked with sincere openness to whatever reactions the clients have, you can get some valuable feedback that can help you improve your performance in future matters. Sometimes a simple phone call after the end of the process may be the most direct, cost-effective way of getting meaningful feedback. Some lawyers use a surrogate, such as a trained legal secretary or another attorney, to get more candid information from the client. Appendix W is a sample client questionnaire that can be used for surveys or interviews.

You can also solicit feedback from professionals with whom you have worked on a case, possibly including judges. In some Collaborative Practice communities, the professionals routinely debrief each other after each meeting and after finishing a case together. Even where this is not a normal practice, you can take the initiative to ask colleagues for observations and ideas about how you might perform better in the future. It may seem inappropriate or feel uncomfortable to ask judges, colleagues, and even opposing counsel to provide such feedback. Indeed, you should consider carefully whether the risks outweigh the likely benefits. Taking some risks can pay off with valuable insights and strengthened relationships, however, so this is worth considering.

A safer option might be to participate in peer or supervised consultation groups with lawyers and other dispute resolution professionals. Such groups provide the opportunity to deeply explore challenging problems in a confidential environment.[1] For example, Los Angeles mediator and Collaborative lawyer Forrest Mosten leads such a group, and the ADR Program of the U.S. District Court for the Northern District of California runs a number of such groups. Although these groups cater to mediators, similar groups can focus on lawyers' work.

Some Collaborative Practice groups provide formal or informal mentoring for members. One lawyer thinks that these groups can help lawyers train themselves and each other to develop a more intentional practice. As a trainer, she encourages clients to go through a continuing process of self-awareness, observation, and self-correction. Having a support system can provide feedback and hold you accountable in an ongoing learning process. The goal would be to make your decisions more self-conscious and explicit. Over time, you can change default behavior and embed new skills and habits in your practice.

Revising Your Practices

Based on input from clients and professionals, you can revise your case management and negotiation procedures. This may include issues such as information provided on your website or directly to clients, procedures used by support staff, explanation of options for client decision making, explanation of lawyers' actions, explanations of legal procedures, negotiation procedures, and use of particular professionals, among others.

You can also work with your courts to develop good *court* case management systems involving a partnership between lawyers, judges, court administrators, and other professionals. Judges are usually respected leaders who can motivate others in their community to work together. They can convene representatives of stakeholder groups to design systems for handling the issues they regularly encounter. These systems might involve some or all of the following: case assessment and referral protocols, educational materials and resource directories for parties (especially unrepresented parties), procedural rules, standard forms, training and mentoring for professionals, ADR programs, and informal mechanisms to deal with professionals' problems.

Court rules requiring cooperation can be an important part of such systems, although it is unlikely that mere promulgation of rules will change lawyers' and parties' behavior. To be effective, lawyers and parties need to believe that the courts take the goals seriously, support those who "get with the program," and sanction those who don't. In serious cases, legal sanctions may be appropriate, but in many cases, public or private admonishments may be at least as effective. Such rules are likely to be most effective if judges are available to help lawyers work through problems informally as appropriate. Courts and local bar associations can co-sponsor continuing education programs and training to promote effective service to parties.

As an example, the family court in Morguson County, Indiana, has a court rule promoting a cooperative system. The rule requires lawyers and parents to "act with the Courts as co-problem-solvers, not mere problem-reporters." It sets an expectation that lawyers and parents consistently display personal responsibility, cooperation, courtesy, and are "focused attention on the children's needs." Parents with children under age 20 are required to use designated websites (such as www.UpToParents.org) to write out commitments they would make about parenting. Parents and counsel are required to make reasonable efforts to resolve problems so that they avoid contested court hearings except in rare circumstances. If both parents are represented, their lawyers are required to consult with each other to resolve any issue before seeking relief from a court.[2] Obviously, this rule is tailored to family court issues, and courts handling other types of cases can fashion rules suiting their particular issues.

Endnotes

1. For a description of peer consultation groups for mediators, *see* Howard Herman & Jeannette P. Twomey, *Training Outside the Classroom: Peer Consultation Groups*, DISPUTE RESOLUTION MAGAZINE, Fall 2005, at 15.

2. Family Court Website, Morguson County, Ind., http://www.familycourtwebsite.org/.

Dealing with Ethical Issues[1] **10**

It's important for lawyers to comply with their ethical rules for many reasons. Clients rely heavily on their lawyers because the clients normally do not have the knowledge, skills, and experience to effectively handle complex, confusing, and risky issues affected by the law. Clients often are "one-shotters" who feel stressed about the legal issues, whereas lawyers are "repeat players" who are professionally detached and don't live with the consequences the way that clients do.

This chapter highlights challenges involved in selected issues that are particularly relevant to planned negotiations. It refers to the Model Rules of Professional Conduct issued by the American Bar Association, which virtually all states have adopted, albeit with some variations. Because the situations are so varied, the ethical rules often are limited to general principles whose application requires careful judgment based on the particular facts in a case. Although the Model Rules reflect generally accepted principles, you should consult the specific ethical rules and opinions applicable in your jurisdiction.

Diligence and Loyalty in Representing Clients' Interests

Based on the 1969 Model Code of Professional Responsibility, many lawyers wrongly believe that they have a duty to represent clients "zealously within the bounds of the law," which they think requires them to be adversarial. This is a misinterpretation of that provision, and in any case it has been superseded in the Model Rules, which were first adopted in 1983.

Model Rule 1.3 requires lawyers to act with "reasonable diligence" in representing clients. A Comment to the Rule states that lawyers must act with "commitment and dedication to the interests of the client and with zeal in advocacy upon the client's behalf. A lawyer is not bound, however, to press for every advantage that might be realized for a client. . . . The lawyer's duty to act with reasonable diligence does not require the use of offensive tactics or preclude the treating of all persons involved in the legal process with courtesy and respect." Certainly some clients may believe that it is in their interest for their lawyers to take tough positions, but others want their lawyers to be conciliatory toward the other side with a goal of reaching an agreement that is in the parties' mutual interests. As the Comment makes clear, lawyers are not required to be adversarial and litigate every possible issue. It is certainly ethical for lawyers to negotiate reasonably and reach agreements.

Loyalty is an "essential element" in lawyers' relationships with their clients, according to a Comment to Rule 1.7, which prohibits conflicts of interests. Inherent in the duties of loyalty and diligence is a clear understanding of who is the client. In a negotiation context, there can be some confusion about lawyers' duties to their clients and the other parties. This may be of particular concern in Collaborative or Cooperative processes where the parties have committed to working together in their mutual interest. Some Collaborative lawyers in divorce cases have identified themselves as lawyers for the family. A Pennsylvania ethics opinion rejects that perspective, stating that lawyers must begin by identifying the specific clients that they represent and that lawyers may not identify themselves as lawyers "for the situation."[2] If clients decide that it is in their interest to resolve issues in a way that the other side believes to be in its interest, lawyers may seek such resolutions. They do so because their clients decide that such solutions are *in the clients' interests*, however, and not because the lawyer owes a duty to the other side. To avoid confusion, many Collaborative and Cooperative lawyers include provisions in negotiation participation agreements stating that each lawyer represents only his or her own client and not the other party.

David Hoffman, of the Boston Law Collaborative, says that biggest challenge he faces is finding the appropriate balance between loyalty to his client's partisan interests and loyalty to his clients' interest in getting a resolution. In practice, this challenge is not so much about the ethical duty of loyalty to the client. Rather, it reflects the difficulty in practical judgment about how best to advance clients' interests, recognizing that clients often have several interests that may conflict. Chapters 2 and 7 suggest strategies for dealing with these difficulties.

Client Decision Making and Informed Consent

Model Rules 1.2 and 1.4 require lawyers to identify and follow clients' wishes about the goals of the representation, communicate regularly with clients, specifically consult with clients about the methods to be used to achieve the clients' goals, and obtain the clients' informed consent regarding specified matters. Rule 1.2(a) states, in relevant part:

[A] lawyer shall abide by a client's decisions concerning the objectives of representation and, as required by Rule 1.4, shall consult with the client as to the means by which they are to be pursued. A lawyer may take such action on behalf of the client as is impliedly authorized to carry out the representation. A lawyer shall abide by a client's decision whether to settle a matter.

Rule 1.4 states:

(a) A lawyer shall:

    (1) promptly inform the client of any decision or circumstance with respect to which the client's informed consent, as defined in Rule 1.0(e), is required by these Rules;

    (2) reasonably consult with the client about the means by which the client's objectives are to be accomplished;

    (3) keep the client reasonably informed about the status of the matter;

    (4) promptly comply with reasonable requests for information; . . .

(b) A lawyer shall explain a matter to the extent reasonably necessary to permit the client to make informed decisions regarding the representation.

Lawyers often define clients' objectives in terms of maximizing recovery or minimizing liability because legal remedies are usually limited to monetary relief, and clients usually want to protect their financial positions. Many clients have important objectives in a matter instead of or in addition to financial goals. These may include protecting reputations, protecting privacy, maintaining relationships, receiving apologies or vindication, and changing policies and procedures, among others. Some lawyers dismiss non-monetary objectives because courts may not be authorized to grant such relief, even though the parties might agree to things that the courts could not order. You should accurately identify how clients define their objectives, which are not necessarily limited to the scope of remedies that courts could order. For example, if clients have an objective of obtaining an apology, lawyers should recognize this.

Moreover, some clients may have objectives about the way a matter is to be handled. Some clients want lawyers to take aggressive positions to express their feelings, punish the other side, or deter other potential adversaries by developing a reputation for hard bargaining. Conversely, some clients may want to start by dealing with the other side through negotiation in the hope of reaching agreements that they consider to be fair to both sides. In both these situations, the clients' preferred approach reflects their objectives and not merely the means of pursuing their objectives. Thus, when inquiring about clients' goals, you should ask about a wide range of objectives and abide by their decisions.

Sometimes lawyers may be tempted to ignore clients' wishes or attempt to dissuade them from pursuing what they believe are unrealistic goals and expectations. In these situations, you should carefully discuss with clients what is realistic to expect. You may or may not conclude that clients have good reasons to pursue their objectives. Given lawyers' duty to abide by their clients' objectives, if you believe that, after consultation, clients have unrealistic objectives that you do not want to pursue, you should follow the procedures for withdrawing from the matter. Ideally, you and your prospective clients would have candid conversations at the outset about potential objectives, and you should decline the representation if you do not wish to pursue the prospective clients' objectives. It is not always possible to anticipate and avoid such conflicts, however, as lawyers' and clients' assessments often change during the course of a matter.

Lawyers usually can distinguish between the objectives of a representation and the means for achieving them, as described in Rule 1.2. There are many decisions that clearly do not set client objectives but simply implement a legal strategy to achieve them. For example, decisions about whether to request or grant time extensions for filing papers, what information to request from or provide to the other side, and what motions, objections, and arguments to make are usually matters of implementing objectives rather than setting them. Although Rule 1.2 requires lawyers to consult clients about implementation, it also authorizes lawyers to take actions that are impliedly authorized by the clients, presumably even without specific consultation. When in doubt, it is generally a good idea to consult with your clients about their preferences.

Informed Consent Generally. The Model Rules require lawyers to obtain clients' informed consent about various decisions. Rule 1.0(e) defines informed consent as "the agreement by a person to a proposed course of conduct after the lawyer has communicated adequate information and explanation about the material risks of and reasonably available alternatives to the proposed course of conduct." Comment 6 to Rule 1.0 states:

The communication necessary to obtain such consent will vary according to the Rule involved and the circumstances giving rise to the need to obtain informed consent. The lawyer must make reasonable efforts to ensure that the client or other person possesses information reasonably adequate to make an informed decision. Ordinarily, this will require communication that includes a disclosure of the facts and circumstances giving rise to the situation, any explanation reasonably necessary to inform the client or other person of the material advantages and disadvantages of the proposed course of conduct and a discussion of the client's or other person's options and alternatives. . . . In determining whether the information and explanation provided are reasonably adequate, relevant factors include whether the client or other person is experienced in legal matters generally and in making decisions of the type involved, and whether the client or other person is independently represented by other counsel in giving the consent.

When the Model Rules require clients' informed consent, they specify the general subjects that lawyers must discuss with clients. Considering that there may be a number of advantages, disadvantages, material risks, and alternative actions for any course of action, informed consent requirements may require substantial discussion. These requirements are appropriate because the decisions requiring informed consent may pose significant risks for clients and/or deviate from general expectations about what lawyers do or do not do. Decisions in which a lawyer is required to obtain clients' informed consent include:

- limiting the scope of representation (Rule 1.2(c))
- revealing information about a client's representation (Rule 1.6(a))
- representing a client when there is a concurrent conflict of interest (Rule 1.7(b))
- entering a business transaction with a client or knowingly acquiring a pecuniary interest adverse to a client (Rule 1.8(a))
- using information relating to a client's representation to the client's disadvantage (Rule 1.8(b))
- representing a person in a matter in which that person's interests are materially adverse to a former client's interests (Rule 1.9(a))

- representing a person in a matter that the lawyer's former firm had previously represented a client with an adverse interest to the person and the lawyer had acquired certain protected information (Rule 1.9(b); see also Rule 1.11(a) for former government lawyers and Rule 1.18 regarding communications with prospective clients)
- representing anyone in connection with a matter in which the lawyer "participated personally and substantially" as a third-party neutral (Rule 1.12(a))
- providing an evaluation of a matter that the lawyer knows or reasonably should know is likely to materially and adversely affect a client's interests (Rule 2.3(b))

Informed Consent for Settlement Counsel and Collaborative Practice. Limiting the scope of representation is particularly relevant to planned early negotiation because the Settlement Counsel and Collaborative Practice processes both limit lawyers' representation by precluding the lawyers from litigating the matters. Informed consent is appropriate for these procedures because they are different from the general perception of lawyers as being available to litigate and because clients face some risk from these procedures. In particular, when clients need to hire new counsel to represent them in litigation, the other side could take advantage of this fact to try to extract significant bargaining advantage, even if the other side has the same limited-scope representation.

David Hoffman described cases where he represented parties as Settlement Counsel, his client did not simultaneously have Litigation Counsel, and the other side had counsel who presumably did not have a limited scope of representation. He and his client had to decide whether to disclose to the other side that he was engaged solely for negotiation. He said that they usually didn't disclose this arrangement because they feared that they would try to take advantage of the fact that his client would need to hire new counsel to litigate. If you undertake a representation as Settlement Counsel or Collaborative lawyer, you should discuss this risk with your clients and proceed only if they give informed consent.

Although there are apparently no ethics opinions specifically dealing with Settlement Counsel process, several ethics opinions discuss informed consent requirements for Collaborative Practice and set high standards for informed consent to use a Collaborative process.[3] For example, a Kentucky opinion requires Collaborative lawyers to advise clients about certain potential risks.

> The client must consent to the limited representation, which means he or she must be advised of the limited nature of the relationship and the implications of the arrangement. For example, obtaining new counsel will entail additional time and cost; the client may feel pressured to settle in order to avoid having to obtain new counsel; and the failure to reach a settlement, necessitating new counsel, is not within the exclusive control of the client—the opponent can effectively disqualify both counsel. The client may be willing to assume these and other risks of the collaborative process but, as previously discussed, the lawyer must communicate sufficient information so that the client has an adequate basis upon which to base such a decision.[4]

A New Jersey opinion also notes significant risks in Collaborative Practice, indicates that Collaborative lawyers have a heightened duty of disclosure, and warns Collaborative lawyers that they must provide clients with a reasonable analysis of the clients' interests regarding possible use of Collaborative Practice, even if this conflicts with the lawyers' interests in getting Collaborative cases:

> [I]t is easy to imagine situations in which a lawyer who practices collaborative law would be naturally inclined to describe [the] risks and benefits to the client in a way that promotes the creation of the relationship, even if the client's interests might be better served by a more traditional form of legal representation. . . . We are not prepared to conclude categorically at this juncture that lawyers who engage in collaborative law would be unable to deal with those conflicts honorably, or could not give the client the information necessary to decide whether to consent to the limitation. But informed consent regarding the limited scope of representation that applies in the collaborative law process is especially demanded, and the lawyer's requirement of disclosure of the potential risks and consequences of failure is concomitantly heightened, because of the consequences of a failed process to the client, or, alternatively, the possibility that the parties could become "captives" to a process that does not suit their needs.[5]

The Kentucky opinion indicates that mere signing of a Collaborative participation agreement is insufficient to constitute informed consent, and that Collaborative lawyers should discuss the Collaborative process with clients and provide an opportunity for them to ask questions.

> Although the collaborative law agreement may touch on these matters [such as advantages and risks of different processes], it is unlikely that, standing alone, it is sufficient to meet the requirements of the rules relating to consultation and informed decision making. The agreement may serve as a starting point, but it should be amplified by a fuller explanation and an opportunity for the client to ask questions and discuss the matter. Those conversations must be tailored to the specific needs of the client and the circumstances of the particular representation. The Committee recommends that before having the client sign the collaborative agreement, the lawyer confirm in writing the lawyer's explanation of the collaborative process and the client's consent to its use.[6]

For discussion of specific factors that suggest the clients may be at risk and that lawyers should discuss with clients, see Chapter 6.[7]

Discussing ADR Options

Although there is no requirement in the Model Rules that lawyers obtain clients' informed consent before proceeding to litigate, lawyers normally should carefully discuss with clients the benefits and risks of litigation and other options for resolving disputes. It is indisputable that litigation poses significant risks. Parties can invest enormous sums in legal costs, plaintiffs may recover nothing, defendants can incur huge liability, the process can drag on for years, litigation can divert parties' attention from more profitable or satisfying activities, parties can be publicly humiliated, relationships can be shattered, etc.

David Hoffman notes that when filing suit, plaintiffs can "open a can of worms with unpredictable consequences because even if they dismiss their suit, the other side may have filed a counterclaim, in which case the plaintiffs cannot unilaterally extricate themselves from the fray." Moreover, the amount of parties' legal costs are affected to a great degree by their adversaries' decisions about how intensely to fight in litigation. Of course, sometimes the expected benefits of litigation outweigh the foreseeable risks, and parties may prefer litigation over other options for handling their disputes. Considering the substantial risks of litigation, you should carefully consult with clients before proceeding.

Under the Model Rules, there is no explicit general requirement for lawyers to discuss ADR options with clients, although it is generally good practice to do so whenever ADR might be appropriate. In a thorough analysis of this issue, Professor Marshall Breger noted four rules implying that lawyers should discuss ADR options with clients. In addition to Rules 1.2(a) and 1.4(b), discussed above, Rule 3.2 states that "[a] lawyer shall make reasonable efforts to expedite litigation consistent with the interests of the client," and Rule 2.1 provides that "[i]n representing a client, a lawyer shall exercise independent professional judgment and render candid advice. In rendering advice, a lawyer may refer not only to law but to other considerations such as moral, economic, social and political factors that may be relevant to the client's situation."[8] Although these provisions do not explicitly *require* lawyers to advise clients about ADR, they certainly suggest that it is appropriate for lawyers to do so.

Some jurisdictions have rules about lawyers' advice to clients regarding dispute resolution options. Such rules typically do not require as much consultation as the informed consent provision of Model Rule 1.2(c). For example, some rules only "encourage" lawyers to discuss dispute resolution options and some rules require such advice only when there is an actual settlement opportunity. Moreover, these rules may not require the careful analysis of advantages, disadvantages, and risks of various dispute resolution options.[9] Of course, you should comply with the letter of any applicable rules in your jurisdiction. Better yet is to comply with the spirit of engaging clients in decisions about how they want to resolve their disputes.

Screening Cases for Appropriateness

Even if clients give informed consent to use a Settlement Counsel or Collaborative process, lawyers can undertake such engagements only if it would be "reasonable" to do so. Rule 1.2(c) states, "A lawyer may limit the scope of the representation if the limitation is reasonable under the circumstances and the client gives informed consent." The Kentucky ethics opinion states, "A lawyer cannot advise a client to use the collaborative process without assessing whether it is truly in the client's best interest." Similarly, a Pennsylvania opinion states that Collaborative lawyers "must consider each client's situation (especially those who are victims of domestic violence) when deciding whether a Rule 1.2(c) limitation on the scope of representation is reasonable and whether [they] can, indeed, provide competent representation to a client under the limited scope of representation."[10] A New Jersey opinion elaborates as follows:

> Whether the limitation that forbids a lawyer engaged in Collaborative Practice from participation in adversarial proceedings is "reasonable" within the meaning of [Rule] 1.2(c) is a determination that must be made in the first instance by the lawyer, exercising sound professional judgment in assessing the needs of the client. If, after the exercise of that judgment, the lawyer believes that a client's interests are likely to be well-served by participation in the collaborative law process, then this limitation would be reasonable and thus consistent with [Rule] 1.2(c). . . .
>
> However, because of the particular potential for hardship to both clients if the collaborative law process should fail and an impasse result, we think it appropriate to give some more specific guidance to the Bar as to when this limitation upon representation is "reasonable" under the circumstances. Thus, given the harsh outcome in the event of such failure, we believe that such representation and putative withdrawal is not "reasonable" if the lawyer, based on her knowledge and experience and after being fully informed about the existing relationship between the parties, believes that there is a significant possibility that an impasse will result or the collaborative process otherwise will fail.[11]

David Hoffman takes this admonition very seriously in assessing clients' ability to bear the cost of hiring successor counsel if a Collaborative case ends without agreement. He advises clients not to choose a Collaborative process if they can't afford to hire successor counsel. So far, he hasn't had to overrule a client's preference for a Collaborative process, but he is prepared to do so if necessary.

Books written by Collaborative experts identify factors regarding appropriateness of Collaborative Practice, including: (1) the motivation and suitability of the parties to participate effectively in a Collaborative process, (2) the trustworthiness of the parties, (3) whether a party is intimidated from participating effectively in the Collaborative process, (4) whether there has been a history of domestic violence between the parties, (5) whether a party has a mental illness, (6) whether a party is abusing alcohol or other drugs, (7) whether the lawyers are suitable for handling the case collaboratively, (8) whether the parties would use professional services in addition to Collaborative legal services, (9) the parties' ability to afford to retain new lawyers if the Collaborative process terminates without agreement, and (10) the parties' views about the risks of disqualification of lawyers and other professionals in the case.[12] The presence of any of these factors does not necessarily preclude lawyers from undertaking a Collaborative representation. Rather, this list can help guide you to comply with your ethical duties in these cases. Indeed, some factors may lead in opposite directions. For example, if one party has a mental illness, that might suggest use of a different process, but if the parties would use skilled Collaborative lawyers and mental health professionals, Collaborative Practice might be the best option under the circumstances.

Lawyers may disagree whether Collaborative Practice is appropriate in difficult cases. Some are more cautious, wanting to protect their clients, and others are more open to clients who have gone through a thorough informed-consent process trying a Collaborative process out of concern that the litigation alternative would be very destructive. These judgments depend on the facts and context of each case, and there is no clear general standard.

The ethical rules suggest that Collaborative lawyers should continue to assess the appropriateness of Collaborative Practice at all times throughout a case. If continued use of the process becomes unreasonable at any time, you may be required to reassess whether the representation is permissible and terminate it if you conclude that it is no longer reasonable. For example, it may not be appropriate to continue in a Collaborative process if the parties have invested substantial time and money, it seems unlikely that they will settle, and if they do not settle, your client would not be able to afford litigation. Another example would be when the lawyers do not realize that a party has a serious mental health problem at the outset of a Collaborative case but discover the problem during the process, and the party refuses to get treatment and act cooperatively. In these situations, under Rule 1.2, lawyers would presumably be required to reassess the case and terminate their representation if it would be unreasonable for their clients to continue.

Avoiding Impermissible Conflicts of Interest

Rule 1.7 of the Model Rules of Professional Conduct requires Collaborative lawyers to screen cases to avoid potential conflicts of interest and obtain clients' informed consent prior to beginning representation. Rule 1.7 provides, in relevant part:

(a) Except as provided in paragraph (b), a lawyer shall not represent a client if the representation involves a concurrent conflict of interest. A concurrent conflict of interest exists if: . . . (2) there is a significant risk that the representation of one or more clients will be materially limited by the lawyer's responsibilities to . . . a third person . . . .

(b) Notwithstanding the existence of a concurrent conflict of interest under paragraph (a), a lawyer may represent a client if:

(1) the lawyer reasonably believes that the lawyer will be able to provide competent and diligent representation to each affected client; . . . ; and

(4) each affected client gives informed consent, confirmed in writing.

Comment 8 to Rule 1.7 states that "a conflict exists if there is a significant risk that a lawyer's ability to consider, recommend or carry out an appropriate course of action for the client will be materially limited by the lawyer's other responsibilities or interests."

An ABA ethics opinion is consistent with this analysis, stating that a "contractual obligation to withdraw [in Collaborative cases] creates on the part of each lawyer a 'responsibility to a third party' within the meaning of Rule 1.7(a)(2)" and concluding that "[r]esponsibilities to third parties constitute conflicts with one's own client only if there is a significant risk that those responsibilities will materially limit the lawyer's representation of the client."[13]

Many Collaborative lawyers use participation agreements to establish contractual obligations to "third persons," namely the other lawyer and party. First, virtually all Collaborative participation agreements include provisions prohibiting lawyers from withholding or misrepresenting relevant information. As noted in Chapter 6, many participation agreements require disclosure of much more information than would be legally discoverable, thus Collaborative lawyers may undertake considerable disclosure obligations to the other party. Second, many Collaborative participation agreements also require Collaborative lawyers to correct mistakes made by the other side. For example, lawyers may be required to inform the other side if the person believes that the other side has made numerical miscalculations or typographical errors, inaccurate factual assumptions, or has relied on legal authorities that have been overruled or superseded. Third, by definition, lawyers obligate themselves to withdraw from a representation if any party, including the opposing party, terminates the Collaborative negotiation. Thus, Collaborative lawyers undertake obligations to third persons, and Rule 1.7 requires lawyers to consider whether they can provide competent and diligent representation to their clients in a Collaborative case.

In some cases, Collaborative lawyers would have an impermissible conflict of interest because they would not be able to provide competent and diligent representation. The appropriateness factors listed in the preceding section would be relevant to this analysis. For example, if you represent a victim of domestic violence who seeks a divorce from her abuser, who has proven to be untrustworthy and would likely seek to take advantage of a Collaborative process, Rule 1.7 would presumably prohibit you from representing the client in a Collaborative process. In that situation, you would be caught in a conflict between protecting the client, who may be harmed by participating in a Collaborative process, and complying with obligations under the Collaborative participation agreement. For some vulnerable clients, merely participating in a process with an intimidating opponent may seriously undermine their ability to assert their interests. Abusers can send subtle signals to victims, which everyone else may miss, threatening the victims if they do not submit to the abusers' demands. In such situations, you might have a difficult problem diligently representing your clients' interests in negotiating an agreement with an unscrupulous adversary. Although it is possible that you could avoid an impermissible conflict of interest, it is a significant risk that you should consider seriously.

Although Rule 1.7 requires a client's informed consent for a lawyer to represent the client in a conflict of interest situation, the client's consent is not sufficient to authorize the representation if the lawyer cannot provide competent and diligent representation. If you can reasonably address the concerns described in this section are reasonably addressed, however, you can undertake a Collaborative representation.

Confidentiality

Rule 1.6 requires that, with only a few exceptions, lawyers protect the confidentiality of "information relating to the representation of a client" unless clients give informed consent to disclose the information. This rule reflects the fact that disclosure of information can have a substantial effect on clients' interests, and it generally prohibits disclosure to anyone. It is particularly important to avoid disclosure to the other side in a matter, as their interests presumably conflict with the clients' interests. Normally, lawyers are very cautious about disclosing information to the other side in a case, sometimes even when it is clearly legally discoverable.

Planned negotiations may reverse the requirement of confidentiality in that parties typically agree to share information, sometimes committing to full disclosure. When such negotiations are appropriate, voluntary disclosure of information makes a lot of sense, as it can build trust and promote efficient resolution of the matter.

Although parties may commit to disclose relevant information, lawyers are still bound by the ethical duty to protect client confidences. Thus, if clients instruct you not to disclose relevant information, you are required to follow your clients' instruction regardless of the agreement with the other side. If, after you discuss with the clients their commitment to disclose the information and they decline to do so, the negotiation agreement may require you to withdraw from your representation, which the ethical rules may permit, as described below.

Various statutes and rules protect against use in litigation of communications in negotiations and mediation, which can enhance the spirit of open disclosure and discussion. Of course, sometimes parties do not reach settlements and they litigate matters that they discussed in negotiation or mediation. You should be familiar with the applicable statutes and rules in your jurisdiction, paying particular attention to any exceptions to these protections.

You should also be aware that merely by participating negotiating sessions with their lawyers, clients may waive the attorney-client evidentiary privilege. Normally, this isn't a problem in traditional arm's-length negotiations, where both sides are very cautious about making disclosures that might be used against them in court. In negotiations where the parties commit to full disclosure, the clients effectively waive the attorney-client privilege regarding statements they make in negotiation that the other side can hear. Although lawyers generally are not called to testify as witnesses about matters where they represent clients, it happens at times, and clients should be aware of and consent to the waiver of this privilege. Appendix G is an information sheet for clients about various privacy issues in Collaborative Law cases.

Truthfulness to Others

Lawyers are generally required to tell the truth, including in negotiation with adverse parties. Rule 4.1 states:

> In the course of representing a client a lawyer shall not knowingly:
>
> (a) make a false statement of material fact or law to a third person; or
>
> (b) fail to disclose a material fact to a third person when disclosure is necessary to avoid assisting a criminal or fraudulent act by a client, unless disclosure is prohibited by Rule 1.6.

Rule 4.1 has a major loophole in that a "material fact" does not include what is generally considered "puffing." A Comment to the Rule states:

> Whether a particular statement should be regarded as one of fact can depend on the circumstances. Under generally accepted conventions in negotiation, certain types of statements ordinarily are not taken as statements of material fact. Estimates of price or value placed on the subject of a transaction and a party's intentions as to an acceptable settlement of a claim are ordinarily in this category. . . .

Similarly, statements of opinion (as opposed to material fact) are not covered by Rule 4.1.

As noted in Chapter 6, parties in planned negotiations may make different agreements about the scope of information that they will exchange and whether they will use an interest-based approach to negotiation. If parties commit to full, voluntary disclosure, in some practice cultures, this may include a commitment not to puff but rather to candidly disclose certain things. These might include parties' assessments of particular issues, willingness to accept certain positions, interests in the matter, expectations and intentions about the future that could affect the other party (such as future business or employment plans), and even some facts that are not legally relevant or discoverable (such as, in a divorce case, whether a party had an affair). Thus, parties may commit to making disclosures greater than lawyers are required to make under the ethical rules. This is relevant to disclosure of information, which requires clients' informed consent, as described above. Compliance with ethical rules and parties' process commitments to be truthful is also relevant to protecting clients' interests, which can be seriously harmed if the other side believes that you or your client have violated on agreement to negotiate and deceived them.

Conflicts with Collaborative Practice Norms

The Collaborative Practice movement has developed extensive written and unwritten protocols, which provide benefits of increased consistency and predictability. These protocols can create some significant ethical challenges when a party wants to do something contrary to the local protocols or unwritten norms that are not reflected in the party's participation agreement.

For example, Los Angeles mediator and Collaborative lawyer Forrest Mosten described a case where his client was thinking of getting out of a Collaborative case and wanted to consult a litigator. Under the norms and standard protocols of the Collaborative community, parties cannot consult litigation counsel during a Collaborative process without disclosing this to the other side. In Mosten's case, the participation agreement did not address this issue, and the client instructed him not to disclose to the other side her consultation with litigation counsel. Under the legal ethics rules governing confidentiality as described above, he was required not to disclose this fact, notwithstanding a contrary protocol or expectation of the Collaborative team members. Theoretically, the lawyer could seek to withdraw from the representation, although the client had not violated her commitment under the participation agreement and the Collaborative lawyer's withdrawal at that point would presumably have been against the client's interest.

Whether a Collaborative lawyer can continue to advise a client or participate as a settlement consultant after a Collaborative process ends is another example of activity contrary to norms in the Collaborative community. Collaborative disqualification agreements generally preclude representation in litigation, although norms in many Collaborative communities would prohibit any further legal service in the matter, including as a Settlement Counsel or advisor who is not involved in the litigation. These norms would preclude a Collaborative lawyer from serving in these roles, although there may be no legal duty preventing the lawyer from doing so. Such lawyers could avoid the ethical dilemma simply by declining to undertake the later representation. However, declining this representation would prevent clients who did not agree to these norms from receiving legal services they would value.

One lawyer said that lawyers should generally respect clients' autonomy about procedural decisions even if this deviates from Collaborative Practice norms. Thus she said that if the parties want to make an informed choice, for example, to permit continued engagement of professionals after the Collaborative case ends, their lawyers should support them in doing so even if contrary to local practice norms.

A Collaborative lawyer notes another norm within communities of Collaborative practitioners that poses ethical issues. He has heard Collaborative lawyers say that it is important that they preserve their relationships with their Collaborative colleagues. These lawyers suggest that some lawyers act in a particular way in order to avoid a negative reaction from their colleagues. Obviously, lawyers may legitimately make tactical judgments that some such actions would not advance their clients' interests. It is also clear that lawyers should not make such decisions if the reason is to protect their ability to get referrals from other Collaborative professionals rather than to advance their client's interest.

Advertising and Membership in a Negotiation Practice Organization

Lawyers who are members of organizations promoting Collaborative and Cooperative Practice sometimes have cases in which they represent "opposing" parties in the same case. This common membership, similar to membership in various bar associations, does not violate Rule 1.10(a) regarding conflicts of interest as long as the organization is does not constitute a "firm" providing legal services. If the relationship between lawyers might interfere with their ability to provide independent professional judgments required by Rule 2.1, they should proceed only with the informed consent of all parties.

Some of these organizations include members who are nonlawyers, and this structure does not violate Rule 5.4(b) against forming partnerships with nonlawyers as long as the organization does not engage in legal practice. For example, if the organization provides education for the public and professionals, this activity does not violate this rule. When parties retain nonlawyer professionals in negotiation, lawyers should comply with Rule 5.4(a) prohibiting fee-sharing with nonlawyers by having the clients separately pay each professional.[14]

Information provided about a lawyer's services by negotiation organizations must comply with Rules 7.1 et seq. regarding information about legal services. For example, Rule 7.1 prohibits lawyers from making false or misleading communications about themselves or their services.

Withdrawal from Representation

Lawyers must comply with Rule 1.16 governing withdrawal from representation when applicable. Withdrawal is not necessary when a representation ends due to termination of the matter, in litigation or negotiation, or when clients discharge their lawyers. When lawyers have been engaged solely for negotiation—as Settlement Counsel or Collaborative lawyers—and the negotiation ends without agreement, it is unclear whether the lawyers are required to follow applicable law regarding notice to courts or obtaining court permission to withdraw. From one perspective, if representations terminate simply because the parties decide to end negotiation, the clients may be considered to have discharged the lawyers following the terms of a representation agreement, and thus the lawyers are not required to withdraw. Lawyers who have not appeared in litigation of the matter presumably should not be required to seek court approval to withdraw. On the other hand, if lawyers have appeared in litigation (such as to initiate a divorce proceeding), it is more likely that they would need court approval to withdraw. Moreover, lawyers who initiate the termination of the negotiation, perhaps in the belief that one of the parties has breached the participation agreement, may need to seek court permission, depending on the applicable laws and rules.[15]

Lawyers are not permitted to withdraw merely because clients do not accept the lawyers' advice about settlement. Under Rule 1.16(b)(4), however, they may withdraw if clients insist on taking an action that the lawyers consider "repugnant" or with which the lawyers have a "fundamental disagreement."

When a representation ends, lawyers must take reasonable steps to protect clients' interests, such as giving reasonable notice to the client, returning clients' papers and property, and returning unearned fees.

Endnotes

1. Some material in this chapter has been adapted from my articles, especially John Lande & Forrest S. Mosten, *Collaborative Lawyers' Duties to Screen the Appropriateness of Collaborative Law and Obtain Clients' Informed Consent to Use Collaborative Law*, 25 OHIO ST. J. ON DISP. RESOL. 347 (2010). For an excellent summary of ethics rules governing Collaborative Law, see Collaborative Law Committee, Section of Dispute Resolution, American Bar Association, Summary of Ethics Rules Governing Collaborative Practice (2009), *available at* http://meetings.abanet.org/webupload/commupload/DR035000/sitesofinterest_files/EthicsPaper%2820091010%29.pdf.

2. Pa. Bar Ass'n Comm. on Legal Ethics and Prof'l Responsibility, Informal Op. 2004-24, 2004 WL 2758094 (May 11, 2004).

3. Although the Uniform Collaborative Law Act does not establish legal ethical rules, it can be helpful to refer to it. Section 14 requires lawyers to make certain disclosures, provide prospective clients with information needed to make an informed choice of dispute resolution process, and inquire about and discuss the appropriateness of Collaborative Law in their case. *See* Uniform Law Commission, Uniform Collaborative Law Act, http://www.nccusl.org/Update/CommitteeSearchResults.aspx?committee=279.

4. Ky. Bar Ass'n Ethics Comm., Op. E-425, 7–8 (2005), *available at* http://www.kybar.org/documents/ethics_opinions/kba_e-425.pdf.

5. N.J. Ethics Op. 699, 2005 WL 3890576, at *5 (2005).

6. Ky. Bar Ass'n Ethics Comm., Op. E-425, 4 (2005).

7. For detailed discussion of informed consent requirements in Collaborative Practice, *see* Lande & Mosten, *supra* note 1.

8. *See* Marshall J. Breger, *Should an Attorney Be Required to Advise a Client of ADR Options?*, 13 Geo. J. Legal Ethics 427, 428–36 (2000) (footnotes omitted).

9. *See* Cole et al., Mediation: Law, Policy and Practice § 4:3 (2d ed. 2008).

10. Pa. Informal Op. 2004-24, 2004 WL 2758094 (2004).

11. N.J. Ethics Op. 699, 14 N.J.L. 2474, 182 N.J.L.J. 1055, 2005 WL 3890576 (2005).

12. *See* Lande & Mosten, *supra* note 1. Section 15 of the Uniform Collaborative Law Act creates a presumption against using Collaborative Law in cases involving a history of a coercive or violent relationship unless the parties request to use the process and the Collaborative lawyers reasonably believe that the parties' safety can be adequately protected during the process.

13. ABA Formal Ethics Op. 07-447 (2007).

14. For a good discussion of these issues, see N.J. Eth. Op. 699, 14 N.J.L. 2474, 182 N.J.L.J. 1055, 2005 WL 3890576.

15. For discussion of these issues, see Pa. Bar Ass'n Comm. on Legal Ethics and Prof'l Responsibility, Informal Op. 2004-24, 2004 WL 2758094 (2004).

APPENDIXES

The following appendixes provide models you might use or adapt in your practice based on your clients' needs. These appendixes do not constitute legal advice, and you should consider any applicable legal authorities in your jurisdiction that might bear on the issues in your case.

Appendix A.
Conflict Analysis
Questionnaire
for Clients

Berkeley, California, mediator Ron Kelly developed the following questionnaire for parties to complete before they mediate with him. You may want to ask your clients to answer some or all of these questions early in your representation for your initial assessment as well as to prepare clients for a negotiation or mediation. This questionnaire is designed for contract disputes but could be adapted for other kinds of issues. For further discussion, see Chapter 2.

Key Questions Before You Meet

You may be heading for a nasty fight, but you're going to meet first.

You want the problem solved sooner—not later. You'd rather spend your time and money on better things.

BE PREPARED. You'll be making the very best use of your time by working through these questions before you meet. Even better—give these questions to both sides (all sides if there are several of you). This questionnaire has been used all over California to help settle tough court cases, and to train lawyers, mediators, and business professionals. Nearly everyone who's written out serious answers to these questions has developed a way to settle their fight themselves—on terms that both sides could live with.

You can use your time and money for much better things than battling each other.

A. YOUR INTERESTS:

1. List your basic interests, and then number their order of importance to you. (For instance: time, money, security, get even, get on with life, minimize risk, fairness, future plans, maintain a working relationship, etc.). To help identify your real interest in each area, ask yourself—"Suppose they agree to what I want—exactly what will that do for me?"

2. How do you think they see their interests? List and rank them.

3. Any voluntary agreement will have to satisfy both your interests and theirs. Both of you will have to decide it's a better choice than fighting. Where could you cooperate to do this, if you both decided you wanted to?

4. What significant things do you think you already agree about?

5. Where do you think you disagree most strongly?

6. In these areas, what objective criteria could you use together to develop fair and constructive voluntary resolutions?

7. How will you know when a potential agreement is a better choice than fighting it out? What criteria will you use to measure how well it satisfies the interests you've identified?

B. YOUR UNDERSTANDINGS:

8. From your perspective, what important understandings did you think you had when you originally got involved together? (Time,

money, working conditions, rights and duties, decision-making, who was responsible for what, who was on the hook for the unforeseen risks, methods for resolving differences, etc.)

9. What important shifts in these understandings happened as the situation developed, and where do you think their perspective differs from yours?

10. What feelings of trust and goodwill supported your original agreements?

11. Exactly when and over what did you first have any feelings of betrayal, bad faith, or loss of confidence? How strong are these still? Do you feel like they might owe you something to specifically make up for this?

C.   YOUR RESOLUTION:

12. In areas where you have sharply different perspectives, what useful evidence can you bring in that will be credible to them, to help them see your view? (Receipts, photographs, witnesses, notes, written industry standards, copies of laws or rules, expert reports, etc.)

13. What could they say or do in your meeting that would really push your buttons all over again? How will you keep things on track if this happens?

14. In resolving this, how will you balance your shorter term emotional interests with your longer term financial interests? (For instance: Are you willing to risk your future financial interests to avoid uncomfortable discussions now? Will you accept a satisfactory offer, even if you're very resentful about how you've been treated? etc.)

15. If you're unable to agree on a voluntary settlement, what do you currently believe is your next best alternative in the real world? You can make an informed choice between 1) the best voluntary agreement available and 2) your next best alternative—but only if you have a clear picture of each one. List as much as you can about potential risks and benefits of your next best alternative.

16. What are their next best alternatives?

17. List every issue which might reasonably be disputed if this is argued before a court, arbitrator, boss, etc. (Verbal representations,

unforeseen problems, mistakes, different versions of facts, breaches of agreements, contract language, delay, scope and quality of work, interpretations of law, methods of calculating direct and consequential damages, coverage issues, etc.)

18. List the possible consequences of not reaching agreement. Suppose you're unable to settle it between yourselves, you end up in the lengthiest and most costly alternative, and the judge, jury, boss, board, or arbitrator eventually agrees completely with the other side's arguments. For instance, what's the maximum amount of your financial risk for:
    a) the difference between your likely claims,
    b) everyone's attorneys' fees, expert witness fees, and procedural costs,
    c) the value of your time lost from work and family?
       If you don't know, go get the most accurate information you can. It's important.

19. What are two different potential settlements that 1) you believe will satisfy their main interests as you understand them, 2) you can live with, and 3) will address all your key issues? (Important note: You can kill the best possible resolution by putting it out too early. It's often seen as a threatening demand instead of a possible solution to a joint problem. Almost any solution will feel better to them if you both develop it together.)

20. How could a neutral third party help you develop your best voluntary settlement? (Defuse emotions, and take some of the heat? Be a confidential sounding board to help you evaluate your options and approaches? Provide for safe and productive direct negotiations? Help you to break logjams, and generate creative options? Help you develop specific written language to ensure a lasting resolution?)

Appendix B.
Early Case Assessment
Guidelines

The International Institute for Conflict Prevention & Resolution (CPR) developed the following Early Case Assessment (ECA) Guidelines. CPR focuses particularly on conflicts involving the largest corporations and the law firms that serve them. This document includes a "short form" on page 188 and a "long form." For further suggestions, see Chapters 1, 2, and 4.

© 2009 International Institute for Conflict Prevention & Resolution, 575 Lexington Ave., New York, NY 10022; (212) 949-6490, www.cpradr.org. Reprinted with permission of CPR. The CPR Institute is a nonprofit initiative of 500 general counsel of major corporations, leading law firms, and prominent legal academics whose mission is to install alternative dispute resolution (ADR) into the mainstream of legal practice.

CPR

RESOURCES FOR NAVIGATING COMPLEX BUSINESS DISPUTES

Corporate Early Case
Assessment Toolkit

CPR assembled a commission of leading corporate counsel, attorneys and academics to collaborate in the production of an Early Case Assessment tool which could be used across a broad spectrum of commercial disputes. The organization gratefully acknowledges the individuals who contributed their expertise and insights to this project.

Lawrence N. Chanen
Senior Vice President &
Associate General Counsel
JPMorgan Chase

Dan S. Dunham
Senior Corporate Counsel
Pfizer, Inc.

Anurag Gulati
Assistant General Counsel
General Mills, Inc.

J. Andrew Heaton
Associate General Counsel
Ernst & Young LLP

Paula A. Johnson
Senior Counsel
ConocoPhillips

Janet S. Kloenhamer
President, Discontinued Operations
Fireman's Fund Insurance Co.

Patrick Lamb
Valorem Law Group

Prof. John Lande
Director, Program in Dispute Resolution
University of Missouri School of Law

Melanie Lewis
Director, Solutions Program
Coca-Cola Enterprises, Inc.

Duncan R. MacKay
Assistant General Counsel,
Dispute Resolution
Northeast Utilities

Deborah Masucci
Vice President & Director of
Dispute Resolution
American International Group Inc.

Julie S. Mazza
Senior Counsel
Citigroup Inc.

Barbara McCormick
Assistant General Counsel
Johnson & Johnson

Richard N. Papper
Vice President &
Senior Litigation Counsel
Bank of New York/Mellon

Roland Schroeder
Senior Counsel, Litigation &
Legal Policy
General Electric Company

Beth Trent
Legal Director
Schering-Plough Corporation

Patricia Caycedo-Smith
Associate General Counsel, Litigation
Duke Energy Corporation

Nancy L. Vanderlip
Vice President & General Counsel
Electronic Components
ITT Corporation

Jennifer Boyens Victor
The Victor Law Firm

Thomas R. Woodrow
Holland & Knight LLP

CPR Staff:

Kathy Bryan
President & CEO

Cathy Cronin-Harris
Senior Consultant

Thomas L. Aldrich
Senior Consultant

Fundamentals of Early Case Assessment

CPR Definition: Early Case Assessment

CPR's Early Case Assessment Toolkit (ECA) outlines a simple conflict management process designed to facilitate more informed and expedited decision-making at the early stages of a dispute. The process calls for a team working together in a specified time frame to gather the key facts of the dispute, identify the key business concerns, assess the various risks and costs the dispute poses for the company, and make an informed choice or recommendation on how to handle the dispute.

While one of the possible recommendations could be to settle or resolve the dispute, CPR wishes to emphasize that these Guidelines are not about settlement, although that could be one possible outcome of Early Case Assessment. Instead, these Guidelines focus on evaluating the dispute so that an appropriate strategy can be formulated, whether that is settlement, full-bore litigation, or something in between, with an eye toward reducing or eliminating disputes as soon and as inexpensively as possible.

Benefits of Using Early Case Assessment

In today's highly litigious business climate there are numerous business and legal trends supporting the use of Early Case Assessment. These trends include an increasing volume of claims and litigation, the increasing complexity and protraction of claims, and the resulting higher legal fees and settlements. In this climate, many legal departments have worked to develop new definitions of "value" and "win" by treating disputes as a business process, and protracted litigation as a defect to be remedied. One effective tool for controlling disputes and reducing or eliminating litigation is the ECA process.

There are numerous potential benefits of implementing an Early Case Assessment program, including:

- Enhanced, early case analysis
- Enhanced, early risk identification and analysis
- Enhanced, early evaluation of potential end-game solutions
- Enhanced ability to gauge business needs and solutions, and improved client relations
- A reduction in legal costs and expenses
- A reduction in settlement and resolution costs
- A reduction in the "claim-through-resolution" cycle time

Setting the Stage for Successful Early Case Assessment

The growing adoption of Early Case Assessment programs arises from the mandate of in-house legal departments to better and more effectively manage litigation, in terms of outcome and cost, and to do so with better calculation of the business interests and objectives implicated by that litigation.

In addition, in-house legal departments have at their disposal more and better tools for gathering necessary data to assess litigation risks and solutions, measure progress, communicate lessons learned, and track successful strategies and solutions. Early identification of risks, business prerogatives, likely outcomes, and potential alternative resolutions should be a part of every Early Case Assessment program.

Using CPR's ECA Toolkit

CPR's ECA Guidelines provide a structured approach for conducting early evaluation of a dispute. It is intended to be a flexible tool that may be adjusted by in-house counsel to meet the particular needs of their business. It can be applied in whole or part depending on dispute circumstances to conduct early, rapid and consistent analysis of a dispute to find the most effective resolution path geared toward limiting corporate expenditures, serving business concerns and utilizing the most appropriate conflict resolution process.

Many companies employ a computerized matter management system for purposes of tracking litigation, claims, government investigations, and related legal matters. The ECA is not intended to take the place of a matter management system; however, one may usefully become a component of the other. Therefore, corporate users are encouraged to tailor these guidelines and tools to their particular needs and requirements.

CPR's ECA Toolkit comprises:

- A detailed, step-by-step guide for users who are less familiar with the concept of ECA and seek a comprehensive analytical model.

- A short Executive Summary form for sophisticated users who are familiar with the elements of the ECA process. See Appendix A.

For more assistance with your ECA process, contact info@cpradr.org. To download materials in an electronic format, please visit CPR's website at www.cpradr.org.

About CPR

The International Institute for Conflict Prevention and Resolution (CPR) is an independent, nonprofit think tank that promotes innovation in commercial dispute prevention and resolution. By harnessing the expertise of leading minds in ADR and benchmarking best practices, it is the resource of choice for multinational corporations with billions of dollars at risk. CPR is also a trusted and respected destination for lawyers seeking superior arbitrators and mediators and cutting-edge ADR tools and training. Our elite membership includes General Counsel from global corporations, attorneys from the top law firms in the world, sitting and retired judges, highly-experienced neutrals and ADR practitioners, and leading academics.

CPR

ECA Step-by-Step Analysis

1	Capture Matter Information & Assemble Team
2	Informal Factual Review
3	Business Concerns
4	Forum & Adversary Analysis
5	Risk Management Analysis
6	Legal Analysis
7	Cost / Benefit Analysis
8	Determine Settlement Value
9	Establish Settlement Strategy
10	Develop Preliminary Litigation Plan
	Post-Resolution: Loop-Back Process (Prevention)

STEP 1
Capture Matter Information
& Assemble Team

Describe the Matter

- Parties: Claimant/Plaintiff; Respondent/Defendant; Third Parties

- Nature of dispute

- Apparent amount at risk

- Background and relationships of parties

- How company learned of matter

- Status of insurance and any related indemnity agreements

- Identification of other applicable contracts, pre-dispute agreements, and agreements regarding how disputes may be handled

Identify the Stage of Development and Contractual Requirements

Note: Do not duplicate matter management system which may contain some of this data.

- Status of negotiations

- Review relevant dispute resolution provisions of contract
  - Negotiation
  - Two-tiered negotiation in company
  - Mediation
  - Arbitration
  - Other

1	Capture Matter Information & Assemble Team
2	Informal Factual Review
3	Business Concerns
4	Forum & Adversary Analysis
5	Risk Management Analysis
6	Legal Analysis
7	Cost / Benefit Analysis
8	Determine Settlement Value
9	Establish Settlement Strategy
10	Develop Preliminary Litigation Plan
	Post-Resolution: Loop-Back Process (Prevention)

- If arbitration will commence, identify
  - ADR provider
  - Applicable arbitration rules
  - Arbitrators
  - Commencement date
  - Causes of action
  - Damages/remedies

- If litigation filed, attach the complaint and identify:
  - Court/Location
  - Judge
  - Docket no.
  - Date filed *(By whom)*
  - Cause(s) of action
  - Damages/other remedies sought *(Claim for Injunctive/Prelim.Relief)*
  - Court-ordered mediation required/completed
  - Dispositive motions filed (*When/Outcome?*)
  - Filing deadlines approaching
  - Jury trial matter

Note: *May be omitted if the Complaint is attached or if the matter is a repeating matter, such as a class action or mass tort.*

Identify Counsel and Team for Company, Other Party and Third Parties

- Inside counsel

- Outside counsel

- Business unit/person(s) involved/affected

- Insurance representatives

Assign Duties and Time Frame to Complete ECA Process

The key benefit of a systematic ECA review is to assemble the information and focus the team on the issues that may be most relevant to settlement before the astronomical costs of discovery and motion practice begin. How early can it be done? Depending on the complexity of the case, the lawyers who use these methods regularly believe that the review should be completed within the first 30-90 days.

The purpose of the ECA is not to conduct an exhaustive legal and factual analysis, but to collect essential information, understand the basic strengths and weakness of the legal positions and use that information to conduct an early cost/benefit analysis. The ECA redefines what the essential information is in order to value the case quickly and as effectively as possible.

With an ECA policy in place, it is even better if all the parties can agree to stay discovery and the filings in the case until the ECA is complete. In pattern cases, or situations where both sides are willing to have further discussions before discovery, an agreement to postpone discovery may be more likely.

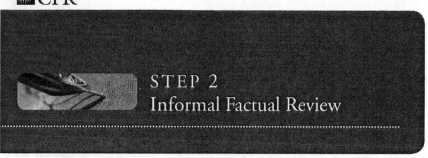

STEP 2
Informal Factual Review

1 Capture Matter Information & Assemble Team
2	Informal Factual Review
3 Business Concerns
4 Forum & Adversary Analysis
5 Risk Management Analysis
6 Legal Analysis
7 Cost / Benefit Analysis
8 Determine Settlement Value
9 Establish Settlement Strategy
10 Develop Preliminary Litigation Plan
Post-Resolution: Loop-Back Process (Prevention)

Conduct Internal Interviews

• Information gathered from discussions with company, law firm, and other lawyers with knowledge of the matter

• Information gathered from client business contacts with knowledge of the matter

Collect Internal Documents

• Hard copy documents

• Electronic documents, including number, type, format, media, cost of storage and production, and possible role for e-discovery expert

Identify Witnesses and Experts

• Identify the fact witnesses and their location

• Evaluate role of experts, if any

• Provide a summary of the interviews with witnesses

• Assess witness capability and credibility

Contacts with Opposing Counsel

- Information garnered
- Agreements on informal discovery or information exchange

Review Relevant Company and Industry Historical Information

- History of similar claims in the company (if any)
- Average number of days to resolution of such claims
- Special circumstances differentiating this case from other similar cases
- In-house, law firm, and other lawyers with relevant experience on similar matters
- Business client contacts with knowledge of similar matters
- Relevant company files and/or databases
- Similar matters in the industry/industry concerns/history
- Damages awards and settlements
- Length of litigation process and procedural issues
- Other relevant public data/records or information that might be available

Identify Essential Information Needed

- If key information is currently unavailable that is essential in selecting resolution strategy, describe informal routes to acquire that information

STEP 3
Business Concerns

1 Capture Matter Information & Assemble Team
2 Informal Factual Review
3 I Business Concerns
4 Forum & Adversary Analysis
5 Risk Management Analysis
6 Legal Analysis
7 Cost / Benefit Analysis
8 Determine Settlement Value
9 Establish Settlement Strategy
10 Develop Preliminary Litigation Plan
Post-Resolution: Loop-Back Process (Prevention)

Identify Client's Priority Business Concerns and Interests

- Protecting sensitive data

- Legal *(E.g., Need new precedent; need TRO or PI; etc.)*

- Economic: short term, long term

- Timing

- Relationships (including confidentiality)

- Publicity and reputation

- Psychological *(E.g., understand occurrences; receive apology; be heard by authority figures; vindicate action; clear name; change policies for others in similar situation; etc.)*

- Other special/unique/sensitive concerns affecting disposition strategy:
  - Corporate survival/treasury at risk
  - Business relationship at stake
  - Reputation/public relations/stock price
  - Repetitive claim/floodgates issue/class action
  - New product under scrutiny
  - New or existing legal precedent
  - Technical issue, e.g. intellectual property
    Location of proceedings: forum, venue, jury issues
  - Industry concerns; possible co-defendants
  - Possible criminal liability; corporate governance; compliance; government oversight; RICO
  - International matter, FCPA, or foreign political concerns
  - High level executive testimony required

Assess Opponent's Likely Priority Business Concerns and Interests

- Protecting sensitive data

- Legal *(E.g., Precedent; PI; etc.)*

- Economic: short term, long term

- Timing

- Relationships (including confidentiality)

- Reputation

- Psychological *(E.g., understand occurrences; receive apology; be heard by authority figures; vindicate action; clear name; change policies for others in similar situation; etc.)*

- Other

Define Successful Resolution from a Business Perspective

NOTE: Identification of mutual concerns and interests may lead to dialogue with opponent and possible Early Case Resolution through collaborative negotiation.

A good ECA process should evaluate the business interests of both parties in the resolution of the dispute. Interest-based questions, which typically give rise to opportunities to find common ground, are often not explored until actual settlement discussions were underway. Lawyers using the usual adversarial practices often fail to uncover elements of the dispute that might be relevant to settlement but may be unrelated to the legal claims in front of them. For example, considerations which focus on the relationship of the parties and business strategy and goals should be analyze and reviewed.

STEP 4
Forum & Adversary Analysis

| 1 Capture Matter Information & Assemble Team |
| 2 Informal Factual Review |
| 3 Business Concerns |
| 4 I Forum & Adversary Analysis |
| 5 Risk Management Analysis |
| 6 Legal Analysis |
| 7 Cost / Benefit Analysis |
| 8 Determine Settlement Value |
| 9 Establish Settlement Strategy |
| 10 Develop Preliminary Litigation Plan |
| Post-Resolution: Loop-Back Process (Prevention) |

Forum Analysis

- Judge's profile *(including circuit or state court rulings out of sync with majority on relevant issues)*

- Potential jury pool

- Mediator's profile

- Arbitrator's profile

Opposing Counsel Analysis

- Reputation or experience of opposing counsel:
  - Negotiation reputation
  - Trial reputation

- Counsel's incentives to settle early

- Similar claims litigated against the opposing lawyer? What was outcome and what approach was used by opponent?

Opposing Party Analysis

- Any continuing business relationship with adversary *(Anything over $_____ requires business or other higher level approval of case strategy)*

- Specify financial and legal resources of the adversary

- Immediate needs of adversary that might support use of an early settlement process *(E.g., financial crisis; etc.)*

- Signatory to CPR Pledge©?

STEP 5
Risk Management Analysis

Legal Hold Notice Issuance, Date and List of Recipients

- Documents

- E-mails

- Length of hold; renewal reminders

- Expansion of document custodians

Insurance

- Is the claim insured or self-insured?

- If insured, has the carrier been notified? Has the carrier accepted coverage, disputed coverage or issued a reservation of rights?

- If the carrier has not been notified, who is responsible for giving notice and when will notice be given?

- Have all potentially applicable policies been located?

- Who is responsible for locating all potentially applicable policies?

1	Capture Matter Information & Assemble Team
2	Informal Factual Review
3	Business Concerns
4	Forum & Adversary Analysis
5 I Risk Management Analysis
6	Legal Analysis
7	Cost / Benefit Analysis
8	Determine Settlement Value
9	Establish Settlement Strategy
10	Develop Preliminary Litigation Plan
Post-Resolution: Loop-Back Process (Prevention)

STEP 6
Legal Analysis

Ascertain and Narrow Scope of Claims and Defenses

Conduct Risk Assessment of Each Claim and Defense

Estimate Possible Damages Spectrum

Identify Additional Information Necessary to Evaluate Damages

Determine Whether and Type of Damages Experts that will be Required

Estimate Costs to Completion

- Outside counsel fees

- Other litigation expenses and "hard" costs

- Anticipated expenditure of internal resources and "soft" costs, including
  - In-house lawyer time
  - Business professional time
  - Witness time

STEP 7
Cost/Benefit Analysis

DISPOSITION STRATEGY AS APPLICABLE	Percentage Likelihood of Success/Loss	External Legal Costs	Internal Costs High (H); Medium (M); Low (L)	Time to Complete	Does Strategy Advance Priority Business Concerns or Not?
Dispositive Motion					
Negotiate (without any mediator)					
Mediate (with a mediator)					
Arbitrate					
Discovery or E-Discovery & E-Discovery Vendor Use, If any					
Experts					
Trial					
Other: Dual Track; Appeal; etc.					
TOTALS					

STEP 8
Determine Settlement Value

1	Capture Matter Information & Assemble Team
2	Informal Factual Review
3	Business Concerns
4	Forum & Adversary Analysis
5	Risk Management Analysis
6	Legal Analysis
7	Cost / Benefit Analysis
8	Determine Settle Value
9	Establish Settlement Strategy
10	Develop Preliminary Litigation Plan
	Post-Resolution: Loop-Back Process (Prevention)

Identify the range of monetary settlement that would be a good result and identify any non-monetary solutions with the potential to resolve the dispute. Consider attaching a decision-tree or similar analysis. A detailed overview of Decision-Trees can be found <u>here</u>.

STEP 9
Establish Settlement Strategy

Review Negotiation History and Current Demand/Offer

Assess Settlement Barriers to Determine if Mediation is Warranted

- The following common settlement barriers can be effectively addressed via mediation:
  - Unassisted negotiations have already failed
  - Communication difficulties and past history foreclose dialogue
  - Emotional barriers to settlement exist between parties or counsel
  - Psychological barriers exist such as partisan perceptions, attribution biases, face-saving needs, reactive devaluation, etc.
  - Process barriers exist such as no settlement event, lack of settlement authority, positional bargaining limitations, etc.
  - Cultural barriers to effective dialogue exist
  - Merit barriers exist such as unrealistic expectations, insufficient key information to settle, etc.

- The following more difficult settlement barriers often foreclose settlement. However, even these barriers have been overcome in mediation:
  - Fundamental corporate or other principle at stake that cannot be settled
  - Need for new precedent is critical
  - Managerial responsibility at center of matter including corporate finance or reorganization cannot be settled
  - Public message needed including defending claims that may open the floodgates to similar claims

1 Capture Matter Information & Assemble Team
2 Informal Factual Review
3 Business Concerns
4 Forum & Adversary Analysis
5 Risk Management Analysis
6 Legal Analysis
7 Cost / Benefit Analysis
8 Determine Settlement Value
9 I Establish Settlement Strategy
10 Develop Preliminary Litigation Plan
Post-Resolution: Loop-Back Process (Prevention)

- Public vindication sought
- Extreme power disparities between parties foreclose ability to bargain
- Absence of resources that can be used for trade-offs in negotiation

Determine Form of Early Resolution Best Suited to Advance Interests and Business Concerns

The final step is to use the information and analysis gathered through the process to evaluate whether the matter can be settled through one of many ADR techniques, which can include any of the following, alone or in combination:

- Negotiation by:
  - management
  - in-house counsel
  - outside litigation or settlement counsel
  - collaboratively trained lawyer(s)
  - other third-party skilled or technical facilitator

- Early Neutral Evaluation

- Early Discovery Exchange

- Competitive Mock Trial

- Shared Focus Study

- Mediation
  - Court conducted mediation
  - Private mediation
    - General or technically trained mediator

- Summary Jury Trial

- Arbitration
  - Non-binding
  - Binding for all or some of the claims

Alternatively, the case could simply be kept on a litigation track heading toward a court trial on the merits.

Secure Resolution Authority

STEP 10
Develop Preliminary
Litigation Plan

Plan Adjudication Route if Settlement Path is Not Successful

Identify Future Opportunities to Reconsider Settlement

Establish Initial Budget and Timeline of Activities

1	Capture Matter Information & Assemble Team
2	Informal Factual Review
3	Business Concerns
4	Forum & Adversary Analysis
5	Risk Management Analysis
6	Legal Analysis
7	Cost / Benefit Analysis
8	Determine Settlement Value
9	Establish Settlement Strategy
10	Develop Preliminary Litigation Plan

Post-Resolution: Loop-Back Process (Prevention)

POST-RESOLUTION
Loop-Back Process
(Prevention)

1	Capture Matter Information & Assemble Team
2	Informal Factual Review
3	Business Concerns
4	Forum & Adversary Analysis
5	Risk Management Analysis
6	Legal Analysis
7	Cost / Benefit Analysis
8	Determine Settlement Value
9	Establish Settlement Strategy
10	Develop Preliminary Litigation Plan
	Post-Production: Loop-Back Process (Prevention)

Once a dispute is resolved, the collaborative team may well benefit by engaging in a "lessons learned" exercise, not only to capture the valuable insights gained from any dispute for application to another, but also to identify appropriate business practice corrections, which may include contract or policy or procedure revisions, enhanced training programs or revised business processes to prevent recurrence.

Appendix A:
Executive Summary

Date prepared: _____   Date last updated: _____

Matter/Dispute

Claimant

Type of Claim

Amount of Claim

Business Unit(s) Affected

Current Status: ☐ *Court*   ☐ *Arbitration*   ☐ *Mediation*   ☐ *Unassisted Negotiation*
☐ *Other (specify):* _____

Assessment of Issues and Outcomes including Rationale
(Include goals and objectives for all parties to the dispute)

Identification of Interests: Ours/Theirs/Joint

Assessment of Settlement Value
(Identify the range of monetary settlement that would be a good result and identify any non-monetary solutions with the potential to resolve the dispute)

Proposed Resolution Strategy and Rationale including Special Circumstances Affecting Strategy

Use decision tree analysis or summarize:
– Resolution phases
– Time frames
– Preliminary litigation management plan
– Budget/costs including counsel fees, forum fees, and liability estimates
  (Total budget for short matters; 12 month budget with "ballpark" totals for prolonged matters)

(Optional: Attach Decision Tree Analysis, if appropriate)

Appendix C.
Factors Affecting Appropriateness of Mediation, Collaborative Law, and Cooperative Law Procedures

This chart was developed by Milwaukee lawyer Gregg Herman and me to help parties and professionals compare processes that might be used in divorce cases. It can be adapted for other types of cases. For further discussion, see Chapters 1, 2, 4, 6, and 10.

This is adapted from John Lande & Gregg Herman, Fitting the Forum to the Family Fuss: Choosing Mediation, Collaborative Law, or Cooperative Law for Negotiating Divorce Cases, *42 FAM. CT. REV. 280, 286–87 (2004). Reprinted with permission.*

Factors	Unassisted Negotiation is appropriate if	Mediation* is appropriate if	Collaborative Law is appropriate if	Cooperative Law is appropriate if	Traditional Litigation is appropriate if
Parties' capabilities					
Ability of parties to assert their interests	parties are able to assert their interests well.	(a) parties are able to assert their interests well and/or (b) lawyers can participate in mediation.	one or more parties need or want a lawyer to advocate their interests.	one or more parties need or want a lawyer to advocate their interests.	one or more parties need or want a lawyer to advocate their interests.
Parties' attitudes about professional services					
Parties' resources and willingness to pay for substantial professional services	parties cannot afford and/or desire professional service, possibly because they want to maximize their own decision making.	parties can afford and/or desire a limited level of professional service, possibly because they want to maximize their own decision making.	parties are willing and able to pay for substantial professional services and willing to pay cost of hiring new litigation lawyers if there is no agreement in collaborative law.	parties are willing and able to pay for substantial professional services.	parties are willing and able to pay for substantial professional services.

Factors	Unassisted Negotiation is appropriate if	Mediation* is appropriate if	Collaborative Law is appropriate if	Cooperative Law is appropriate if	Traditional Litigation is appropriate if
Parties desire for neutral third party to manage the process	parties do not want neutral third party to manage the process.	parties want neutral third party to manage the process.	(a) parties do not want neutral third party to manage the process or (b) are willing to hire mediator in addition to lawyers.	(a) parties do not want neutral third party to manage the process or (b) are willing to hire mediator in addition to lawyers.	(a) parties do not want neutral third party to manage the process or (b) are willing to hire mediator in addition to lawyers.
Parties willingness to hire lawyers	parties are reluctant or unwilling to hire lawyers at all or to take the lead in negotiation.	parties are reluctant or unwilling to hire lawyers at all or to take the lead in negotiation.	both parties are willing to hire lawyers.	both parties are willing to hire lawyers.	at least one party is willing to hire a lawyer.
Parties desire to keep their lawyer if the case involves contested litigation	not applicable	parties want to be able to keep their lawyers in contested litigation.	parties are willing to risk losing their collaborative lawyers if the parties litigate.	parties want to be able to keep their lawyers in contested litigation.	parties want to be able to keep their lawyers in contested litigation.

Factors	Unassisted Negotiation is appropriate if	Mediation* is appropriate if	Collaborative Law is appropriate if	Cooperative Law is appropriate if	Traditional Litigation is appropriate if
Parties desire for well-established dispute resolution procedure and practice	parties are not concerned about using a well-established dispute resolution procedure and practice.	parties want a procedure that has been studied extensively and that is the subject of well-developed norms and practices.	parties want a procedure that is the subject of well-developed norms and practices.	parties are willing to use an innovative procedure that has not been studied extensively and that is not the subject of well-developed norms and practices.	parties want a procedure that is the subject of well-developed norms and practices.

Factors	Unassisted Negotiation is appropriate if	Mediation* is appropriate if	Collaborative Law is appropriate if	Cooperative Law is appropriate if	Traditional Litigation is appropriate if
Parties' risk assessments and preferences					
Risk that a party would take advantage of another	(a) there is a low risk that parties will try to take advantage of each other, and/or (b) parties are capable of representing themselves effectively, and/or (c) parties may hire professionals if needed.	(a) there is a low risk that parties will try to take advantage of each other, and/or (b) parties are capable of representing themselves effectively, and/or (c) parties use mediator skilled in managing conflict, and/or (d) lawyers participate in mediation.	(a) there is a low risk that parties will try to take advantage of each other or (b) there is a significant risk of parties trying to take advantage and they are willing to risk that the other party would terminate collaborative law as an adversarial tactic.	there may be a significant risk that one party would take advantage of another.	there may be a significant risk that one party would take advantage of another.

Factors	Unassisted Negotiation is appropriate if	Mediation* is appropriate if	Collaborative Law is appropriate if	Cooperative Law is appropriate if	Traditional Litigation is appropriate if
Risk that a party may want to use litigation	parties are unwilling to make an investment to reduce risk of contested litigation.	parties are willing to make a limited investment to reduce risk of contested litigation.	there is a low risk that a party will want to use contested litigation.	there may be a significant risk that a party will want to use contested litigation.	there may be a significant risk that a party will want to use contested litigation.
Need for threat of litigation to motivate a party to act reasonably	a party does not need threat of litigation to motivate another party to act reasonably.	a party may need threat of litigation to motivate another party to act reasonably.	a party does not need threat of litigation to motivate another party to act reasonably.	a party may need threat of litigation to motivate another party to act reasonably.	a party may need threat of litigation to motivate another party to act reasonably.
Parties desire to avoid contested litigation	parties prefer to avoid litigation but are willing to use it if needed to protect their interests.	parties prefer to avoid litigation but are willing to use it if needed to protect their interests.	parties strongly prefer to avoid litigation and are willing to use it only as a last resort.	parties prefer to avoid litigation but are willing to use it if needed to protect their interests.	parties prefer to avoid litigation but are willing to use it if needed to protect their interests.

Factors	Unassisted Negotiation is appropriate if	Mediation* is appropriate if	Collaborative Law is appropriate if	Cooperative Law is appropriate if	Traditional Litigation is appropriate if
Relative preference of settlement pressure and litigation pressure	parties are wary of settlement and litigation pressure but willing to risk litigation pressure.	parties are wary of settlement pressure and willing to risk greater litigation pressure.	parties are wary of litigation pressure and willing to risk greater settlement pressure.	parties are wary of settlement pressure and willing to risk greater litigation pressure.	parties are wary of settlement pressure and willing to risk greater litigation pressure.

* This table assumes that any lawyers for mediation participants do not attend mediation sessions except as noted.

Appendix D.
Client Information
about Collaborative
Representation

This chart was developed by Los Angeles mediator and Collaborative lawyer Forrest Mosten to help parties consider the benefits and risks of using a Collaborative process. It is designed for divorce cases and could be adapted for other types of cases. For more information, see Chapters 1, 2, 6, and 10.

This chart was published in Forrest S. Mosten, Collaborative Law Practice: An Unbundled Approach to Informed Client Decision-Making, *2008 J. DISP. RESOL. 163, 190–93. Reprinted with permission.*

Elements of Collaborative representation	Benefits	Risks
Collaborative guidelines and principles The Collaborative process involves treating each other respectfully and satisfying the interests of all family members rather than trying to gain individual advantage.	• The Collaborative process sets a positive tone so that you and your spouse can work to satisfy your interests. • The process can reduce unnecessary and destructive conflict and avoid litigation.	• This process may not produce a constructive agreement if your spouse will respond only to threats, litigation, or a decision by a judge. • The Collaborative process may not be appropriate if you or your spouse do not have the ability to participate effectively. • Domestic violence, substance abuse, or mental illness may make the process inappropriate. • You may feel unprotected if you want your Attorney to advocate strongly to protect your interests (including your concerns about your children).

Elements of Collaborative representation	Benefits	Risks
Participation agreement requiring disqualification of attorneys in litigation Clients and Attorneys sign a Participation Agreement that includes a Court Disqualification Clause, which states that if the parties do not resolve the matter in the Collaborative process, neither attorney will represent the parties in any contested litigation between you. If you would want to hire an attorney to represent you in court, you would need to hire another attorney.	• The process can increase the motivation of all parties and Attorneys to reach a settlement. If negotiations break down and a law suit is filed, both parties need to hire new Attorneys and the Collaborative Attorneys are out of a job. As a result, everyone in the Collaborative process focuses exclusively on reaching agreement. • All parties and Attorneys focus on negotiation from the very beginning of the process. • Collaborative Attorneys work to negotiate constructively and avoid attacking the other side.	• If the Collaborative representation ends, you and your spouse will need to spend additional time and money to hire new Attorneys and may lose some information or momentum during a transition of Attorneys. After developing a relationship of trust and confidence with your Collaborative Attorney, you might feel abandoned emotionally and/or strategically at a time of contentious conflict. • You may feel a lot of pressure if your spouse is willing to terminate the process and you want to stay in it. • You should be cautious about using a Collaborative process if you do not trust that your spouse will negotiate honestly and sincerely.

Elements of Collaborative representation	Benefits	Risks
Trained Collaborative professionals The Collaborative process may involve a team of Collaborative professionals who have specialized training in Collaborative divorce skills. Separate divorce coaches help each party to deal with emotional, relationship, and parenting issues. Child development specialists and financial professionals may be hired jointly to provide unbiased information and advice.	• You and your spouse may benefit from using a team of Collaborative professionals with different skills. • Collaborative professionals usually have had special training to help promote constructive settlements. • By investing the time and money for professional training, Collaborative professionals demonstrate a commitment to constructive negotiation.	• You or your spouse may feel some pressure to use more professionals that you want or feel that you can afford.

Elements of Collaborative representation	Benefits	Risks
Direct communication and decisionmaking by the parties Parties are the key decision makers and you communicate directly with each other and the Attorneys.	• You and your spouse control the decisions that affect your lives and families. • You and your spouse can discuss both non-legal and legal issues. • You and your spouse can develop communication skills and learn how to communicate more effectively in the future.	• You and your spouse might increase conflict without making any progress if your communication styles are disrespectful or harmful to each other and you cannot work together constructively.

Elements of Collaborative representation	Benefits	Risks
Voluntary disclosure of assets, obligations, and important information You and your spouse make a binding commitment that you will fully disclose assets and will not to hide important relevant information.	• You and your spouse agree to provide each other with full information of marital and separate assets so that you can make informed decisions. • The Collaborative process can include a protection against parties' failure to disclose fully. If either party does not make the required disclosures, the agreement can be set aside. • The Collaborative process does not use formal court "discovery" processes to investigate the facts of your case. This can save money and avoid conflicts. Discovery does not necessarily produce full information.	• Your spouse may hide assets and other critical information unless you use a formal discovery process.

Elements of Collaborative representation	Benefits	Risks
Confidentiality of Collaborative process Communications in the Collaborative process are generally confidential and inadmissible in court.	• Confidentiality can encourage you and your spouse to talk openly and reach creative solutions. • Confidentiality permits your family business to remain private by avoiding public testimony in court and keeping sensitive documents out of the public records.	
Divorce process may save time and money The Collaborative process may save you and your spouse time and money in handling your divorce. Some courts give Collaborative cases priority within their court system and cases may not have to follow strict court schedules.	• The Collaborative process can help you reduce the length of negotiations and the cost of your divorce. • You may save money by avoiding litigation procedures. Specialized Collaborative professionals can help resolve disputes that might otherwise go to court. • Settlements can be processed quickly in court so that you can move on with your life.	• Collaborative cases can take a long time if there are no court deadlines to keep the process moving. • The use of a team of professionals can increase the cost of your divorce.

I have read this chart and I understand Collaborative representation and its benefits and risks.

I have had an opportunity to discuss any concerns and questions I may have with my attorney before signing an Attorney-Client Engagement Agreement and before signing a Collaborative Participation Agreement with my spouse.

I also understand that if I have additional questions or concerns about the Collaborative representation after it begins, I am encouraged to discuss them with my attorney.

Date _____

_____

CLIENT

Appendix E.
Client Information about Cooperative Representation

This chart is adapted from one developed by Los Angeles mediator and Collaborative Lawyer Forrest Mosten. It is designed to help clients consider whether to use a Cooperative Process.. For more information, see Chapters 1, 2, 6, and 10.

This is adapted, with permission, from Forrest S. Mosten, Collaborative Law Practice: An Unbundled Approach to Informed Client Decision-Making, *2008 J. DISP. RESOL. 163, 190–93.*

Elements of Cooperative representation	Benefits	Risks
Cooperative approach to negotiation The Cooperative process involves treating each other respectfully and satisfying the interests of all parties rather than trying to gain individual advantage.	• The process sets a positive tone so that the parties can work together to satisfy your interests. • The process can reduce unnecessary and destructive conflict and avoid litigation.	• This process may not produce a constructive agreement if a party will respond only to threats, litigation, or a decision by a judge. • The process may not be appropriate if a party does not have the ability to participate effectively. • Domestic violence, substance abuse, or mental illness may make the process inappropriate.

Elements of Cooperative representation	Benefits	Risks
Direct communication and decisionmaking by the parties Parties are the key decision makers and you communicate directly with each other and your lawyers.	• The parties control the decisions that affect your situation. • The parties can decide how much you want to participate in face-to-face meetings and how much you want your lawyers to handle the negotiations. • The parties can discuss both non-legal and legal issues. • The parties can develop communication skills and learn how to communicate more effectively in the future.	• The parties might increase conflict without making any progress if your communication styles are disrespectful or harmful to each other and you cannot work together constructively.

Elements of Cooperative representation	Benefits	Risks
Voluntary disclosure of information The parties arrange to provide information needed to make good decisions in your case.	• The process involves a voluntary and efficient way to exchange information the parties need to make informed decisions. • The process can include a protection against parties' failure to disclose relevant information. If either party does not make disclosures as agreed, the agreement can be set aside. • The process does not use formal court "discovery" processes to investigate the facts of your case. This can save money and avoid conflicts. Discovery does not necessarily produce full information.	• The parties may hide critical information unless you use a formal "discovery" process.

Elements of Cooperative representation	Benefits	Risks
Confidentiality of the process Communications in the process are generally confidential and inadmissible in court.	• Confidentiality can encourage the parties to talk openly and reach creative solutions. • Confidentiality permits the parties to keep your situation private by avoiding public testimony in court and keeping sensitive documents out of the public records.	
Process may save time and money The process may save the parties time and money in handling your case.	• The process can help you reduce the length of negotiations and the cost of your case. • You may save money by avoiding litigation procedures. Specialized professionals can help resolve disputes that might otherwise go to court. • Settlements can be processed quickly in court so that you can move on with your life and business.	• Cooperative cases can take a long time if there are no court deadlines to keep the process moving. • The use of a team of professionals can increase the cost of your case.

I have read this chart and I understand Cooperative representation and its benefits and risks.

I have had an opportunity to discuss any concerns and questions I may have with my attorney before signing an Attorney-Client Engagement Agreement and before signing a Cooperative Participation Agreement with my spouse.

I also understand that if I have additional questions or concerns about the Cooperative representation after it begins, I am encouraged to discuss them with my attorney.

Date _____   _____

CLIENT

Appendix F.
Client Information
about Settlement
Counsel

This chart is adapted from one developed by Los Angeles mediator and Collaborative Lawyer Forrest Mosten. It is designed to help clients consider whether to use a Settlement Counsel process. For more information, see Chapters 1, 2, 4, 6, and 10.

This is adapted, with permission, from Forrest S. Mosten, Collaborative Law Practice: An Unbundled Approach to Informed Client Decision-Making, *2008 J. DISP. RESOL. 163, 190–93.*

Elements of Settlement Counsel process	Benefits	Risks
Deliberate approach to negotiation The negotiation process involves treating each other respectfully and trying to reach an agreement that both parties are satisfied with.	• The process involves a systematic procedure to negotiate as quickly and successfully as possible. • The process sets a positive tone so that the parties can work together to satisfy your interests. • The process can reduce unnecessary and destructive conflict and avoid litigation.	• This process may not produce a constructive agreement if a party will respond only to threats, litigation, or a decision by a judge. • The process may not be appropriate if a party does not have the ability to participate effectively. • Domestic violence, substance abuse, or mental illness may make the process inappropriate.

Elements of Settlement Counsel process	Benefits	Risks
Limitation of Settlement Counsel's services to negotiation Settlement Counsel focus only on trying to reach an agreement, quickly and efficiently.	• The process can increase the motivation of all parties and lawyers to reach a settlement. If the negotiation breaks down, litigation may be expensive, time-consuming, and divisive. If you are prepared to litigate vigorously, this may motivate the other party to negotiate with your Settlement Counsel. • Settlement Counsel work to negotiate constructively and avoid attacking the other side.	• If the Settlement Counsel negotiation ends, you will spend additional time and money for litigation. • If you hire both Settlement Counsel and Litigation Counsel at the same time, this could increase your expense. It could also cause conflict or confusion in coordinating between the lawyers. • If you do not hire both Settlement Counsel and Litigation Counsel at the same time, the other side could try to take advantage by dragging out the negotiation and pressuring you to settle on its terms so that you don't have to hire a new lawyer. You should be cautious about using a Settlement Counsel process if you do not trust that the other party will negotiate sincerely.

Elements of Settlement Counsel process	Benefits	Risks
Direct communication and decision making by the parties Parties are the key decision makers and you communicate directly with each other and your lawyers.	• The parties control the decisions that affect your situation. • The parties can decide how much you want to participate in face-to-face meetings and how much you want your lawyers to handle the negotiations. • The parties can discuss both non-legal and legal issues. • The parties can develop communication skills and learn how to communicate more effectively in the future.	• The parties might increase conflict without making any progress if your communication styles are disrespectful or harmful to each other and you cannot work together constructively.

Elements of Settlement Counsel process	Benefits	Risks
Voluntary disclosure of information The parties arrange to provide information needed to make good decisions in your case.	• The process involves a voluntary and efficient way to exchange information the parties need to make informed decisions. • The process can include protection against parties' failure to disclose relevant information. If either party does not make disclosures as agreed, the agreement can be set aside. • The process does not use formal court "discovery" processes to investigate the facts of your case. This can save money and avoid conflicts. Discovery does not necessarily produce full information.	• The parties may hide critical information unless you use a formal "discovery" process.

Elements of Settlement Counsel process	Benefits	Risks
Confidentiality of the process Communications in the process are generally confidential and inadmissible in court.	• Confidentiality can encourage the parties to talk openly and reach creative solutions. • Confidentiality permits the parties to keep your situation private by avoiding public testimony in court and keeping sensitive documents out of the public records.	
Process may save time and money The process may save the parties time and money in handling your case.	• The process can help you reduce the length of negotiations and the cost of your case. • You may save money by avoiding litigation procedures. Specialized professionals can help resolve disputes that might otherwise go to court. • Settlements can be processed quickly in court so that you can move on with your life and business.	• Settlement Counsel cases can take a long time if there are no court deadlines to keep the process moving. • The use of separate Settlement Counsel and Litigation Counsel or a team of professionals can increase the cost of your case.

I have read this chart and I understand Settlement Counsel representation and its benefits and risks.

I have had an opportunity to discuss any concerns and questions I may have with my attorney before signing an Attorney-Client Engagement Agreement.

I also understand that if I have additional questions or concerns about the Settlement Counsel representation after it begins, I am encouraged to discuss them with my lawyer.

Date _____   _____

                                        CLIENT

Appendix G.
Client Information about Privacy in Collaborative Cases

Los Angeles mediator and Collaborative lawyer Forrest Mosten and I developed the following handout to provide a basic explanation of privacy issues to clients in Collaborative cases, based on the provisions of the Uniform Collaborative Law Act. You should adapt this material to reflect the applicable statutes, rules, protocols, and norms in your community. This form can be adapted for Cooperative or Settlement Counsel cases, though there are no rules specifically relating to comparable privacy issues for these processes. For further discussion, see Chapters 1, 2, and 6.

This is reprinted with permission from Forrest S. Mosten & John Lande, The Uniform Collaborative Law Act's Contribution to Informed Client Decision Making in Choosing a Dispute Resolution Process, *38 HOFSTRA LAW REVIEW 611, 631-33 (2010).*

In the Collaborative process, parties agree to share all relevant information so that they can make fully informed decisions that are fair for everyone involved. To make it easier for parties to share this information, there are rules protecting the privacy of these discussions. This handout is designed to provide you a general explanation of these arrangements. To help you understand these issues and avoid providing more information than you might want, this handout does not provide all the detailed rules. If you have any questions about these issues, please be sure to ask your attorney or member of the lawyer's staff.

Collaborative Law Privilege in General

In general, "communications" (things you say and offers you make) in a Collaborative process generally cannot be used in court if you do not settle the case. You have a "privilege" (an important right) to prevent "Collaborative law communications" from being used in court or other legal procedures. This means that if one party tries to introduce a Collaborative law communication in a court hearing, the other party can object and prevent the communication from being used. Parties sometimes hire some other professionals to participate in the process, such as financial or mental health experts, and these professionals can object to the use of their statements in court. If an expert prepares a report for the Collaborative process, the report may not be used in court. So if you do go to court, you might need to hire new experts to testify (possibly separately for each party), which could cost you substantial additional fees.

Communications Protected by the Privilege

The communications protected under the law can be spoken, written, or even involve nonverbal conduct intended to communicate something, such as nodding one's head. They include communications made from the time the parties sign a Collaborative law participation agreement until the time that the process ends. Therefore, until a participation agreement is signed, you should be careful about statements that you make to the other party or documents that you might provide. Some communications are protected even if they are not made during face-to-face meetings, such as conversations between professionals between these meetings. Conversations between clients and their lawyers are also generally protected from disclosure (though this is protected under the general attorney-client privilege, not the Collaborative law privilege).

The privilege does not apply to communications or documents that currently exist or that are not made for or within the Collaborative process, such as tax returns. Just because some information is used in a Collaborative process does not mean that it can't be used in court if the information can be produced in some way other than a Collaborative law communication. For example, if accounting records are kept in the regular course of business, the fact that they are used during a Collaborative process does not prevent them from also being used in court.

Waiver of Privilege

Parties can give up ("waive") their privileges if they want. If there is a court hearing, a Collaborative law communication can be used if all parties waive their privilege. If the communication involves a statement by a non-party, such as an expert hired in the process, the expert would also need to waive the privilege for the communication to be used in court.

Exceptions to the Privilege

Certain communications are not protected by the privilege and thus they may be used in court. Some of the major exceptions to the privilege include threats to physically harm another person, plans to commit a crime, statements indicating child abuse or neglect, and complaints of professional misconduct.

Preventing Use of Communications in Non-court Situations

The privilege described above prevents use of Collaborative law communications in court and other legal procedures. It *does not provide confidentiality protection in other situations,* such as sharing Collaborative law communications with other family members, professionals you use outside the Collaborative process (including accountants, realtors, or therapists), business associates, friends, or members of your community. It also does not prevent you or the other party from sharing communications publicly, for example, by posting them on the Internet or giving information to the news media.

You and the other party can agree to prohibit use of these communications outside of court. These agreements normally will be made in the participation agreement as agreed in the first joint session, though you can also make agreements about this later in the process. Before the first session, consider what information you would want to share (or prevent from being shared) at all or with particular individuals. If you are in a divorce and you have children, you should plan to reach an agreement about what should or should not be told to the children, when and how it should be done, etc. You might also plan to discuss what should be told, if anything, to other relatives and friends.

Extent and Limits of Duty of Full Disclosure

An essential part of the Collaborative process is that each party must fully disclose all relevant information. There is no clear definition of what is "relevant," which depends on the facts of each case. For example, in some cases, parties may—or may not—be required to disclose a past or current romantic relationship, or employment or financial opportunity. If you do not provide full disclosure, the process may be terminated before an agreement is reached, and the other party may not trust you or cooperate in settlement negotiation. In some situations, if you fail to disclose an asset, the settlement agreement could be set aside, and the court could award the entire asset to the other party as punishment for non-disclosure. If you have any questions about what you would or would not need to disclose, discuss this with your lawyer or any member of the lawyer's staff.

Appendix H.
Attorney Retainer Agreement for Collaborative and Cooperative Cases

This is language to include in retainer agreements for Collaborative or Cooperative cases. It is designed as an addendum to an attorney retainer agreement but you could incorporate some of this language into a single document as the complete retainer agreement.

In Collaborative cases, the lawyer's representation ends if any party decides to litigate the matter, and this form includes a provision to that effect for Collaborative cases.

Lawyers and parties should modify this form to fit their particular situations. Some optional language is in brackets, and there may be variations depending on whether this is used in a family or other type of case. For further discussion, see Chapters 1, 2, and 6.

This is adapted from forms developed by the Mid-Missouri Collaborative and Cooperative Law Association, © 2006. Reprinted with permission. For more information, see http://www.mmccla.org/.

ADDENDUM TO LAWYER RETAINER AGREEMENT FOR PARTICIPATION IN COOPERATIVE OR COLLABORATIVE NEGOTIATION PROCESSES

Client agrees to retain Lawyer in a [Cooperative *or* Collaborative] Negotiation Process (the "Process") regarding the matter identified in the Lawyer Retainer Agreement. In consideration of the mutual promises contained in this Addendum, Client and Lawyer agree as follows:

1. Client is committed to resolve disputes in the Process without using litigation if possible. Lawyer will not file documents in court during the Process except as provided in the Negotiation Agreement with the other Party in this matter (the "Negotiation Agreement").

[*In Collaborative cases:* 1a. During the Collaborative Process, Lawyer shall not represent Client in litigation except as provided in the preceding paragraph. Lawyer's representation of Client is therefore limited to this purpose, which also precludes Lawyer from representing Client in litigation regarding this matter or in any related contested matter. During this Process, Client will not be able to get court orders requiring the other party to provide information or take any other action in this case (such as orders about parenting and child support). **If any party decides to litigate this matter, Lawyer's representation ends, even if the other party makes the decision to litigate.** Client seeks to limit the objectives and purpose of this representation to gain the benefits of using a lawyer who will provide services related only to negotiation. Client consents to this limitation.]

2. Client understands that the Process requires the Client to disclose [all relevant *or* certain] information to the other Party and the other Party's lawyer. Disclosures to and discussions with them are subject to the confidentiality provisions of the Negotiation Agreement, including certain exceptions.

3. Client will have confidential communications with Lawyer that are protected by attorney-client privilege, which generally protects clients from having their lawyers disclose information that the clients provide to the lawyers. Client understands that communications in the presence of others (including negotiation with the other party or lawyer) are not confidential and so are not protected by the attorney-client privilege. Even so, Client's statements may be protected from disclosure by the Negotiation Agreement and legal rules. If Client is not sure about the confidentiality of particular communications, Client will ask Lawyer for an explanation.

4. If, after consulting with Client, Lawyer believes that Client is withholding or misrepresenting information that Client has agreed to provide to the other party, Client consents to Lawyer's withdrawal from representation of Client. If Client withholds or misrepresents information, this is effectively Client's decision to terminate this representation. In this situation, Lawyer shall not disclose to the other Party or the other Party's lawyer the reason for this withdrawal. Client understands that Client may incur additional expense if the Process terminates without a settlement and Client hires a new lawyer.

5. Client understands that there is no guarantee that the Process will successfully resolve all issues. Nothing in this agreement and nothing in Lawyer's statements to Client is a promise or guarantee about the outcome of any matter. Client understands that the Process cannot eliminate concerns about the trustworthiness of the other Party or relationship between the parties. [*In family cases:* Client understands that the Process is not personal therapy or marriage counseling.]

Date _____   _____

                                 CLIENT

Date _____   _____

                                 LAWYER

Appendix I.
Provisions for Attorney Retainer Agreement for Settlement Counsel Cases

This is a model form agreement for clients who want to hire lawyers to serve as Settlement Counsel. This form is designed as an addendum to an attorney retainer agreement, but you could incorporate some of this language into a single document as the complete retainer agreement. This might be in the form of a letter rather than an agreement. Because of the ethical rule requiring informed consent for limited-scope representation, you should obtain your client's signature on whatever document you use. The client's signature, in itself, does not necessarily establish that the client has given informed consent but it can be helpful in focusing the client's attention and documenting the provision of information.

Lawyers and parties should modify this form to fit their particular situations. Some optional language is in brackets and there may be variations depending on whether this is used in a family or other type of case. For further discussion, see Chapters 1, 2, 4, and 6.

This is adapted from forms developed by the Mid-Missouri Collaborative and Cooperative Law Association, © 2006. Reprinted with permission. For more information, see http://www.mmccla.org/.

ADDENDUM TO LAWYER RETAINER AGREEMENT
FOR SETTLEMENT COUNSEL SERVICES

Client agrees to retain Lawyer in the Negotiation (the "Negotiation") of the matter identified in the Lawyer Retainer Agreement. In consideration of the mutual promises contained in this Addendum, Client and Lawyer agree as follows:

1. Lawyer's representation of Client is limited to negotiation and Lawyer shall not represent Client in litigation. Client seeks to limit the objectives and purpose of this representation to gain the benefits of using a lawyer who shall provide services related only to negotiation. Client consents to this limitation.

2. If Client retains separate Litigation Counsel in this matter, Lawyer shall coordinate [his *or* her] activities with Litigation Counsel. If the other side raises an issue with Lawyer related to litigation, Lawyer shall refer them to Litigation Counsel. Client shall instruct Litigation Counsel that if the other side raises an issue with Litigation Counsel related to negotiation, Litigation Counsel shall refer the other side to Lawyer. If Lawyer and Litigation Counsel disagree about any issue in this matter, Lawyer shall inform Client and abide by Client's decision about the issue.

3. Client understands that the Negotiation requires the Client to disclose [all relevant *or* certain] information to the other Party and the other Party's lawyer. Client agrees to provide this information.

4. Client will have confidential communications with Lawyer that are protected by attorney-client privilege, which generally protects clients from having their lawyers disclose information that the clients provide to the lawyers. Client understands that communications in the presence of others (including negotiation with the other party or lawyer) are not confidential and so are not protected by the attorney-client privilege. Even so, Client's statements may be protected from disclosure by agreement with the other party and by legal rules. If Client is not sure about the confidentiality of particular communications, Client will ask Lawyer for an explanation.

5. If, after consulting with Client, Lawyer believes that Client is withholding or misrepresenting information that Client has agreed to provide to the other party, Client consents to Lawyer's withdrawal from representation of Client. In this situation, Lawyer shall not disclose to the other Party or the other Party's lawyer the reason for this withdrawal. Client

understands that Client may incur additional expense if the Negotiation terminates without a settlement and Client hires a new lawyer.

6.   Client understands that there is no guarantee that the Negotiation will successfully resolve all issues. Nothing in this agreement and nothing in Lawyer's statements to Client is a promise or guarantee about the outcome of any matter. Client understands that the Negotiation cannot eliminate concerns about the trustworthiness of the other Party or relationship between the parties.

Date _____   _____

                            CLIENT

Date _____   _____

                            LAWYER

Appendix J.
Attorney
Compensation Clauses

The following are sample clauses defining the attorneys' fee arrangements to be included in retainer agreements. You may include several of these clauses in a single agreement. For example, you may include a retainer, hourly rate, and contingent fee in the same agreement. These clauses generally do not address charges for costs, time period of representation, or other provisions in the retainer agreement. For discussion of attorney fee arrangements, see Chapter 3.

Retainer

Client shall pay Lawyer $_____ as a deposit no later than _____.
This payment shall be deposited in Lawyer's trust account to pay for legal
services and expenses in this matter. Lawyer shall withdraw funds from this
account to pay for these charges incurred.

[*For "evergreen" retainer add:* Each month, Lawyer shall send Client
a statement of the charges incurred in the prior month. To maintain the
amount of the deposit in the Lawyer's trust fund, Client shall pay the
amount of the statement within __ days of the date of the statement. In
the last month of Lawyer's services in this matter, Lawyer shall deduct the
charges from the deposit and refund any balance to Client. If the amount of
the charges is greater than the deposit, Client shall pay Lawyer the difference
between the charges and the amount in Client's account.]

Straight Hourly Billing

Client shall pay Lawyer $_____ per hour for legal services performed in
this matter. Fees will be charged in increments of _____ [minutes *or* tenths
of an hour].

Plaintiff's Contingency Fee

Option A (based on percentages of recovery)

*The following clause includes an optional "trigger" provision, providing that
a plaintiff's lawyer would recover only if the gross recovery exceeds a specified
amount.*

Client shall pay Lawyer a percentage of the net amount recovered in
the matter for legal services performed in this matter [*if there is a "trigger"
for recovery, add:* if the gross recovery exceeds $_____]. The percentage shall
depend on when the matter is completed. The percentage shall be ___%
if settled without filing suit, ___% after suit is instituted but before trial,
___% after trial has begun but before the filing of a notice of appeal, or
___% after the filing of a notice of appeal. The net amount recovered shall
be calculated by deducting from the recovery the reasonable costs incurred
in this matter including, but not limited to, telephone, copying, postage,
travel expenses, expert and witness fees, and transcript expenses.

Option B (based on hourly rates)

This clause is suitable for a "double or nothing" fee, where the lawyer gets twice the normal hourly rate if successful, but no fees if unsuccessful. You can use any multiple of your normal hourly rate. This provision necessarily includes a trigger, since it would not be appropriate for lawyers to earn a premium rate unless the results met some minimum standard.

If the gross recovery exceeds $_____, Client shall pay Lawyer $_____ per hour for legal services performed in this matter. If the gross recovery does not exceed this amount, Client shall not pay Lawyer any fees for legal services. In any case, Client shall pay Lawyer the reasonable costs incurred in this matter including, but not limited to, telephone, copying, postage, travel expenses, expert and witness fees, and transcript expenses.

Defendant's Contingency Fee

Option A (based on percentages of recovery)

The following clause includes an optional "trigger" provision, providing that a defendant's lawyer would recover only if the "amount saved" does not exceed a specified amount. The amount saved is calculated by deducting the gross damages from an amount agreed by the Lawyer and Client.

For legal services performed in this matter, Client shall pay Lawyer a percentage of the amount saved in the matter [*if there is a "trigger" for recovery, add:* if the amount saved exceeds $_____]. The percentage shall depend on when the matter is completed. The percentage shall be ___% if settled without filing suit, ___% after suit is instituted but before trial, ___% after trial has begun but before the filing of a notice of appeal, or ___% after the filing of a notice of appeal. The amount saved is calculated by deducting the gross liability to plaintiffs from $_____.

Option B (based on hourly rates)

This clause is suitable for a "double or nothing" fee, where the lawyer gets twice the normal hourly rate if successful, but no fees if unsuccessful. You can use any multiple of your normal hourly rate. This provision necessarily includes a trigger, since it would not be appropriate for lawyers to earn a premium rate unless the results met some minimum standard.

If the gross liability to plaintiffs does not exceed $_____, Client shall pay Lawyer $_____ per hour for legal services performed in this matter.

If the gross liability to plaintiffs exceeds this amount, Client shall not pay Lawyer any fees for legal services. In any case, Client shall pay Lawyer the reasonable costs incurred in this matter including but not limited to telephone, copying, postage, travel expenses, expert and witness fees, and transcript expenses.

Fixed Fees

Client shall pay Lawyer $_____ for legal services in this matter.

Task Fees

Client shall pay Lawyer for services performed as follows: [*specify tasks and fees, such as:* Factual investigation – $_____; Preparation of a decision tree – $_____; Conducting a settlement meeting – $_____].

Value Billing

Option A (based on percentages of hourly rates)

Client shall pay Lawyer at least ___% but no more than ___% of Lawyer's normal hourly rate (of $_____ per hour) for legal services in this matter. Throughout this matter, Lawyer shall send Client bills for services rendered based on the lower percentage. At the conclusion of this matter, Lawyer will send Client a final bill showing the additional amount that would be paid based on the higher percentage. Client shall pay Lawyer any portion of this amount based on Client's assessment of the value of the services. Client has the sole discretion about what portion of this amount, if any, to pay Lawyer.

Option B (based on dollar amounts)

This clause provides that the client would pay a certain amount by a specified date. This may be the full amount of the minimum fee or some portion of it. After completion of the matter, the client may pay an additional amount based on the client's degree of satisfaction.

Client shall pay Lawyer at least $_____ but no more than $_____ for legal services in this matter. Client shall pay Lawyer $_____ no later than _____. Within __ days after the conclusion of this matter, Client shall pay Lawyer an amount within this range based on Client's assessment of the value of the services. Client has the sole discretion about what amount, if any, to pay Lawyer in excess of $_____ [*the minimum fee*].

Premiums for Early Settlement

Client shall pay Lawyer ___% of Lawyer's normal hourly rate (of $_____ per hour) for legal services in this matter. Throughout this matter, Lawyer shall send Client bills for services rendered based on this percentage. The difference between the amounts actually billed and what would be billed at 100% of Lawyer's normal hourly rate shall be considered the "bonus fund." If Client receives an offer that [exceeds *or* does not exceed] $_____, Client shall pay Lawyer a bonus in addition to the fees previously billed, as follows. If Client receives such an offer before _____, Client shall pay Lawyer __ times the amount of the bonus fund. If Client receives such an offer after _____ and before _____, Client shall pay Lawyer __ times the amount of the bonus fund. If Client receives such an offer after _____ and before _____, Client shall pay Lawyer __ times the amount of the bonus fund.

Appendix K.
Letter to Clients about Lawyer's Philosophy of Practice

The following is a letter that Fort Myers, Florida, family lawyer and mediator Shelly Finman sends to all his legal clients. This sets out his philosophy and expectations about dealing with family law matters. You can avoid some misunderstandings and disagreements with clients by sending such a letter to them at the outset so that they have clear understandings of how you approach matters and what is expected of them. This is a very personal document, and if you want to draft such a letter, obviously it should reflect your philosophy and be tailored to the kind of cases you handle. For discussion of different philosophies of practice, see Chapter 2.

SHELDON E. FINMAN, P.A.
ATTORNEY AT LAW
BOARD CERTIFIED BY THE FLORIDA BAR
IN MARITAL AND FAMILY LAW

Street Address: 2134 McGregor Boulevard Fort Myers, Florida 33901	Telephone (239) 332-4543 Facsimile (239) 334-7828 E-Mail seflaw@comcast.net

Mailing Address:
Post Office Box 1380
Fort Myers, Florida 33902-1380

TO: ALL CLIENTS

FROM: SHELDON E. FINMAN

I have engaged in divorce practice since 1971. **I have found the adversarial system is unworkable, unproductive, inefficient, overly expensive,** and only continues to fuel the fire of acrimony and bitterness. I, therefore, expect all of my clients to take the high road, if you will, and ask that you pay specific heed to the following standards of conduct which I require and which will ultimately serve your best interests:

Each person in a divorce (attorney and client) has the absolute obligation to operate properly, regardless of the behavior of the other. You must avoid stooping to his/her level. That is, try to do the right thing regardless of how the other behaves.

Fighting accomplishes nothing. Fighting only sets up another fight.

No matter how weird or outrageous another's actions, their behavior makes sense to them and that person can justify it, no matter how misguided or incorrect it seems to us.

In a marriage, all disagreements finally come down to giving in or giving up. If you insist on being stubborn, in always being right, or demanding your own way, you doom your divorce to never-ending conflict. All harmonious human relationships <u>require compromise</u>, even in divorce.

Arguments are usually caused by fear. Jealousy is fear of loss. Anger is fear of domination or control. Resistance is fear of being overpowered.

In order to overcome fear, you must show courage. Willingness to be open-minded and view your spouse's behavior in light of new information is evidence of courage. To show courage the first thing you must do is temporarily give in -- surrender pride, stubbornness, vindictiveness, contentiousness or a desire for revenge.

I will expect you to show courage, respect and rational behavior.

In divorce, punishment in any form, particularly keeping power and control, is likely to make unwanted behavior continue.

Also, dirty looks, insults, bringing up past mistakes, and shouting are all forms of punishment. Why should you stop punishing your spouse? Because:

1. You will feel better about yourself.
2. You will look better.
3. You will show goodwill.
4. You will generate goodwill.
5. Tension will be reduced.

It is only human for each party to see the rightness of his/her side and to deny the rightness of the offending party. Both can conjure up all kinds of arguments and find support for their side in books and with friends, but usually the truth is that there is some right on both sides. When two people are right and each tries to make the other see his/her side, they rarely succeed. Only by trusting and conceding can the deadlock be broken.

It is respectful to try to satisfy your spouse's wishes if they are reasonable and possible.

If you want to convince your partner of your goodwill, don't tell him or her, show your good behavior. Do something you <u>know</u> he or she will consider nice. Remember: actions speak louder than words. Kindness and understanding can repair anger and hurt.

Even if your spouse is really as bad as you think he or she is, describing his or her defects is not going to cure him or her, and, certainly, repeating old criticisms or past mistakes is not going to undo them. In fact, if you find the right opportunity, you might seriously consider validating and acknowledging some of your spouse's good qualities (especially a spouse who shows signs of bitterness and anger toward you).

A productive divorce is a function of mutual cooperation or reciprocity. Equals treat each other fairly and with justice. They expect the same treatment in return. If you are unfair to your spouse, mistreat or look down on him or her, you are not treating him or her as an equal. This will only lead to conflict. The following is a brief list of ways to make people feel unequal:

1. Criticize them.
2. Compare them unfavorably.
3. Ridicule them.
4. Act superior or arrogant.
5. Ignore them.
6. Fault-find.

Do you have to be right, do you have to prove your correctness, do you have to have your own way, do you have to win? If so, you may have the pleasures of your short-gained victories at the expense of totally unsatisfactory long-term results.

Finally, if I suggest therapy to assist you in being more productive, more constructive and more objective, please do yourself a favor and follow my advice. Often, the emotional adjustment in the divorce process is extremely difficult and will determine whether or not a case is settled.

Over the past few years, I have only taken one or two cases to trial per year. I expect, even almost demand, every case be settled. If you want to fight and punish your spouse, do not hire me.

Sincerely,

Appendix L.
Letter to Other Party
Inviting Negotiation

The following is a letter developed by Columbia, Missouri, lawyer Mary Carnahan, of Brown, Willbrand, Simon, Powell & Lewis, P.C. This letter invites the other party in a divorce to use a Collaborative or Cooperative process. It refers to a brochure of the Mid-Missouri Collaborative and Cooperative Law Association to provide more information. The brochure is available at http://mmccla.org/wp-content/uploads/mmccla-brochure-07-07.pdf. The website also includes an information sheet comparing Collaborative and Cooperative practice at http://mmccla.org/wp-content/uploads/choosing_ccl.pdf.

This letter assumes that the other party has not retained a lawyer. If the other party already has a lawyer, under the ethics rules, you must not contact the party and you should contact the lawyer instead. You could adapt this letter for the lawyer of the other party, though it may make more sense to call the lawyer instead of sending a letter. You should adapt this form for the circumstances of your case. For further discussion, see Chapter 4.

BROWN, WILLBRAND, SIMON, POWELL & LEWIS, P.C.

ATTORNEYS AT LAW

601 EAST BROADWAY, SUITE 203

P.O. BOX 1304

COLUMBIA, MISSOURI

TELEPHONE (573) 442-3181   65205-1304   FACSIMILE (573) 874-3796

E. M. BROWN (1926-1980)

H. C. WILLBRAND

B. DANIEL SIMON

JAMES M. POWELL

MARJORIE M. LEWIS

KAREN E. HAJICEK

MARY E. CARNAHAN

Name

Address

RE: Petition for Dissolution of Marriage

Dear Mr. _____:

As you may know, _____ has hired me to file her Petition for Dissolution of Marriage.

This letter describes some legal matters about the petition and our request for your cooperation in acknowledging that you received the petition (called "service of process"), but before I get into that, I want to address how you and _____ might handle your divorce.

There are several ways to proceed through the dissolution process, including the traditional process where each spouse has his or her own lawyer. This traditional process involves formal legal procedures and paperwork and, generally, the parties do not meet together with each other and their attorneys.

Another approach is mediation, where the parties meet with an impartial mediator to help them reach an agreement. This method gives people direct control over the decisions in their own case but the mediator cannot give legal advice to either party.

There are also some relatively new processes, called Collaborative and Cooperative Law, wherein each party has a lawyer and the lawyers and parties work together to resolve all the issues.

The goal in mediation, Collaborative Law, and Cooperative Law is to reach an agreement that most nearly satisfies the interests of both parties.

I practice Collaborative and Cooperative Law, which are described in more detail in the enclosed brochure. If you are interested in using either a Collaborative or Cooperative Law approach, you might contact one of the lawyers listed on the brochure or another lawyer who is interested in this process.

I encourage you to hire your own attorney and have that attorney answer any questions you may have and contact me. If you do not want to use an attorney, feel free to contact me if you have any questions. Although I cannot give you legal advice because I represent _____, I would be willing to try to answer general questions you may have regarding this case.

I recently filed the following documents in the Circuit Court of Boone County:

1. Petition for Dissolution of Marriage
2. Party Information Sheet
3. Notice and Acknowledgment for Service by Mail
4. Certificate of Dissolution of Marriage.

In order to avoid having the Sheriff of Boone County serve you personally, I am enclosing a Notice and Acknowledgment for Service by Mail for you to sign and return to the Circuit Clerk of Boone County.

You will note that in my cover letter to the Circuit Clerk, I asked that personal service to you by the Sheriff be delayed to allow you time to sign and return the Notice and Acknowledgment for Service by Mail.

If you sign the Notice and return it to the Circuit Clerk prior to the date specified on the Notice and Acknowledgment for Service by Mail, the Sheriff will not be required to deliver the summons and Petition to you personally.

If you do not return the Notice and Acknowledgment within the designated time, the Sheriff has been instructed to serve a summons and the Petition to you personally as directed in my cover letter to the Circuit Clerk.

You will have thirty (30) days from the date you acknowledge service or are served by the Sheriff to file your Answer to the Petition or you will be deemed to be in default and the matter can proceed without further notice to you.

_____ would like to work out your divorce in a way that is fair to you both and that keeps the legal costs to the minimum. That would require cooperation with you and your attorney, if you have one. I hope that we can proceed in this way. I look forward to your response.

Very truly yours,
Mary E. Carnahan

Enclosure

Appendix M.
Checklist for
Conversation with
Other Lawyers

You are likely to do a better job in a case—and enjoy it more—if you develop a good relationship with the other lawyer from the outset of the case. If you are working on a case with a lawyer you have never met or worked with before, it is very helpful to start by getting to know each other personally. If you are working on a case with a lawyer you already know, you obviously don't need to start from scratch, but it still may be helpful to catch up with each other before you focus on the case. Ideally, you should have this conversation face-to-face, perhaps over coffee or lunch. You might want to discuss some of the following topics in your first conversation. Of course, this should feel like a personal conversation rather than an interview. So you will presumably want to discuss many of the following issues from your perspective as well as hearing from the other lawyer. For further suggestions, see Chapter 4.

Personal Background

❑ Information about their practice (e.g., how long they have practiced, types of cases they handle, types of processes they offer, description of their firm, their philosophy of practice).

❑ Where they went to law school and college.

❑ Mutual acquaintances.

❑ Where they grew up and have lived.

❑ Members of their family.

❑ Personal interests such as travel, hobbies, sports, etc.

Background about the Parties and the Case

❑ Description of their client and the case

❑ How their client sees the problem.

❑ What their client really wants in the matter.

❑ Ways that the lawyers might work together to make the case go as smoothly as possible.

❑ Problems that they anticipate might arise and how you might work together to avoid or deal with these problems.

❑ Any "hot buttons" of their client that you should try to avoid pushing.

Plans for Working Together

❑ Ask what you can do to help them in this case.

❑ Ask what information that they will want. Offer to share information informally (if your client has authorized this) or to seek client's permission to provide the information.

❑ Ask them for information that you will want and whether they would provide this information informally (with their client's permission).

❑ Ask what types of professionals would be helpful or needed, if any, and whether it would make sense to hire joint neutral professionals. Ask if there are professionals whom they respect and would recommend.

❑ Ask what they see as the key legal issues in the case.

❑ Ask about their ideas for the best way to proceed in the case and when they think that negotiation might be appropriate.

☐   Ask whether they think that a face-to-face meeting with clients would be helpful early in the case.

☐   Ask if they would agree that you would both call each other before filing motions in court (other than in emergencies), initiating discovery requests, and doing anything that the other side would consider as an unwelcome surprise.

Appendix N.
Checklist for Preparing Clients for First Negotiation Session

This checklist is to help you prepare your clients for the first negotiation session. Your negotiations will generally be more successful if clients are well prepared. It is often difficult for clients to absorb all the information you provide, so you might ask them periodically to summarize their understanding of key points. If you ask them only if they understand what you have told them, they may simply affirm that they do because they are embarrassed to say that they don't. Even if they aren't embarrassed, they may misunderstand things, so it is helpful to check what they understand from your conversation. You should adapt this checklist based on your particular clients and cases. For further discussion, see Chapter 6.

❏ Ask about their expectations, hopes, and fears about the negotiation session.

❏ Explain your expectation about the procedure for the first meeting, including your conversations with the other lawyer about this. If you expect that you will spend a substantial amount of time discussing the process, including reviewing an agreement to negotiate, explain this to the client and why you think that this is helpful.

❏ Review the agreement to negotiate. Ask clients to explain their understanding of it and if they have any questions or concerns.

❏ Describe interest-based negotiation and how this approach can be used most effectively. Compare it with positional negotiation and describe the advantages and disadvantages of both approaches.

❏ Explain the items you expect to be on the agenda and ask what the client would like to put on the agenda. If appropriate, explain that certain issues may be discussed at a later meeting.

❏ Discuss the information and documents that would be needed for the negotiation. Confirm that clients are willing to provide the information and documents necessary for a successful negotiation. Ask what information they want to receive from the other side. Ask if there is any information or document that they do not want to disclose to the other side.

❏ If appropriate, identify the individuals from each side who are expected to attend the negotiation. Ask if there are people who definitely should or should not attend.

❏ Discuss whether it would be necessary or helpful to use any additional professionals.

❏ Discuss the roles of the lawyer and client in the negotiation and how you each can participate in the discussion most constructively.

❏ Describe your expectations about the process and results if the parties do not reach agreement.

❏ Ask what might happen that would upset clients during the meeting. Explain that it is perfectly normal for parties to run into problems during negotiation, so they shouldn't be surprised if and when that happens. Ask what they might do to get through an upset as easily as possible. Ask what could you do to help them if they get upset.

☐   Ask what might happen that would upset *the other party* during the meeting. Ask what you or they might do to avoid unnecessarily upsetting the other party.

☐   Ask what strengths they have that could help them work through any problems in the negotiation.

☐   Explain that sometimes parties say things that don't help them or the negotiation, such as calling the other side names, harshly criticizing them, bickering, etc. Explain that when that happens, it is usually helpful for lawyers to discuss this with their clients, sometimes in a meeting with the other side and sometimes privately. Assure them that you will always be "on their side" and that if you have such a conversation with them, you would do so because you want to help them achieve their goals.

☐   Ask how you could be most helpful to them in the negotiation session.

☐   Ask if they have any remaining questions or concerns about the negotiation.

Appendix O.
Checklist for First
Negotiation Session

This is a checklist for things to do at the first negotiation session. It is adapted from a form developed by the Mid-Missouri Collaborative and Cooperative Law Association for divorce cases. In these cases, there are often multiple negotiation sessions, and this checklist contemplates that there may be more than one session. You should adapt this form to fit your cases.

It is important that the parties understand the process as well as possible, so you might ask them periodically to summarize their understanding of key points. If you ask them only if they understand what you have told them, they may simply affirm that they do because they are embarrassed to say that they don't. Even if they aren't embarrassed, they may misunderstand things, so it is helpful to check what they understand from the discussion.

At the first meeting, parties may not be sure whether they want to use a Planned Early Negotiation process and may want to see how the first meeting goes before deciding. This is particularly relevant if the parties are considering a Collaborative process, because the disqualification of lawyers is generally considered irrevocable.

Following the meeting, you should discuss with your clients what they thought worked well during the meeting and what might be done differently in later meetings. After both lawyers have had these discussions, you should have a similar conversation with the other lawyer. For further discussion, see Chapters 2, 6, and 10.

This is adapted from a form developed by the Mid-Missouri Collaborative and Cooperative Law Association, © 2006. Reprinted with permission. For more information, see http://www.mmccla.org/.

☐ Set the agenda for the meeting.

☐ Arrange for a lawyer to make notes and distribute minutes of the meeting.

☐ Review the agreement to negotiate, answer any questions, and have the parties sign the agreement if they are ready to do so.

☐ Identify parties' interests.

☐ Discuss general process issues, such as:

  ☐ the goal is to reach agreement satisfying the interests of the parties (and, if applicable, their children).

  ☐ description of interest-based negotiation.

  ☐ what the parties should (and shouldn't) expect from their lawyer and the other lawyer.

  ☐ behavioral guidelines, such as treating each other respectfully and having only one person speak at a time.

  ☐ what the parties agree should or shouldn't be discussed with others (such as kids, parents, and friends).

  ☐ whether parties should communicate directly between meetings.

  ☐ principle of not taking provocative action—ACBD principle (always consult before deciding).

  ☐ what to do if problems arise between meetings.

  ☐ documents and additional information needed.

  ☐ what additional professionals, if any, to hire (such as financial or mental health professionals).

  ☐ dates for one or more additional meetings.

☐ Identify issues that need to be addressed immediately (such as support, housing, transportation of children).

☐ Discuss specific issues.

☐ Identify tasks to be completed before the next meeting, specifying who will perform the tasks and when they will be completed (including who will write a memo summarizing the meeting).

Appendix P.
Agreement to Negotiate in Collaborative Cases

This is a model agreement to negotiate (sometimes called a "participation agreement") for lawyers and clients in a Collaborative divorce case, adapted from a form developed by the Mid-Missouri Collaborative and Cooperative Law Association.

This agreement includes a disqualification provision that would be needed for this to be a Collaborative case. Because of the significance of this provision, this form includes lines for parties to initial that they intend to agree to it.

This agreement creates a presumption that, in the event of litigation or administrative agency proceeding, any professionals retained in the process would be disqualified as witnesses or advisors for either party, and their work product will be inadmissible as evidence. The provision contemplates that the parties might agree otherwise.

If desired, you could reverse the presumption and require an agreement for disqualification or preclusion of admissibility of work product. Appendix S is a model agreement for joint retention of a neutral professional, which addresses these issues.

Under norms of Collaborative Practice, all substantive negotiation occurs in face-to-face meetings with the parties. This form contemplates that some of the negotiation may take place between the lawyers without the parties present. If you want to conform to the Collaborative norms, you should modify this provision.

This agreement provides for protection against use of settlement negotiations in later litigation. Such protections may be affected by statutes or court rules in your jurisdiction, so you should make sure that the agreement is not inconsistent with any such statutes or rules.

This agreement provides that parties would bring certain documents to the first meeting. It also includes a broad definition of "relevant" information that goes beyond legally relevant information. These provisions may not be appropriate in some cases; if not, you should modify them.

The lawyers sign this agreement to approve the form but are not themselves parties to the agreement. Some Collaborative lawyers believe that it is important for them to sign these agreements as a commitment to abide by the process. Others are concerned that signing the agreement creates obligations to the other side that could create ethical problems of conflict of interest.

Lawyers and parties should modify this form to fit their particular situations. Some optional language is in brackets, and there may be variations depending on whether this is used in a family or other type of case. For further discussion, see Chapter 6.

This is adapted from forms developed by the Mid-Missouri Collaborative and Cooperative Law Association, © 2006. Reprinted with permission. For more information, see http://www.mmccla.org/.

AGREEMENT TO NEGOTIATE

This Agreement ("Agreement") is made between _____ and _____ (the "Parties"). The Parties commit to use our best efforts in a Collaborative Negotiation Process ("the Process") to negotiate a fair and reasonable agreement about _____.

Our goal is to reach a fair and reasonable agreement and avoid prolonged and harmful conflict without using the courts. We promise to listen carefully, honestly provide all information required under this Agreement, try to understand the interests of both Parties, seek solutions that satisfy the interests of both Parties, and treat everyone in the Process with respect. We shall not disparage each other to family members, colleagues, or mutual friends and acquaintances. We understand the Process and how it differs from other dispute resolution processes. Therefore, in consideration of our mutual promises, we agree to use the Process as follows.

I.   Focus on Direct Negotiation

By making this Agreement, we agree to work hard to negotiate a reasonable agreement in this matter and we direct our lawyers to do so as well. As we go through the Process, we shall decide the best way to proceed *[possibly include the following language:* , such as using meetings with all Parties and lawyers, conversations just between the lawyers, conversations just between the Parties, and inclusion of other professionals in our discussions, among others].

II.   Disqualification of Lawyers and Other Employed Professionals. Limited Scope of Representation

A.   If either of us files a document with a court or administrative agency related to or in connection with this matter (other than as agreed upon in writing), both of our lawyers (including any lawyers in association who would have a conflict of interest according to the Rules of Professional Conduct) are disqualified from representing us in the court or administrative agency proceeding. Lawyers disqualified under this provision shall be disqualified from representing us in any related contested matter involving both Parties, including but not limited to any subsequent action such as modification, enforcement, and appeals.

B.   We understand that each lawyer is hired only for negotiation in this Process and filing court documents as described in this Agreement.

Therefore each lawyer's representation of his or her client is a "limited representation," preventing each lawyer from representing his or her client in litigation about this matter or in any related contested matter.

C. Unless otherwise agreed to in writing, all other professionals employed in this Process (including consultants and experts) are disqualified as witnesses or advisors for either party in the event of litigation or administrative agency proceeding in this matter. Unless otherwise agreed to in writing, the other professionals' work product will be inadmissible as evidence in any court or administrative agency proceeding.

D. We understand that actual or potential disqualification of lawyers and other professionals could have an influence on our negotiation process and could result in additional cost and delay if we need to retain new lawyers or other professionals. We believe that the benefits of the Process outweigh the risks for us. We indicate our understanding of the Process and our desire to use it by initialing the next line.

Initials: _____   _____

III. Lawyers' Duty to Serve Their Own Clients

A. Each Party has retained an independent lawyer to provide legal advice. We understand that each lawyer has a professional duty to diligently represent his or her own client and that our lawyers represent only their own clients and not the other Party. There is no lawyer-client relationship between one Party and the other Party's lawyer.

B. We shall each direct our lawyers to listen carefully to other Party and lawyer, try to understand their interests, seek solutions that satisfy the interests of both Parties, and treat everyone in the Process with respect. We shall each ask our lawyers to advise us privately if they believe that it is in our interest to use a different approach than we want. We understand that our lawyers are trying to represent our individual interests when they consider how others' interests may affect us and when they give advice that we may not agree with.

IV. Confidentiality

Except as we agree in writing, any and all statements made and information provided by Parties and lawyers during the Process shall be considered as settlement negotiations, with all the confidentiality protections provided by law. We agree to broaden this confidentiality protection by precluding the use of any statement or information for any purpose to the extent allowed by law, except as follows. Statements or information cannot be protected as confidential if they (a) assist a criminal or fraudulent act, or (b) give reasonable cause to suspect that a child has been or may be subjected to abuse or neglect. We agree that, if we litigate this case, no Party will: (a) introduce as evidence in court any communications made or information disclosed in this Process unless it is otherwise admissible, (b) disclose to the court any settlement offer or responses to a settlement offer made in this Process, (c) subpoena any lawyer or expert in this Process to testify in any court proceeding, or (d) seek the production in any court proceedings of any notes, records, or documents in the possession of the lawyers or any experts in this Process unless they are otherwise discoverable.

V.   Information Exchange

We agree to completely and honestly disclose all relevant documents and information in this matter. At least three days before our first meeting in the Process, we shall each provide to the other the following statements notarized under oath: (1) Statement of Marital and Non-Marital Property and Liabilities, (2) Income and Expense Statement, and (3) copies of any existing documents that substantiate each answer made. After the first meeting, we shall give complete responses within agreed deadlines to all requests for other relevant documents and information. Relevant information is information needed to make an informed decision. (In other words, we agree to provide all information that we would want to know if in the other Party's position.) We shall not take advantage of miscalculations or inadvertent mistakes of fact or law. If we or our lawyers discover such miscalculations or other mistakes, we shall promptly inform each other and direct our lawyers to do the same.

VI. Use of Experts

If experts are needed, we shall consider retaining them jointly and sharing their work product. If we jointly retain an expert, the retention agreement shall describe the use of the work product and expectations about confidentiality. If such a retention agreement does not address confidentiality, the expert's work product shall not be admissible in court. Either Party may consult an expert separately. If a Party separately consults an expert, the Party need not share that expert's work product with the other Party [*optional provision:* but must notify the other Party, in advance, that the expert is being consulted].

VII. Maintaining a Reasonable Environment during the Process

At the beginning of the Process, we shall negotiate interim arrangements to maintain a fair and reasonable environment while we negotiate in the Process. We may agree to submit interim agreements to court. We shall begin the Process by discussing the need for interim agreements to achieve the following goals:

    A. Ensure frequent and meaningful contact between parents and children;

    B. Ensure adequate financial support for the care of the children [*add, if applicable:* and the Parties];

    C. Refrain from transferring, encumbering, concealing or in any way disposing of any property, except in the usual course of business or for the necessities of life and then with a full accounting, if requested;

    D. Refrain from harassing, abusing, molesting or disturbing the peace of each other or of any child; and

    E. Maintain without change in coverage or beneficiary designation, all existing contracts of insurance covering the life, health, dental or vision of the children and/or the spouse.

VIII. Termination

The following events and actions shall terminate the Process, although the provisions of this Agreement related to disqualification and confidentiality shall continue in effect even if the Process terminates. Termination occurs by serving a written notice of termination to the other party (or his or her lawyer). If the Process terminates, we understand that all lawyers in this Process shall withdraw from representing us and we shall direct them to transfer our files to our new lawyers.

    A. Either of us may terminate the Process at any time and for any reason by serving notice of the intent to terminate the Process. This termination is subject to a [30]-day "cooling off" period beginning on the date of service of the notice. During this period, neither party may file any action in any court or with any administrative agency except in emergency. During this period, we shall reflect on what caused the problems in negotiation, discuss with our lawyers every plausible idea for negotiating an appropriate resolution, and discuss the hiring of a mediator or neutral evaluator to help resolve the problems. Such mediation or neutral evaluation would be voluntary and take place only by our agreement. We shall share equally the costs of mediation or neutral evaluation unless otherwise agreed.

B. Either of us may discharge a Collaborative lawyer to hire another Collaborative lawyer, who would be bound by all the terms of this Agreement. If we discharge a Collaborative lawyer, we (or our lawyer) shall provide prompt written notice to the other party. The opportunity to retain a new Collaborative lawyer shall be available for a period of [30] days from the date of service of the notice. Failure to retain a substitute Collaborative lawyer within the [30]-day period shall constitute a termination of the Process.

C. We have directed our lawyers to withdraw from the Process if one of them believes that his or her client is withholding or misrepresenting relevant information or otherwise undermining the Process. In this situation, the lawyer will not disclose to the other party or the other party's attorney who decided to terminate the process or the reason for the termination.

IX. Acknowledgment

We have read this Agreement, understand its terms, and agree to comply with it. We understand that by agreeing to this Process, we may give up certain rights, including formal court procedure rules for discovery of information. We understand that there is no guarantee that we will reach agreement in this Process. We voluntarily enter into this Agreement.

Date _____   Party: _____

Approved as to Form by His/Her Lawyer:

_____

Date _____   Party: _____

Approved as to Form by His/Her Lawyer:

_____

Appendix Q.
Agreement to Negotiate in Cooperative Cases

This is a model agreement to negotiate (sometimes called a "participation agreement") for lawyers and clients in a Cooperative case, adapted from a form developed by the Mid-Missouri Collaborative and Cooperative Law Association. This form can be adapted when a party uses Settlement Counsel.

This agreement is similar to the one in the preceding appendix for Collaborative cases. Refer to the introduction to that agreement for more information.

This agreement differs from the Collaborative agreement in that it does not include the disqualification provision, and thus the related provisions for termination of the process also differ. It contemplates that the Cooperative process may continue during litigation. In that situation, the parties direct their lawyers to focus solely on the merits of the issues and avoid tactics that would unnecessarily aggravate the conflict.

This agreement provides includes optional provisions for family and non-family cases. It also includes alternative provisions about the scope of information that each party would provide. One provision includes a broad definition of "relevant" information that goes beyond legally relevant information. The other provision calls for agreement about the particular information to be exchanged.

Lawyers and parties should modify this form to fit their particular situations. Some optional language is in brackets, and there may be variations depending on whether this is used in a family or other type of case. For further discussion, see Chapter 6.

This is adapted from forms developed by the Mid-Missouri Collaborative and Cooperative Law Association, © 2006. Reprinted with permission. For more information, see http://www.mmccla.org/.

AGREEMENT TO NEGOTIATE

This Agreement ("Agreement") is made between _____ and _____ (the "Parties"). The Parties commit to use our best efforts in a Cooperative Negotiation Process ("the Process") to negotiate a fair and reasonable agreement about _____.

Our goal is to reach a fair and reasonable agreement and avoid prolonged and harmful conflict without using the courts. We promise to listen carefully, honestly provide all information required under this Agreement, try to understand the interests of both Parties, seek solutions that satisfy the interests of both Parties, and treat everyone in the Process with respect. We shall not disparage each other to [family members, colleagues, or mutual friends and acquaintances]. We understand the Process and how it differs from other dispute resolution processes. Therefore, in consideration of our mutual promises, we agree to use the Process as follows.

I. Focus on Direct Negotiation

By making this Agreement, we agree to work hard to negotiate a reasonable agreement in this matter and we direct our lawyers to do so as well. As we go through the Process, we shall decide the best way to proceed, such as using meetings with all Parties and lawyers, conversations just between the lawyers, conversations just between the Parties, and inclusion of other professionals in our discussions, among others.

II. Lawyers' Duty to Serve Their Own Clients

A. Each Party has retained an independent lawyer to provide legal advice. We understand that each lawyer has a professional duty to diligently represent his or her own client and that our lawyers represent only their own clients and not the other Party. There is no lawyer-client relationship between one Party and the other Party's lawyer.

B. We shall each direct our lawyers to listen carefully to other Party and lawyer, try to understand their interests, seek solutions that satisfy the interests of both Parties, and treat everyone in the Process with respect. We shall each ask our lawyers to advise us privately if they believe that it is in our interest to use a different approach than we want. We understand that our lawyers are trying to represent our individual interests when they consider how others' interests may affect us and when they give advice that we may not agree with.

III. Confidentiality

Except as we agree in writing, any and all statements made and information provided by Parties and lawyers during the Process shall be considered as settlement negotiations, with all the confidentiality protections provided by law. We agree to broaden this confidentiality protection by precluding the use of any statement or information for any purpose to the extent allowed by law, except as follows. Statements or information cannot be protected as confidential if they (a) assist a criminal or fraudulent act, or (b) give reasonable cause to suspect that a child has been or may be subjected to abuse or neglect. We agree that, if we litigate this case, no Party will: (a) introduce as evidence in court any communications made or information disclosed in this Process unless it is otherwise admissible, (b) disclose to the court any settlement offer or responses to a settlement offer made in this Process, (c) subpoena any lawyer or expert in this Process to testify in any court proceeding, or (d) seek the production in any court proceedings of any notes, records, or documents in the possession of the lawyers or any experts in this Process unless they are otherwise discoverable.

IV. Information Exchange

[Alternative 1—for family cases] We agree to completely and honestly disclose all relevant documents and information in this matter. At least three days before our first meeting in the Process, we shall each provide to the other the following statements notarized under oath: (1) Statement of Marital and Non-Marital Property and Liabilities, (2) Income and Expense Statement, and (3) copies of any existing documents that substantiate each answer made. After the first meeting, we shall give complete responses within agreed deadlines to all requests for other relevant documents and information. Relevant information is information needed to make an informed decision. (In other words, we agree to provide all information that we would want to know if in the other Party's position.) We shall not take advantage of miscalculations or inadvertent mistakes of fact or law. If we or our lawyers discover such miscalculations or other mistakes, we shall promptly inform each other and direct our lawyers to do the same.

[Alternative 2—more likely to be used in non-family cases] We agree to promptly exchange information, documents, and any other materials (hereafter "information") needed to negotiate in this Process. We understand that to negotiate successfully and efficiently, we will not need

all the information that would be produced in litigation. Instead, at the beginning of the Process, we shall agree on what information each Party will initially provide and the deadlines for doing so. After negotiating based on this information, if we need additional information to negotiate, we shall cooperate to provide such information promptly. To provide confidence in the information provided, we may agree that the Parties will sign declarations under the penalty of perjury that the information provided is true and correct. We shall not take advantage of miscalculations or inadvertent mistakes of fact or law. If we or our lawyers discover such miscalculations or other mistakes, we shall promptly inform each other and direct our lawyers to do the same.

V. Use of Experts

If experts are needed, we shall consider retaining them jointly and sharing their work product. If we jointly retain an expert, the retention agreement shall describe the use of the work product and expectations about confidentiality. If such a retention agreement does not address confidentiality, the expert's work product shall not be admissible in court. Either Party may consult an expert separately. If a Party separately consults an expert, the Party need not share that expert's work product with the other Party [*optional provision:* but must notify the other Party, in advance, that the expert is being consulted].

[for family cases]

VI. Maintaining a Reasonable Environment during the Process

At the beginning of the Process, we shall negotiate interim arrangements to maintain a fair and reasonable environment while we negotiate in the Process. We may agree to submit temporary agreements to court. We shall begin the Process by discussing the need for interim agreements to achieve the following goals:

   A. Ensure frequent and meaningful contact between parents and children;
   B. Ensure adequate financial support for the care of the children [*add, if applicable:* and the Parties];
   C. Refrain from transferring, encumbering, concealing or in any way disposing of any property, except in the usual course of business

or for the necessities of life and then with a full accounting, if requested;

D. Refrain from harassing, abusing, molesting, or disturbing the peace of each other or of any child; and

E. Maintain without change in coverage or beneficiary designation, all existing contracts of insurance covering the life, health, dental or vision of the children and/or the spouse.

VII. Dealing with Apparent Impasse; Termination of This Agreement

A. Either Party may terminate this Agreement at any time by giving written notice to the other Party or the Party's lawyer.

B. If either Party wants to use litigation or administrative agency action to resolve any issues in this matter, we shall do so only after a [30]-day "cooling-off" period or in case of an emergency. The cooling-off period begins by serving a written notice to the other Party or the Party's lawyer. During this period, we shall reflect on what caused the problems in negotiation, discuss with our lawyers every plausible idea for negotiating an appropriate resolution, and discuss the hiring of a mediator or neutral evaluator to help resolve the problems. Such mediation or neutral evaluation would be voluntary and take place only by our agreement. We shall share equally the costs of mediation or neutral evaluation unless otherwise agreed.

C. If we use the courts or an administrative agency to resolve any issues in this matter, we may litigate in a cooperative spirit under this Agreement or we may terminate this Agreement. If we litigate under this Agreement, we shall direct our lawyers to focus solely on the merits of the issues and avoid tactics that would unnecessarily aggravate the conflict. If we terminate the Process, we make no such commitment to litigate in a cooperative spirit.

D. Either Party may discharge a Cooperative lawyer to hire another Cooperative lawyer, who would be bound by all the terms of this Agreement. If we discharge a Cooperative lawyer, we (or our lawyer) shall provide prompt written notice to the other Party. The opportunity to retain a new Cooperative lawyer shall be available for a period of [30] days from the date of service of the notice. Failure to retain a substitute Cooperative lawyer within the [30]-day period shall constitute a termination of the Process.

E. We have directed our lawyers to withdraw from the Process if one of them believes that, after discussing the matter with their client, the client is withholding or misrepresenting relevant information, secretly disposing of property in this case, or otherwise undermining the Process. In this situation, the lawyer shall not disclose to the other Party or the other Party's attorney who decided to terminate the process or the reason for the termination.

F.   If the Process is terminated, the provisions of this Agreement related to confidentiality shall continue in effect.

VIII.   Acknowledgment

We have read this Agreement, understand its terms, and agree to comply with it. We understand that by agreeing to this Process, we may give up certain rights, including formal court procedure rules for discovery of information. We understand that there is no guarantee that we will reach agreement in this Process. We voluntarily enter into this Agreement.

Date _____   Party: _____

Approved as to Form by His/Her Lawyer:

_____

Date _____   Party: _____

Approved as to Form by His/Her Lawyer:

_____

Appendix R. Agreement for Joint Retention of Neutral Professional

This agreement establishes the relationship between the parties and a neutral professional, such as a mediator, financial professional, appraiser, technical expert, mental health professional, neutral evaluator, or arbitrator. It includes a provision specifying whether the professional may or may not participate in litigation, be required to provide his or her work product, or engage in any services for the parties after the negotiation ends. You should adapt this form to fit the circumstances of your case. For discussion of these and other issues regarding retention of professionals, see Chapter 8.

AGREEMENT FOR PROFESSIONAL SERVICES

This Agreement ("Agreement") is made between _____ _____ and _____ (the "Parties") and _____ ("Professional"). The Parties retain Professional to provide the following services in Parties' negotiation process: _____ _____.

1.   Professional is retained jointly by both Parties and will serve as a neutral for the benefit of both Parties and not as an advocate or advisor to benefit only one Party.

2.   Parties shall promptly cooperate with all reasonable requests by Professional, including requests for information.

3.   Unless Parties otherwise agree in writing, if Parties engage in litigation or an administrative agency proceeding in this matter: (a) Professional shall [not] be permitted to serve as a witness or advisor for the Parties (including depositions), and (b) Professional's notes and work product shall [not] be admissible as evidence.

4.   [*If applicable:*] Parties understand that Professional may be required to report to legal authorities if [he *or* she] has a reasonable suspicion of child abuse or neglect in this matter.

5.   Professional shall provide information in this matter to the Parties and their lawyers and other professionals engaged in this matter. Except as provided in this agreement, Professional shall not provide information about this matter to others without Parties' written consent.

6.   The joint retention of Professional does not prevent either Party from individually retaining another professional to provide similar services.

7.   Following termination of the negotiation, Professional may [not] work for either or both parties, unless Parties otherwise agree in writing.

8.   Parties agree to pay Professional's fees of $_____ per hour as well as reasonable costs incurred in this matter. Professional's services may include consultation with Parties' lawyers and other professionals in this case outside of negotiation sessions. Parties shall each pay [one half of Professional's charges *or specify other arrangement*].

Date _____   Party: _____

Approved as to Form by His/Her Lawyer:

_____

Date _____   Party: _____

Approved as to Form by His/Her Lawyer:

_____

Date _____   Professional: _____

Appendix S. Stipulation for Confidential Mini-evaluation

Los Angeles mediator and Collaborative lawyer Forrest Mosten uses the following stipulation in divorce cases to quickly obtain an oral report to help with the negotiation rather than having to wait a long time to get a detailed written evaluation. It is reprinted with permission. For further discussion, see Chapter 8.

SUPERIOR COURT OF THE STATE OF CALIFORNIA
IN AND FOR THE COUNTY OF LOS ANGELES

In re Marriage of:

Mother:	**and**	) **Case No. XXXXXXX**
		)
		) **COLLABORATIVE CASE**
Father:		) **PER FAMILY CODE 2031**
		)
		) **STIPULATION for**
		) **Confidential**
		) **Mini-Evaluation (CME)**
		)

IT IS HEREBY STIPULATED between the parties that:

1. The parties are engaged in a Collaborative Process and wish to resolve current parenting issues in an amicable, child-centered, cost-effective, and confidential manner;

2. The parties shall appoint _____,PhD, to conduct the CME, and both parties shall participate and cooperate with the process as set forth in this Stipulation;

3. The CME Evaluator shall meet with the parties, minor children, and other persons agreed upon on or before _____. The CME Evaluator shall have telephone interviews with the children's teachers, coaches, nanny, pediatrician, and other persons agreed upon on or before _____.

4. The CME Evaluator shall not prepare a written report of his/her observations, findings and recommendations which shall be presented orally to the parties and all Collaborative professionals (and mediator) on _____.

5. Following the oral presentation, the parties, Collaborative Professionals, and CME Evaluator shall have a discussion about the content of the CME oral report.

6. Neither party, any Collaborative professional, nor the CME Evaluator shall disclose any observation, finding, or recommendation to the court or to a subsequent Evaluator.

7. Following the CME, either party shall have the right to compel the parties to participate in a Formal Parenting Evaluation that shall be admitted to court.

8. The Court finds that the parties have resolved these issues within a Collaborative Proceeding pursuant to a Collaborative Stipulation filed with the court.

9. If any dispute should arise as to the compliance, interpretation, modification, or enforcement of this Stipulation, at the request of either party, both parties and their attorneys shall participate in a Joint Collaborative Session within 7 days of either party's written request.

10. This Stipulation shall be signed in duplicate originals and held by the counsel and not filed with the court except for the purposes of compliance, interpretation, modification, or enforcement following participation in mediation as provided in this Stipulation.

11. All other issues in this matter are reserved.

IT IS SO STIPULATED:

Dated: _____   _____
                        Mother

Dated: _____   _____
                        Father

Approved as to Form:

Dated: _____   _____
                        Collaborative Attorney for Mother

Dated: _____   _____
                        Collaborative Attorney for Father

IT IS SO ORDERED:

Dated: _____   _____
                        Judge of the Superior Court

Appendix T.
Contract Provision for
Early Negotiation of
Future Disputes

This is adapted from a form developed by Toledo, Ohio, attorney Peter R. Silverman for use in franchise disputes. It is included in franchise agreements and provides for "early active intervention" by lawyers to try to resolve the disputes very soon after they arise. It provides for preliminary negotiation between the lawyers and, if needed, a case facilitator to manage the negotiations. This form is included with permission. For further discussion, see Chapters 7 and 8.

Early active intervention. If one party has a claim against the other, that party may invoke early active intervention (EAI) to negotiate before filing suit or a demand for arbitration. EAI is subject to the following rules:

1. *Initiation of the Process.* A party initiates EAI by sending notice (the "Notice") to the other party that states that the initiating party is initiating EAI and that provides a concise statement of the claim. Normally, before sending the Notice, the initiating party will call the other party to discuss the issue and possibility for negotiation.

2. *Tolling.* Initiation of EAI tolls the statute of limitations on the initiating party's claims. The other party may terminate tolling on [14] days' notice.

3. *Response.* Within [7] days of receiving the Notice, the other party shall send the initiating party a concise statement of whether it would like to use the EAI process. If the other party sends no response, we shall not use the EAI process.

4. *Direct negotiation.* If the responding party would like to use the EAI process, we shall begin negotiations within [3] days of the response. We shall use effective negotiation principles as follows:

    i. *Parties with authority.* We will arrange for attendance at the negotiation of the people on our respective sides who have the authority to resolve the dispute.

    ii. *Goal and principles of negotiation.* The goal of negotiation will be to seek a business resolution of the dispute through cooperative communication. We will focus on each other's most important interests and seek to generate options to satisfy those interests, considering possible objective standards to evaluate interests and options.

    iii. *Need for further information or documents.* If the dispute is not resolved at our initial negotiation session, we shall determine whether any party needs further information or documents to reasonably evaluate the issues. If either side needs such information or documents, we shall set a time period for exchange of information and documents. Normally, this period will be no more than [30] days.

    iv. *Further negotiation.* If we agree to continue negotiation following information and document exchange, negotiations shall begin within [14] days after completion of the information and document exchange.

5. *Facilitated negotiation.*

    i. *Selection of EAI facilitator.* At any time, if we believe that it would be helpful to have a neutral facilitator assist us in negotiation, we shall mutually and promptly select an EAI facilitator.

    ii. *Fees.* We will each be responsible for half of the facilitator's fees.

    iii. *Case facilitation process.* Within [7] days of the facilitator's selection, the facilitator shall hold a case facilitation conference by telephone. The conference shall address the following topics.

        a. *Information and document exchange.* If we have not agreed on exchange of information or documents, the facilitator may decide on the appropriate scope of information and document exchange. The presumption shall be to require only that discovery necessary to give the parties enough information to reasonably evaluate the merits of our respective positions. The facilitator shall set a short time limit to finish exchange of information and documents. Normally, this exchange will be completed no later than [30] days after the initial case facilitation conference.

        b. *Facilitation schedule and site.* The facilitator shall set a date for a face-to-face case facilitation conference. The conference shall be scheduled no later than [30] days after the end of information and document exchange. The facilitator shall decide the place of the conference after consulting with us.

        c. *Facilitation conference.* The facilitator may require us to submit materials to the facilitator that we send confidentially to only the facilitator and/or that we share with each other. We will arrange for the attendance at the conference the people on our respective sides who have the authority to resolve the dispute. The facilitator's role will be to actively mediate the dispute.

        d. *Litigation management.* If we are unable to resolve the dispute at the facilitation conference, the facilitator shall assist us in developing a litigation management agreement to cover discovery, time limits, and other matters to seek to limit the cost and time of suit or arbitration.

6. *Method of written communication.* All written communication shall be by e-mail. For purposes of calculating dates, receipt of written communications will be deemed contemporaneous with sending.

7. *Modification of the process.* If the facilitator believes that it would be appropriate to modify the procedure, he or she may do so after consulting with the parties.

8. *Voluntary termination.* Either party may terminate the EAI process at any time by sending [3] days' notice to the other.

Appendix U.
Self-Assessment Form
—General

This form is designed to help you analyze your professional performance. You will probably want to focus on interactions that didn't go as well as you would have liked, though it would also be helpful to analyze ones that went particularly well—perhaps surprisingly so. The interactions can include portions of negotiation sessions but shouldn't be limited to them. (Appendix V is designed for assessment of negotiation.) For example, you can include interactions with clients, the other lawyer, other professionals, and judges and court staff, among others. You are likely to get the most out of the analysis if you do it as soon as possible after the interaction. For further discussion, see Chapter 9.

1. How well did you perform overall? Use a scale from 1 to 10, where 1 is the worst possible performance and 10 is the best possible performance.
2. What were the key events in the interaction?
3. What went well in this interaction? (Don't skip this question or skimp on your answer.)
4. What was problematic in this interaction? (Be honest and not unduly hard on yourself.)
5. How did you feel during the interaction? (You might include emotions such as anger, embarrassment, and physical reactions such as sweating or tension in your chest.)
6. What were you thinking during the interaction?
7. What were you trying to accomplish?
8. How do you think that the other person saw the interaction?
9. What do you think that the other person was trying to accomplish?
10. Can you pinpoint the behaviors that triggered problematic reactions? (These might be behaviors by you and/or the other person.)
11. What are the most likely reasons for the problems?
12. Does this interaction fit into a recurring pattern of yours and/or the other person? If so, how would you describe the pattern?
13. If you could redo the interaction, what might you do differently?
14. Do you think it would be productive to discuss this interaction with the other person? (In some situations, it can be very helpful to debrief with the other person. This can help you improve your skills and avoid future problems with that person. In some situations, it would be problematic to discuss this with the other person, as it could undermine your ability to function effectively in the matter.)
15. Is there someone who was not involved in the interaction who could help you analyze it?

Appendix V.
Self-Assessment Form
—Negotiation

This form is designed to help you analyze your professional performance in negotiation (or mediation). You will probably want to focus on interactions that didn't go as well as you would have liked, though it would also be helpful to analyze ones that went particularly well—perhaps surprisingly so. You are likely to get the most out of the analysis if you do it as soon as possible after the interaction. For further discussion, see Chapter 9.

1. How well did you perform overall? Use a scale from 1 to 10, where 1 is the worst possible performance and 10 is the best possible performance.
2. How well did you understand <u>your client's interests</u>?
3. How well did you understand the <u>other party's interests</u>?
4. How well did you help your client <u>analyze his or her own interests</u>?
5. How well did you help your client <u>analyze the other party's interests</u>?
6. How well did you help your client <u>analyze the strengths and weaknesses of his or her case</u>?
7. How well did you <u>prepare your client for the negotiation</u>?
8. How well did you <u>plan the negotiation with the other side</u>?
9. How well did you <u>manage the negotiation process</u>?
10. If you used <u>other professionals</u> in the negotiation, <u>how well did you work with them</u>?
11. How well did you <u>deal with problems arising in the negotiation process</u>?
12. How well did you <u>develop options to advance the negotiation process</u>?
13. If the parties settled, how well did <u>the agreement satisfy your client's most important interests</u>?
14. If the parties did not settle, what were the <u>barriers to settlement</u>? What might you have done to <u>overcome these barriers</u>?
15. What did you <u>do particularly well in the negotiation</u>? (Don't skip this question or skimp on your answer.)
16. Based on your analysis of this negotiation, <u>what might you do differently</u> in the future? (Be honest and not unduly hard on yourself.)
17. Do you think it would be productive to discuss this negotiation with others who participated in the negotiation? (In some situations, it can be very helpful to debrief with the other person. This can help you improve your skills and avoid future problems. In some situations, it would be problematic to discuss this with people involved in the case, as it could undermine your ability to function effectively in the matter.)
18. Is there someone who was not involved in the negotiation who could help you analyze it?

Appendix W.
Client Assessment
Interview

This is a protocol for interviewing clients after completion of your work for them on a matter. It is designed to elicit feedback about a range of specific aspects of your services and interactions with clients.

You may not be able to interview all of your clients, and if not, you should develop a plan for selecting which clients to interview. You might limit the interviews to certain types of matters, such as those of a certain size or dealing with particular types of issues (which we will refer to as "qualified cases"). You might then select a fraction of qualified cases, such as a quarter or half, depending on the number of cases and the time available to do the interviews. Decide on a procedure for selecting cases for interviews, such as every fourth qualified case you complete.

This form assumes that your office would interview some of your clients after you have completed work in their matters. Although you might want to conduct the interviews for your own cases, some clients may not feel comfortable being candid with you. So you might arrange for a member of the support staff or another lawyer in your office to do the interviews. In some cases, you might want a consultant to conduct interviews. Using a consultant may increase clients' willingness to be candid. Of course, using a consultant involves some additional expense.

Many clients will want to know who will or will not learn about their answers. Researchers often protect confidentiality—and thus encourage candor— by telling people that their responses will be reported only in combination with others' responses. Although this arrangement encourages candor, it means that you would not learn about clients' reactions in particular matters. If you prefer to get these specific reactions, you cannot promise confidentiality, which may decrease clients' candor to some degree.

This form includes an e-mail to solicit clients' participation and a list of questions for the interview. You should modify this form to fit your situation. For example, you might send the solicitation by postal mail, or you want to adapt this for use in Internet surveys rather than telephone interviews. For further discussion, see Chapter 9.

Solicitation E-mail

Dear _____:

Our law office routinely interviews some of our clients to help improve our services to clients in the future. You have been randomly selected for one of these interviews.

We would appreciate it if we could interview you about how our office handled your case involving _____. We will ask about things you liked and things you didn't like. The interview can take about 15 minutes, though it could take longer if you want to say more.

If applicable: We will combine your answers with those of other clients so that no one will know your particular responses (except the interviewer).

Can we schedule a time to call you for this interview? If so, are there some dates and times that would be especially convenient for you?

Thanks very much for your consideration.

Sincerely,

/s/

Interview Protocol

Thanks very much for taking the time to talk with me today about how our office handled your case involving _____. We would especially appreciate it if you could be <u>as candid as possible</u>—both about things you liked and things you didn't like.

If applicable: We will combine your answers with those of other clients so that no one will know your particular responses except for me, and I won't tell others in our office.

For most of the questions, I will ask you to begin your answer with a numerical rating and then briefly explain in your own words. The numerical ratings will be on a scale from 1 to 5 where 1 means "very dissatisfied," 5 means "very satisfied," and 3 means "neither satisfied nor dissatisfied." Some questions may not be applicable to your case, and please let me know if that's your situation.

Do you have any questions before we begin?

1. Overall, <u>how satisfied were you with the services</u> you received from our office?
   - very dissatisfied
   - somewhat dissatisfied
   - neither satisfied nor dissatisfied
   - somewhat satisfied
   - very satisfied
   Why do you feel this way? _____

2. How satisfied were you that your lawyer(s) <u>understood your goals</u>?
   - very dissatisfied
   - somewhat dissatisfied
   - neither satisfied nor dissatisfied
   - somewhat satisfied
   - very satisfied
   Why do you feel this way? _____

3. How satisfied were you with your lawyer(s)' <u>actions to achieve your goals</u>?
   - very dissatisfied
   - somewhat dissatisfied
   - neither satisfied nor dissatisfied

- somewhat satisfied
- very satisfied

Why do you feel this way? _____

4. How satisfied were you with your lawyer(s)' <u>advice to you</u>?
   - very dissatisfied
   - somewhat dissatisfied
   - neither satisfied nor dissatisfied
   - somewhat satisfied
   - very satisfied

   Why do you feel this way? _____

5. How satisfied were you with the <u>outcome of your case</u>?
   - very dissatisfied
   - somewhat dissatisfied
   - neither satisfied nor dissatisfied
   - somewhat satisfied
   - very satisfied

   Why do you feel this way? _____

6. How satisfied were you with your lawyer(s)' <u>interactions with the other side</u>?
   - very dissatisfied
   - somewhat dissatisfied
   - neither satisfied nor dissatisfied
   - somewhat satisfied
   - very satisfied
   - not applicable

   Why do you feel this way? _____

7 How satisfied were you with your lawyer(s)' <u>performance in litigation</u>?
   - very dissatisfied
   - somewhat dissatisfied
   - neither satisfied nor dissatisfied
   - somewhat satisfied
   - very satisfied
   - not applicable

   Why do you feel this way? _____

8. How satisfied were you with your lawyer(s)' <u>performance in negotiation</u> (including mediation, if applicable)?
   - very dissatisfied
   - somewhat dissatisfied
   - neither satisfied nor dissatisfied
   - somewhat satisfied
   - very satisfied
   - not applicable

   Why do you feel this way? _____

9. How satisfied were you with the <u>accuracy of the communications you received from our office</u>?
   - very dissatisfied
   - somewhat dissatisfied
   - neither satisfied nor dissatisfied
   - somewhat satisfied
   - very satisfied

   Why do you feel this way? _____

10. How satisfied were you with the <u>timeliness of the communications you received from our office</u>?
    - very dissatisfied
    - somewhat dissatisfied
    - neither satisfied nor dissatisfied
    - somewhat satisfied
    - very satisfied

    Why do you feel this way? _____

11. How satisfied were you with your <u>interactions with the support staff in our office</u>?
    - very dissatisfied
    - somewhat dissatisfied
    - neither satisfied nor dissatisfied
    - somewhat satisfied
    - very satisfied
    - not applicable

    Why do you feel this way? _____

For the next two questions, there will be slightly different numerical scales, as I will explain.

12. Would you <u>recommend our office to others</u> who have a case similar to yours? Please answer on a scale from 1 to 5 where 1 means "definitely would <u>not</u> recommend" and 5 means "definitely <u>would</u> recommend."
    * definitely not
    * probably not
    * uncertain
    * probably would
    * definitely would
    Why do you feel this way? _____

13. Considering the value you received from our services, <u>how reasonable were the fees</u>? Please answer on a scale from 1 to 5 where 1 means "very <u>un</u>reasonable" and 5 means "very reasonable."
    * very unreasonable
    * somewhat unreasonable
    * neither reasonable nor unreasonable
    * somewhat reasonable
    * very reasonable
    Why do you feel this way? _____

14. What was the best thing about the services we provided in this case?

15. What might we have done to improve our services in this case?

16. Do you have any other comments?

Thank you very much for giving us your feedback.

Bibliography

There are many resources to learn more about the issues discussed in this book. The following list is far from comprehensive, but it provides a good place to start looking for additional materials. Some publications could fit in several categories.

You might want to read some of my other publications, including those listed below, which you can download from http://www.law.missouri.edu/lande/publications.htm.

The readings are collected in the following categories:

Legal Practice

Harold Abramson, *Problem-Solving Advocacy in Mediations: A Model of Client Representation*, 10 Harv. Negot. L. Rev. 103 (2005).

Phillip M. Armstrong, *Why We Still Litigate*, 8 Pepp. Disp. Resol. L.J. 379 (2008).

Maurits Barendrecht & Berend R. de Vries, *Fitting the Forum to the Fuss with Sticky Defaults: Failure in the Market for Dispute Resolution Services?*, 7 Cardozo J. Conflict Resol. 83 (2005).

Beyond the Billable Hour: An Anthology of Alternative Billing Methods (Richard C. Reed ed., 1989).

Robert M. Bastress & Joseph D. Harbaugh, Interviewing, Counseling, and Negotiating: Skills for Effective Representation (1990).

David A. Binder, Paul Bergman & Susan C. Price, Lawyers as Counselors: A Client Centered Approach (2d ed. 2004).

Lisa Blomgren Bingham, *When We Hold No Truths to Be Self-Evident: Truth, Belief, Trust, and the Decline in Trials*, 2006 J. Disp. Resol. 131 (2006).

Lisa Blomgren Bingham, Tina Nabatchi, Jeffrey M. Senger & Michael Scott Jackman, *Dispute Resolution and the Vanishing Trial: Comparing Federal Government Litigation and ADR Outcomes*, 24 Ohio St. J. on Disp. Resol. 225 (2009).

Gary L. Blasi, *What Lawyers Know: Lawyering Expertise, Cognitive Science, and the Functions of Theory*, 45 J. Legal Educ. 313 (1995).

Marshall J. Breger, *Should an Attorney Be Required to Advise a Client of ADR Options?*, 13 Geo. J. Legal Ethics 427 (2000).

Robert F. Cochran, Jr., John M.A. DiPippa & Martha M. Peters, The Counselor-at-Law: A Collaborative Approach to Client Interviewing and Counseling (2d ed. 2006).

Jonathan R. Cohen, *Advising Clients to Apologize*, 72 S. Cal. L. Rev. 1009 (1999).

Jonathan R. Cohen, *The Culture of Legal Denial*, 84 Neb. L. Rev. 247 (2005).

Jonathan R. Cohen, *The Immorality of Denial*, 79 Tul. L. Rev. 903 (2005).

Susan Daicoff, *Lawyer, Know Thyself: A Review of Empirical Research on Attorney Attributes Bearing on Professionalism*, 46 AM. U.L. REV. 1337 (1997).

Susan Daicoff, *Lawyer, Be Thyself: An Empirical Investigation of the Relationship Between the Ethic of Care, the Feeling Decisionmaking Preference, and Lawyer Wellbeing*, 16 VA. J. SOC. POL'Y & L. 87 (2008).

Susan Daicoff, *Law as a Healing Profession: The "Comprehensive Law Movement,"* 6 PEPP. DISP. RESOL. L.J. 1 (2006).

Robert D. Dinerstein, *Client-Centered Counseling: Reappraisal and Refinement*, 32 ARIZ. L. REV. 501 (1990).

Stephen D. Easton, *My Last Lecture: Unsolicited Advice for Future and Current Lawyers*, 56 S.C. L. REV. 229 (2004).

HENRY W. EWALT & ANDREW W. EWALT, THROUGH THE CLIENT'S EYES: NEW APPROACHES TO GET CLIENTS TO HIRE YOU AGAIN AND AGAIN (3d ed. 2008).

Monroe H. Freedman, *In Praise of Overzealous Representation—Lying to Judges, Deceiving Third Parties, and Other Ethical Conduct*, 34 HOFSTRA L. REV. 771 (2006).

Marc Galanter, *Case Congregations and Their Careers*, 24 LAW & SOC'Y REV. 371 (1990).

Marc Galanter, *Why the "Haves" Come Out Ahead: Speculations on the Limits of Legal Change*, 9 LAW & SOC'Y REV. 95 (1974).

Tracey E. George & Chris Guthrie, *Induced Litigation*, 98 NW. U. L. REV. 545 (2004).

Ronald J. Gilson & Robert H. Mnookin, *Disputing Through Agents: Cooperation and Conflict Between Lawyers in Litigation*, 94 COLUM. L. REV. 509 (1994).

Helaine Scarlett Golann & Dwight Golann, *Why Is It Hard for Lawyers to Deal with Emotional Issues?*, DISP. RESOL. MAG., Winter 2003, at 26.

Jeffrey H. Goldfien & Jennifer K. Robbennolt, *What If the Lawyers Have Their Way? An Empirical Assessment of Conflict Strategies and Attitudes Toward Mediation Styles*, 22 OHIO ST. J. ON DISP. RESOL. 277 (2007).

Samuel R. Gross & Kent D. Syverud, *Don't Try: Civil Jury Verdicts in a System Geared to Settlement*, 44 UCLA L. REV. 1 (1996).

Chris Guthrie, *Better Settle Than Sorry: The Regret Aversion Theory of Litigation Behavior*, 1999 U. ILL. L. REV. 43 (1999).

ROGER S. HAYDOCK & PETER B. KNAPP, HAYDOCK & KNAPP'S LAWYERING: PRACTICE AND PLANNING (2d ed. 2003).

G. NICHOLAS HERMAN & JEAN M. CARY, LEGAL COUNSELING, NEGOTIATING, AND MEDIATING: A PRACTICAL APPROACH (2d ed. 2009).

Robert A. Kagan, *Do Lawyers Cause Adversarial Legalism? A Preliminary Inquiry*, 19 LAW & SOC. INQUIRY 1 (1994).

Russell Korobkin & Chris Guthrie, *Psychology, Economics, and Settlement: A New Look at the Role of the Lawyer*, 76 TEX. L. REV. 77 (1997).

Kenneth Kressel, Kathleen M. Scanlon, Warren Reich & Gary Weiner, *A Field Report on the New CPR Mediation Screen*, 21 ALTERNATIVES TO HIGH COST LITIG. 133 (2003).

STEFAN H. KRIEGER & RICHARD K. NEUMANN, JR., ESSENTIAL LAWYERING SKILLS: INTERVIEWING, COUNSELING, NEGOTIATION, AND PERSUASIVE FACT ANALYSIS (3d ed. 2007).

Herbert M. Kritzer, *Adjudication to Settlement: Shading in the Gray*, 70 JUDICATURE 161 (1986).

Herbert M. Kritzer, *American Adversarialism*, 38 LAW & SOC'Y REV. 349 (2004).

Herbert M. Kritzer, *Contingent-Fee Lawyers and Their Clients: Settlement Expectations, Settlement Realities, and Issues of Control in the Lawyer-Client Relationship*, 23 LAW & SOC. INQUIRY 795 (1998).

Herbert M. Kritzer, *Lawyer Fees and Lawyer Behavior in Litigation: What Does the Empirical Literature Really Say?*, 80 TEX. L. REV. 1943 (2002).

Herbert M. Kritzer & Frances Kahn Zemans, *Local Legal Culture and the Control of Litigation*, 27 LAW & SOC'Y REV. 535 (1993).

John Lande, *The Movement Toward Early Case Handling in Courts and Private Dispute Resolution*, 24 OHIO ST. J. ON DISP. RESOL. 81 (2008).

John Lande, *How Will Lawyering and Mediation Practices Transform Each Other?*, 24 FLA. ST. U. L. REV. 839 (1997).

John Lande & Gregg Herman, *Fitting the Forum to the Family Fuss: Choosing Mediation, Collaborative Law, or Cooperative Law for Negotiating Divorce Cases*, 42 FAM. CT. REV. 280 (2004).

Lisa G. Lerman, *Lying to Clients*, 138 U. PA. L. REV. 659 (1990).

JULIE MACFARLANE, THE NEW LAWYER: HOW SETTLEMENT IS TRANSFORMING THE PRACTICE OF LAW (2008).

LYNN MATHER, CRAIG A. MCEWEN & RICHARD J. MAIMAN, DIVORCE LAWYERS AT WORK: VARIETIES OF PROFESSIONALISM IN PRACTICE (2001).

Barbara McAdoo & Nancy Welsh, *Does ADR Really Have a Place on the Lawyer's Philosophical Map?*, 18 HAMLINE J. PUB. L. & POL'Y 376 (1997).

Craig A. McEwen, *Managing Corporate Disputing: Overcoming Barriers to the Effective Use of Mediation for Reducing the Cost and Time of Litigation*, 14 OHIO ST. J. ON DISP. RESOL. 1 (1998).

Carrie Menkel-Meadow, *The Lawyer as Problem Solver and Third-Party Neutral: Creativity and Non-Partisanship in Lawyering*, 72 TEMP. L. REV. 785 (1999).

Carrie Menkel-Meadow, *Lying to Clients for Economic Gain or Paternalistic Judgment: A Proposal for a Golden Rule of Candor*, 138 U. PA. L. REV. 761 (1990).

Carrie Menkel-Meadow, *When Winning Isn't Everything: The Lawyer as Problem Solver*, 28 HOFSTRA L. REV. 905 (2000).

Michael L. Moffitt, *Customized Litigation: The Case for Making Civil Procedure Negotiable*, 75 GEO. WASH. L. REV. 461 (2007).

Forrest S. Mosten, *Lawyer as Peacemaker: Building a Successful Law Practice Without Ever Going to Court*, 43 FAM. L.Q. 489 (2009).

FORREST S. MOSTEN, UNBUNDLING LEGAL SERVICES: A GUIDE TO DELIVERING LEGAL SERVICES A LA CARTE (2000).

Scott R. Peppet, *Contract Formation in Imperfect Markets: Should We Use Mediators in Deals?*, 19 OHIO ST. J. ON DISP. RESOL. 283 (2004).

Jeffrey J. Rachlinski, *Gains, Losses and the Psychology of Litigation*, 70 S. CAL. L. REV. 113 (1996).

Peter H. Rehm & Denise R. Beatty, *Legal Consequences of Apologizing*, 1996 J. DISP. RESOL. 115.

TAMARA RELIS, PERCEPTIONS IN LITIGATION AND MEDIATION: LAWYERS, DEFENDANTS, PLAINTIFFS, AND GENDERED PARTIES (2009).

Nancy H. Rogers & Craig A. McEwen, *Employing the Law to Increase the Use of Mediation and to Encourage Direct and Early Negotiations*, 13 Ohio St. J. on Disp. Resol. 831 (1998).

Leonard L. Riskin, *The Contemplative Lawyer: On the Potential Contributions of Mindfulness Meditation to Law Students, Lawyers, and Their Clients*, 7 Harv. Negot. L. Rev. 1 (2002).

Leonard L. Riskin, *Mediation and Lawyers*, 43 Ohio St. L.J. 29 (1982).

Mark A. Robertson & James A. Calloway, Winning Alternatives to the Billable Hour: Strategies that Work (3d ed. 2008).

Joshua D. Rosenberg, *Interpersonal Dynamics: Helping Lawyers Learn the Skills, and the Importance, of Human Relationships in the Practice of Law*, 58 U. Miami L. Rev. 1225 (2004).

Peter Salem, Debra Kulak & Robin M. Deutsch, *Triaging Family Court Services: The Connecticut Judicial Branch's Family Civil Intake Screen*, 27 Pace L. Rev. 741 (2007).

Frank E.A. Sander & Stephen B. Goldberg, *Fitting the Forum to the Fuss: A User-Friendly Guide to Selecting an ADR Procedure*, 10 Negot. J. 49 (1994).

Frank E. A. Sander & Lukasz Rozdeiczer, *Matching Cases and Dispute Resolution Procedures: Detailed Analysis Leading to a Mediation-Centered Approach*, 11 Harv. Negot. L. Rev. 1 (2006).

Austin Sarat & William L. F. Felstiner, Divorce Lawyers and Their Clients: Power and Meaning in the Legal Process (1995).

Donna Shestowsky, *Disputants' Preferences for Court-Connected Dispute Resolution Procedures: Why We Should Care and Why We Know So Little*, 23 Ohio St. J. on Disp. Resol. 549 (2008).

Donna Shestowsky & Jeanne Brett, *Disputants' Perceptions of Dispute Resolution Procedures: An Ex Ante and Ex Post Longitudinal Empirical Study*, 41 Conn. L. Rev. 63 (2008).

Mark Spiegel, *Lawyering and Client Decisionmaking: Informed Consent and the Legal Profession*, 128 U. Pa. L. Rev. 41 (1979).

Jean R. Sternlight & Jennifer Robbennolt, *Good Lawyers Should Be Good Psychologists: Insights for Interviewing and Counseling Clients*, 23 Ohio St. J. on Disp. Resol. 437 (2008).

Susan P. Sturm, *From Gladiators to Problem-Solvers: Connecting Conversations about Women, the Academy, and the Legal Profession*, 4 DUKE J. GENDER L. & POL'Y 119 (1997).

RICHARD E. SUSSKIND, THE END OF LAWYERS?: RETHINKING THE NATURE OF LEGAL SERVICES (2008).

Symposium, *Unbundled Legal Services and Unrepresented Family Court Litigants*, 40 FAM. CT. REV. 10 (2002).

J. ALEXANDER TANFORD, THE PRETRIAL PROCESS (2004).

Lee Taft, *Apology Subverted: The Commodification of Apology*, 109 YALE L.J. 1135 (2000).

Nancy A. Welsh, *Looking Down the Road Less Traveled: Challenges to Persuading the Legal Profession to Define Problems More Humanistically*, 2008 J. DISP. RESOL. 45.

Roselle L. Wissler, *Barriers to Attorneys' Discussion and Use of ADR*, 19 OHIO ST. J. ON DISP. RESOL. 459 (2004).

Roselle L. Wissler, *Representation in Mediation: What We Know from Empirical Research*, 37 FORDHAM URB. L.J. 419 (2010).

Roselle L. Wissler, *When Does Familiarity Breed Content? A Study of the Role of Different Forms of ADR Education and Experience in Attorneys' ADR Recommendations*, 2 PEPP. DISP. RESOL. L.J. 199 (2002).

Roselle L. Wissler & Bob Dauber, *Leading Horses to Water: The Impact of an ADR "Confer and Report" Rule*, 26 JUST. SYS. J. 253 (2005).

Mark D. Wolf, *Update: How Value Billing Helps Both the Client and the Law Firm*, 28 ALTERNATIVES TO HIGH COST LITIG. 1 (2010).

J. KIM WRIGHT, LAWYERS AS PEACEMAKERS: PRACTICING HOLISTIC, PROBLEM-SOLVING LAW (2010).

RICHARD A. ZITRIN & CAROL M. LANGFORD, THE MORAL COMPASS OF THE AMERICAN LAWYER: TRUTH, JUSTICE, POWER, AND GREED (1999).

Paul J. Zwier & Ann B. Hamric *The Ethics of Care and Reimagining the Lawyer/Client Relationship*, 22 J. CONTEMP. L. 383 (1996).

Negotiation and Problem-Solving

Robert S. Adler & Elliot M. Silverstein, *When David Meets Goliath: Dealing with Power Differentials in Negotiations*, 5 HARV. NEGOT. L. REV. 1 (2000).

James J. Alfini, *Settlement Ethics and Lawyering in ADR Proceedings: A Proposal to Revise Rule 4.1*, 19 N. ILL. U. L. REV. 255 (1999).

BARRIERS TO CONFLICT RESOLUTION (Kenneth Arrow, Robert H. Mnookin, Lee Ross, Amos Tversky & Robert Wilson eds., 1999).

ROBERT M. AXELROD, THE EVOLUTION OF COOPERATION (1984).

LINDA BABCOCK & SARA LASCHEVER, WOMEN DON'T ASK: NEGOTIATION AND THE GENDER DIVIDE (2003).

Ian Ayres & Barry J. Nalebuff, *Common Knowledge as a Barrier to Negotiation*, 44 UCLA L. REV. 1631 (1997).

Maurits Barendrecht & Jin Ho Verdonschot, *Objective Criteria: Facilitating Dispute Resolution by Information about Going Rates of Justice* (Tilburg University Legal Studies Working Paper No. 011/2008), *available at* http://ssrn.com/abstract=1246697.

John Barkai, *Cultural Dimension Interests, the Dance of Negotiation, and Weather Forecasting: A Perspective on Cross-Cultural Negotiation and Dispute Resolution*, 8 PEPP. DISP. RESOL. L.J. 403 (2008).

Eleanor Barr, *Making Sound Decisions: How to Help Your Client Evaluate Settlement Options*, 24 ALTERNATIVES TO HIGH COST LITIG. 65 (2006).

Thomas D. Barton, *Creative Problem Solving: Purpose, Meaning, and Values*, 34 CAL. W. L. REV. 273 (1998).

MAX H. BAZERMAN & MARGARET A. NEALE, NEGOTIATING RATIONALLY (1992).

MARJORIE L. BENSON, THE SKILLS AND ETHICS OF NEGOTIATION: WISDOM AND REFLECTIONS OF WESTERN CANADIAN CIVIL PRACTITIONERS (2007).

DISPUTE RESOLUTION ETHICS: A COMPREHENSIVE GUIDE (Phyllis Bernard & Bryant Garth eds., 2002).

Richard Birke & Craig R. Fox, *Psychological Principles in Negotiating Civil Settlements*, 4 HARV. NEGOT. L. REV. 1 (1999).

BRINGING PEACE INTO THE ROOM: HOW THE PERSONAL QUALITIES OF THE MEDIATOR IMPACT THE PROCESS OF CONFLICT RESOLUTION (Daniel Bowling & David Hoffman eds., 2003).

Bernard Black, David Hyman & Charles Silver, *The Effects of "Early Offers" on Settlement: Evidence from Texas Medical Malpractice Cases*, 6 J. EMPIRICAL LEGAL STUDIES 747 (2009).

Bernard Black, David A. Hyman & Charles Silver, *O'Connell Early Settlement Offers: Toward Realistic Numbers and Two-Sided Offers*, 7 J. EMPIRICAL LEGAL STUDIES 379 (2010).

Wayne C. Brazil, *Protecting the Confidentiality of Settlement Negotiations*, 39 HASTINGS L. J. 955 (1998).

PAUL BREST & LINDA HAMILTON KRIEGER, PROBLEM SOLVING, DECISION MAKING, AND PROFESSIONAL JUDGMENT: A GUIDE FOR LAWYERS AND POLICYMAKERS (2010).

Jennifer Gerarda Brown, *The Role of Apology in Negotiation*, 87 MARQ. L. REV. 665 (2004).

Jennifer Gerarda Brown, *The Role of Hope in Negotiation*, 44 UCLA L. REV. 1661 (1997).

Anne M. Burr, *Ethics in Negotiation: Does Getting to Yes Require Candor?*, DISP. RESOL. J., July 2001, at 8.

Robert A. Baruch Bush, *What Do We Need a Mediator For?: Mediation's "Value-Added" for Negotiators*, 12 OHIO ST. J. ON DISP. RESOL. 1 (1996).

ROBERT A. BARUCH BUSH & JOSEPH FOLGER, THE PROMISE OF MEDIATION: THE TRANSFORMATIVE APPROACH TO CONFLICT (rev. ed. 2005).

ROBERT B. CIALDINI, INFLUENCE: SCIENCE AND PRACTICE (5th ed. 2008).

Jonathan R. Cohen, *When People Are the Means: Negotiating with Respect*, 14 GEO. J. LEGAL ETHICS 739 (2001).

SARAH RUDOLPH COLE, CRAIG A. McEWEN & NANCY HARDIN ROGERS, MEDIATION: LAW, POLICY, & PRACTICE (2d ed. 2000–2010).

Robert J. Condlin, *"Every Day and in Every Way We Are All Becoming Meta and Meta," or How Communitarian Bargaining Theory Conquered the World (of Bargaining Theory)*, 23 OHIO ST. J. ON DISP. RESOL. 231 (2008).

JOHN W. COOLEY, CREATIVE PROBLEM SOLVER'S HANDBOOK FOR NEGOTIATORS AND MEDIATORS: A PRACADEMIC APPROACH (2005).

John W. Cooley, *Defining the Ethical Limits of Acceptable Deception in Mediation*, 4 PEPP. DISP. RESOL. L. J. 263 (2004).

CHARLES B. CRAVER, EFFECTIVE LEGAL NEGOTIATION AND SETTLEMENT (6th ed. 2009).

CHARLES B. CRAVER, SKILLS & VALUES: LEGAL NEGOTIATING (2009).

Charles B. Craver, *What Makes a Great Legal Negotiator?*, 56 LOY. L.REV. 101 (2010).

THE HANDBOOK OF CONFLICT RESOLUTION: THEORY AND PRACTICE (Morton Deutsch, Peter T. Coleman & Eric C. Marcus eds.) (2d ed. 2006).

Laurie Kratky Doré, *Secrecy by Consent: The Use and Limits of Confidentiality in the Pursuit of Settlement*, 74 NOTRE DAME L. REV. 283 (1999).

Laurie Kratky Doré, *Public Courts Versus Private Justice: It's Time to Let Some Sun Shine in On Alternative Dispute Resolution*, 81 CHI.-KENT L. REV. 463 (2006).

Frank G. Evans, *The ADR Management Agreement: New Conflict Resolution Roles for Texas Lawyers and Mediators*, HOUS. LAW., Sept./Oct. 2007, at 10.

Trevor C. W. Farrow, *The Negotiator-as-Professional: Understanding the Competing Interests of a Representative Negotiator*, 7 PEPP. DISP. RESOL. L.J. 373 (2007).

ROGER FISHER & WILLIAM URY WITH BRUCE PATTON, GETTING TO YES: NEGOTIATING AGREEMENT WITHOUT GIVING IN (2d ed. 1991).

Owen M. Fiss, *Against Settlement*, 93 YALE L.J. 1073 (1984).

JAY FOLBERG & DWIGHT GOLANN, LAWYER NEGOTIATION: THEORY, PRACTICE, AND LAW (2d ed. 2010).

DIVORCE AND FAMILY MEDIATION: MODELS, TECHNIQUES AND APPLICATIONS (Jay Folberg, Ann L. Milne & Peter Salem eds. 2004).

Marc Galanter & Mia Cahill, *"Most Cases Settle": Judicial Promotion and Regulation of Settlements*, 46 STAN. L. REV. 1339 (1994).

Donald G. Gifford, Gifford's Legal Negotiation: Theory and Practice (2d ed. 2007).

Dwight Golann, *'Insulting' First Offers: Why Lawyers Make Them, and How to Respond*, 27 Alternatives to High Cost Litig. 113 (2009).

Dwight Golann, Mediating Legal Disputes: Effective Strategies for Neutrals and Advocates (2008).

Samuel R. Gross & Kent D. Syverud, *Getting to No: A Study of Settlement Negotiations and the Selection of Cases for Trial*, 90 Mich. L. Rev. 319 (1991).

Chris Guthrie, *Panacea or Pandora's Box?: The Costs of Options in Negotiation*, 88 Iowa L. Rev. 601 (2003).

Chris Guthrie, *Principles of Influence in Negotiation*, 87 Marq. L. Rev. 829 (2004).

Chris Guthrie & David Sally, *The Impact of the Impact Bias on Negotiation*, 87 Marq. L. Rev. 817 (2004).

Colleen M. Hancyz, Trevor C.W. Farrow & Frederick H. Zemans, The Theory and Practice of Representative Negotiation (2008).

Joni Hersch, Jeffrey O'Connell & W. Kip Viscusi, *An Empirical Assessment of Early Offer Reform for Medical Malpractice*, 36 J. Legal Studies S231 (2007).

Joni Hersch, Jeffrey O'Connell & W. Kip Viscusi, *Reply to "The Effects of 'Early Offers' in Medical Malpractice Cases: Evidence from Texas,"* 7 J. Empirical Legal Studies 164 (2010).

Milton Heumann & Jonathan M. Hyman, *Negotiation Methods and Litigation Settlement Methods in New Jersey: "You Can't Always Get What You Want,"* 12 Ohio St. J. on Disp. Resol. 253 (1997).

Art Hinshaw & Jess K. Alberts, *Doing the Right Thing: An Empirical Study of Attorney Negotiation Ethics*, (CELS 2009 4th Annual Conference on Empirical Legal Studies Paper, 2009), *available at* http://ssrn.com/abstract=1417666.

David P. Hoffer, Note, *Decision Analysis as a Mediator's Tool*, 1 Harv. Negot. L. Rev. 113 (1996).

Rebecca Hollander-Blumoff, *Just Negotiation*, (Washington U. School of Law Working Paper No. 10-03-10, 2010), *available at* http://ssrn.com/abstract=1577803.

Rebecca Hollander-Blumoff & Tom R. Tyler, *Procedural Justice in Negotiation: Procedural Fairness, Outcome Acceptance, and Integrative Potential*, 33 LAW & SOC. INQUIRY 473 (2008).

David A. Hoffman, *Colliding Worlds of Dispute Resolution: Towards a Unified Field Theory of ADR*, 2008 J. DISP. RESOL. 11.

Randall L. Kiser, Martin A. Asher & Blakeley B. McShane, *Let's Not Make a Deal: An Empirical Study of Decision Making in Unsuccessful Settlement Negotiations*, 5 J. EMPIRICAL LEGAL STUDIES 551 (2008).

Mary Kay Kisthardt, *The Use of Mediation and Arbitration for Resolving Family Conflicts: What Lawyers Think about Them*, 14 J. AM. ACAD. MATRIM. LAW 353 (1997).

DEBORAH M. KOLB & JUDITH WILLIAMS, EVERYDAY NEGOTIATION: NAVIGATING THE HIDDEN AGENDAS IN BARGAINING (2003).

RUSSELL KOROBKIN, NEGOTIATION THEORY AND STRATEGY (2d ed. 2009).

Russell Korobkin, *Against Integrative Bargaining*, 58 CASE W. RES. L. REV. 1323 (2008).

Russell Korobkin & Chris Guthrie, *Heuristics and Biases at the Bargaining Table*, 87 MARQ. L. REV. 795 (2004).

Russell Korobkin & Chris Guthrie, *Opening Offers and Out of Court Settlement: A Little Moderation Might Not Go a Long Way*, 10 OHIO ST. J. ON DISP RESOL. 1 (1994).

Minna J. Kotkin, *Outing Outcomes: An Empirical Study of Confidential Employment Discrimination Settlements*, 64 WASH. & LEE L. REV. 111 (2007).

DAVID A. LAX & JAMES K. SEBENIUS, THE MANAGER AS NEGOTIATOR: BARGAINING FOR COOPERATION AND COMPETITIVE GAIN (1986).

ROY J. LEWICKI, DAVID M. SAUNDERS & BRUCE BARRY, NEGOTIATION (6th ed. 2009).

ROY J. LEWICKI, ALEXANDER HIAM & KAREN WISE OLANDER, THINK BEFORE YOU SPEAK: A COMPLETE GUIDE TO STRATEGIC NEGOTIATION (1996).

David Luban, *Settlements and the Erosion of the Public Realm*, 83 GEO. L.J. 2619 (1995).

BERNARD MAYER, STAYING WITH CONFLICT: A STRATEGIC APPROACH TO ONGOING DISPUTES (2009).

Craig A. McEwen, *Managing Corporate Disputing: Overcoming Barriers to the Effective Use of Mediation for Reducing the Cost and Time of Litigation*, 14 OHIO ST. J. ON DISP. RESOL. 1 (1998).

Carrie Menkel-Meadow, *Whose Dispute Is It Anyway?: A Philosophical and Democratic Defense of Settlement (In Some Cases)*, 83 GEO. L.J. 2663 (1995).

Carrie Menkel-Meadow, *Toward Another View of Legal Negotiation: The Structure of Problem-Solving*, 31 UCLA L. REV. 754 (1984).

CARRIE J. MENKEL-MEADOW, ANDREA KUPFER SCHNEIDER & LELA PORTER LOVE, NEGOTIATION: PROCESSES FOR PROBLEM SOLVING (2006).

ROBERT MNOOKIN, BARGAINING WITH THE DEVIL: WHEN TO NEGOTIATE, WHEN TO FIGHT (2010).

Robert H. Mnookin, *Why Negotiations Fail: An Exploration of Barriers to the Resolution of Conflict*, 8 OHIO ST. J. ON DISP. RESOL. 235 (1993).

Robert H. Mnookin & Lewis Kornhauser, *Bargaining in the Shadow of the Law: The Case of Divorce*, 88 YALE L. J. 950 (1979).

ROBERT H. MNOOKIN, SCOTT R. PEPPET & ANDREW S. TULUMELLO, BEYOND WINNING: NEGOTIATING TO CREATE VALUE IN DEALS AND DISPUTES (2000).

Michael Moffitt, *Contingent Agreements: Agreeing to Disagree About the Future*, 87 MARQ. L. REV. 691 (2004).

Michael Moffitt, *Three Things to Be Against ("Settlement" Not Included)*, 78 FORDHAM L. REV. 1203 (2009).

THE HANDBOOK OF DISPUTE RESOLUTION (Michael L. Moffitt & Robert C. Bordone eds., 2005).

Janice Nadler, *Rapport in Legal Negotiation: How Small Talk Can Facilitate E-Mail Deal Making*, 9 HARV. NEGOT. L. REV. 223 (2004).

Janice Nadler, *Rapport in Negotiation and Conflict Resolution*, 87 MARQ. L. REV. 875 (2004).

Melissa L. Nelken, Understanding Negotiation (2001).

Jacqueline M. Nolan-Haley, *Lawyers, Clients, and Mediation*, 73 Notre Dame L. Rev. 1369 (1998).

Erin Ann O'Hara & Douglas Yarn, *On Apology and Consilience*, 77 Wash. L. Rev. 1121 (2002).

Scott R. Peppet, *Lawyer's Bargaining Ethics, Contract, and Collaboration: The End of the Legal Profession and the Beginning of Professional Pluralism*, 90 Iowa L. Rev. 475 (2005).

Donald R. Philbin, Jr, *The One Minute Manager Prepares for Mediation: A Multidisciplinary Approach to Negotiation Preparation*, 13 Harv. Negot. L. Rev. 249 (2008).

Bennett G. Picker, Mediation Practice Guide: A Handbook for Resolving Business Disputes (2d ed. 2003).

Paul Prestia & Harrie Samaras, *Beyond Decision Trees: Determining Aggregate Probabilities of Time, Cost, and Outcomes*, 28 Alternatives to High Cost Litig. 89 (2010).

Howard Raiffa with John Richardson and David Metcalfe, Negotiation Analysis: The Science and Art of Collaborative Decision Making (2007).

Alan Scott Rau, Edward F. Sherman & Scott R. Peppet, Negotiation (3d ed. 2006).

Peter Reilly, *Was Machiavelli Right? Lying in Negotiation and the Art of Defensive Self-Help*, 24 Ohio St. J. on Disp. Resol. 481 (2009).

John Richardson, *How Negotiators Choose Standards of Fairness: A Look at the Empirical Evidence and Some Steps Toward a Process Model*, 12 Harv. Negot. L. Rev. 415 (2007).

Douglas R. Richmond, *Lawyers' Professional Responsibilities and Liabilities in Negotiations*, 22 Geo. J. Legal Ethics 249 (2009).

Leonard L. Riskin, *Decisionmaking in Mediation: The New Old Grid and the New New Grid System*, 79 Notre Dame L. Rev. 1 (2003).

Jennifer K. Robbennolt, *Apologies and Legal Settlement: An Empirical Examination*, 102 Mich. L. Rev. 460 (2003).

Jennifer K. Robbennolt, *Attorneys, Apologies, and Settlement Negotiation*, 13 Harv. Negot. L. Rev. 349 (2008).

Peter Robinson, *Contending with Wolfes in Sheep's Clothing: A Cautiously Cooperative Approach to Mediation Advocacy*, 50 BAYLOR L. REV. 963 (1998).

Jeswald W. Salacuse, *Ten Ways That Culture Affects Negotating Style: Some Survey Results*, 14 NEGOT. J. 221 (1998).

Andrea Kupfer Schneider, *Shattering Negotiation Myths: Empirical Evidence on the Effectiveness of Negotiation Style*, 7 HARV. NEGOT. L. REV. 143 (2002).

THE NEGOTIATOR'S FIELDBOOK: A DESKBOOK FOR THE EXPERIENCED NEGOTIATOR (Andrea Kupfer Schneider & Christopher Honeyman eds., 2006).

Andrea Kupfer Schneider & Nancy Mills, *What Family Lawyers Are Really Doing When They Negotiate*, 44 FAM. CT. REV. 612 (2006).

Jeffrey R. Seul, *Settling Significant Cases*, 79 WASH. L. REV. 881 (2004).

Jean R. Sternlight, *Lawyers' Representation of Clients in Mediation: Using Economics and Psychology to Structure Advocacy in a Nonadversarial Setting*, 14 OHIO ST. J. ON DISP. RESOL. 269 (1999).

DOUGLAS STONE, BRUCE PATTON & SHEILA HEEN, DIFFICULT CONVERSATIONS: HOW TO DISCUSS WHAT MATTERS MOST (2010).

DEBORAH TANNEN, THE ARGUMENT CULTURE: STOPPING AMERICA'S WAR OF WORDS (1999).

LEIGH L. THOMPSON, THE MIND AND HEART OF THE NEGOTIATOR (4th ed. 2008).

E. WENDY TRACHTE-HUBER & STEPHEN K. HUBER, MEDIATION AND NEGOTIATION: REACHING AGREEMENTS IN LAW AND BUSINESS (2d ed. 2007).

Nancy A. Welsh, *Perceptions of Fairness In Negotiation*, 87 MARQ. L. REV. 753 (2004).

Gerald Wetlaufer, *The Ethics of Lying in Negotiations*, 75 IOWA L. REV. 1219 (1990).

Gerald B. Wetlaufer, *The Limits of Integrative Bargaining*, 85 GEO. L.J. 369 (1996).

GERALD R. WILLIAMS & CHARLES B. CRAVER, LEGAL NEGOTIATING (2007).

Gerald R. Williams, *Negotiation as a Healing Process*, 1996 J. DISP. RESOL. 1.

PAUL J. ZWIER & THOMAS F. GUERNSEY, ADVANCED NEGOTIATION AND MEDIATION THEORY AND PRACTICE (2005).

Collaborative Practice

ABA Section of Dispute Resolution Collaborative Law Committee, http://www.abanet.org/dch/committee.cfm?com=DR035000.

SHERRIE R. ABNEY, AVOIDING LITIGATION: A GUIDE TO CIVIL COLLABORATIVE LAW (2005).

NANCY J. CAMERON, COLLABORATIVE PRACTICE: DEEPENING THE DIALOGUE (2004).

Christopher M. Fairman, *A Proposed Model Rule for Collaborative Law*, 21 OHIO ST. J. ON DISP. RESOL. 73 (2005).

Christopher M. Fairman, *Why We Still Need a Model Rule for Collaborative Law: A Reply to Professor Lande*, 22 OHIO ST. J. ON DISP. RESOL. 707 (2007).

SHEILA M. GUTTERMAN, COLLABORATIVE LAW: A NEW MODEL FOR DISPUTE RESOLUTION (2004).

David Hoffman, *Collaborative Law in the World of Business*, COLLAB. REV., Winter 2004, at 1.

International Academy of Collaborative Professionals,

http://www.collaborativepractice.com/.

Michaela Keet, Wanda Wiegers & Melanie Morrison, *Client Engagement Inside Collaborative Law*, 24 CANADIAN J. FAM. L. 145 (2008).

John Lande, *An Empirical Analysis of Collaborative Practice*, 49 FAM. CT. REV. (forthcoming).

John Lande, *Possibilities for Collaborative Law: Ethics and Practice of Lawyer Disqualification and Process Control in a New Model of Lawyering*, 64 OHIO ST. L.J. 1315 (2003).

John Lande, *Principles for Policymaking about Collaborative Law and Other ADR Processes*, 22 OHIO ST. J. ON DISP. RESOL. 619 (2007).

John Lande & Forrest S. Mosten, *Collaborative Lawyers' Duties to Screen the Appropriateness of Collaborative Law and Obtain Clients' Informed Consent to Use Collaborative Law*, 25 OHIO ST. J. ON DISP. RESOL. 347 (2010).

JULIE MACFARLANE, THE EMERGING PHENOMENON OF COLLABORATIVE FAMILY LAW (CFL): A QUALITATIVE STUDY OF CFL CASES (2005), *available at* http://www.justice.gc.ca/eng/pi/fcy-fea/lib-bib/rep-rap/2005/2005_1/pdf/2005_1.pdf.

FORREST S. MOSTEN, COLLABORATIVE DIVORCE HANDBOOK: HELPING FAMILIES WITHOUT GOING TO COURT (2009).

Forrest S. Mosten, *Collaborative Law Practice: An Unbundled Approach to Informed Client Decision-Making*, 2008 J. DISP. RESOL. 163.

Forrest S. Mosten & John Lande, *The Uniform Collaborative Law Act's Contribution to Informed Client Decision Making in Choosing a Dispute Resolution Process*, 38 HOFSTRA L. REV. 611 (2009).

Scott R. Peppet, *The Ethics of Collaborative Law*, 2008 J. DISP. RESOL. 131.

Ted Schneyer, *The Organized Bar and the Collaborative Law Movement: A Study in Professional Change*, 50 ARIZ. L. REV. 289 (2008).

William H. Schwab, *Collaborative Lawyering: A Closer Look at an Emerging Practice*, 4 PEPP. DISP. RESOL. L.J. 351 (2004).

RICHARD W. SHIELDS, JUDITH P. RYAN & VICTORIA L. SMITH, COLLABORATIVE FAMILY LAW: ANOTHER WAY TO RESOLVE FAMILY DISPUTES (2003).

PAULINE H. TESLER, COLLABORATIVE LAW: ACHIEVING EFFECTIVE RESOLUTION IN DIVORCE WITHOUT LITIGATION (2d ed. 2008).

Uniform Collaborative Law Act, http://www.nccusl.org/Update/CommitteeSearchResults.aspx?committee=279.

Wanda Wiegers & Michaela Keet, *Collaborative Family Law and Gender Inequalities: Balancing Risks and Opportunities*, 46 OSGOODE HALL L.J. 733 (2008).

Cooperative Practice

David A. Hoffman, *Cooperative Negotiation Agreements: Using Contracts to Make a Safe Place for a Difficult Conversation, in* INNOVATIONS IN FAMILY LAW PRACTICE (Kelly Browe Olson & Nancy Ver Steegh eds., 2008).

John Lande, *Learning From "Cooperative" Negotiators in Wisconsin*, DISP. RESOL. MAG. Winter 2009, at 20.

John Lande, *Practical Insights from an Empirical Study of Cooperative Lawyers in Wisconsin*, 2008 J. DISP. RESOL. 203.

Julie O'Halloran, *Cooperative Law: The Practice of Family Law with Civility and Respect*, WIS. J. FAMILY L., July 2004, at 1.

Settlement Counsel

Kathy A. Bryan, *Why Should Businesses Hire Settlement Counsel?*, 2008 J. DISP. RESOL. 195.

William F. Coyne, Jr., *The Case for Settlement Counsel*, 14 OHIO ST. J. ON DISP. RESOL. 367 (1999).

Charles B. Craver, *Negotiation as a Distinct Area of Specialization*, 9 AM. J. TRIAL ADVOC. 377 (1986).

Roger Fisher, *What About Negotiation as a Specialty?*, 69 A.B.A. J. 1221 (1983).

Jim Golden, H. Abigail Moy & Adam Lyons, *The Negotiation Counsel Model: An Empathetic Model for Settling Catastrophic Personal Injury Cases*, 13 HARV. NEGOT. L. REV. 211 (2008).

James E. McGuire, *Why Litigators Should Use Settlement Counsel*, 18 ALTERNATIVES TO HIGH COST LITIG. 107 (2000).

James E. McGuire, *Settlement Counsel: Answers to the FAQs*, NYSBA DISP. RESOL. LAW,. Fall 2010, at 23.

Dispute System Design

Maurits Barendrecht, *Growing Justice: Justice Policies and Transaction Costs*, (TISCO Working Paper Series on Civil Law and Conflict Resolution Systems No. 009/2009; Tilburg University Legal Studies Working Paper No. 013/2009, 2009), *available at* http://ssrn.com/abstract=1475201.

Maurits Barendrecht, *Understanding the Market for Justice*, Tilburg University Legal Studies Working Paper No. 009/2009, 2009), *available at* http://ssrn.com/abstract=1416841.

Lisa Blomgren Bingham, *Designing Justice: Legal Institutions and Other Systems for Managing Conflict*, 24 Ohio St. J. on Disp. Resol. 1 (2008).

John P. Conbere, *Theory Building for Conflict Management System Design*, 19 Conflict Resol. Q. 215 (2001).

Cathy A. Costantino, *Second Generation Organizational Conflict Management Systems Design: A Practitioner's Perspective on Emerging Issues*, 14 Harv. Negot. L. Rev. 81 (2009).

Cathy A. Costantino & Christina Sickles Merchant, Designing Conflict Management Systems: A Guide to Creating Productive and Healthy Organizations (1996).

Catherine Cronin-Harris, Building ADR into the Corporate Law Department: ADR Systems Design (1997).

Catherine Cronin-Harris, Building ADR into the Law Firm: ADR Systems Design (1997).

Hallie Fader, Note, *Designing the Forum to Fit the Fuss: Dispute System Design for the State Trial Courts*, 13 Harv. Negot. L. Rev. 481 (2008).

International Institute for Conflict Prevention and Resolution, How Companies Manage Employment Disputes: A Compendium of Leading Corporate Employment Programs (2002).

John Lande, *Helping Lawyers Help Clients Make Good Decisions About Dispute Resolution*, Disp. Resol. Mag., Fall 2010, at 14.

John Lande, *Using Dispute System Design Methods to Promote Good-Faith Participation in Court-Connected Mediation Programs*, 50 UCLA L. Rev. 69 (2002).

Melanie Lewis, *Systems Design Means Process Precision, but Emphasizes Culture, Value, and Results*, 25 ALTERNATIVES TO HIGH COST LITIG. 113 (2007).

DAVID B. LIPSKY, RONALD L. SEEBER & RICHARD D. FINCHER., EMERGING SYSTEMS FOR MANAGING WORKPLACE CONFLICT: LESSONS FROM AMERICAN CORPORATIONS FOR MANAGERS AND DISPUTE RESOLUTION PROFESSIONALS (2003).

MARYLAND MEDIATION AND CONFLICT RESOLUTION OFFICE, THE USE OF ALTERNATIVE DISPSUTE RESOLUTION (ADR) IN MARYLAND BUSINESS: A BENCHMARKING STUDY (2004), *available at* http://www.courts.state.md.us/macro/pdfs/macro-busstudy.pdf.

KARL A. SLAIKEU & RALPH H. HASSON, CONTROLLING THE COSTS OF CONFLICT: HOW TO DESIGN A SYSTEM FOR YOUR ORGANIZATION (1998).

Stephanie Smith & Janet Martinez, *An Analytic Framework for Dispute Systems Design*, 14 HARV. NEGOT. L. REV. 123 (2009).

What Corporations Need to Know About How to Install an Integrated Conflict Management System, 27 ALTERNATIVES TO HIGH COST LITIG. 99 (2009).

WILLIAM L. URY, JEANNE M. BRETT & STEPHEN B. GOLDBERG, GETTING DISPUTES RESOLVED: DESIGNING SYSTEMS TO CUT THE COSTS OF CONFLICT (1988).

Jin Ho Verdonschot, Maurits Barendrecht, Laura Klaming & Peter Kamminga, *Measuring Access to Justice: The Quality of Outcomes*, (Tilburg University Legal Studies Working Paper No. 014/2008, 2008), *available at* http://papers.ssrn.com/sol3/papers.cfm?abstract_id=1298917.

Promoting Quality of Dispute Resolution

There have been efforts to improve the quality of mediation that can be adapted to negotiation and legal practice generally.

Judith Cohen, *Reflective Practice: How Veterans Can Benefit from Rookie Training*, 21 ALTERNATIVES TO HIGH COST LITIG. 49 (2003).

Robert B. Davidson & Deborah Gage Haude, *Shadowing: The Key to Developing Strong Mediation Skills*, Disp. Resol. Mag., Fall 2005, at 13.

Dwight Golann, *What Can Training Do for an Experienced Mediator?*, Disp. Resol. Mag., Fall 2005, at 9.

Howard Herman & Jeannette P. Twomey, *Training Outside the Classroom: Peer Consultation Groups*, Disp. Resol. Mag., Fall 2005, at 15.

Art Hinshaw & Roselle L. Wissler, *How Do We Know That Mediation Training Works?*, Disp. Resol. Mag., Fall 2005, at 21.

John Lande, *Doing the Best Mediation You Can*, Disp. Resol. Mag., Spring/Summer 2008, at 43.

John Lande, *Improving Mediation Quality: You, Too, Can Do This in Your Area*, 26 Alternatives to High Cost Litig. 89 (2008).

Julie Macfarlane, *Mediating Ethically: The Limits of Codes of Conduct and the Potential of a Reflective Practice Model*, 40 Osgoode Hall L.J. 49 (2002).

Julie Macfarlane & Bernard Mayer, *What's the Use of Theory?: Integrating Theory and Research into Training*, Disp. Resol. Mag., Fall 2005, at 5.

Maryland Mediator Quality Assurance Committee, Maryland Mediation and Conflict Resolution Office, Final Report: Meeting the Challenge Of Mediator Excellence (2004), *available at*

http://www.courts.state.md.us/macro/pdfs/reports/meetingthechallenge ofmediatorexcellence2004report.pdf.

David Matz & Roni Lipton, *Choosing Between a Training Program and a Graduate ADR Program*, Disp. Resol. Mag., Fall 2005, at 17.

Michael L. Moffitt, *The Four Ways to Assure Mediator Quality (and why none of them work)*, 24 Ohio St. J. on Disp. Resol. 191 (2009).

Charles Pou, Jr., *Assuring Excellence, or Merely Reassuring? Policy and Practice in Promoting Mediator Quality*, 2004 J. Disp. Resol. 303.

Roselle L. Wissler & Robert W. Rack, Jr., *Assessing Mediator Performance: The Usefulness of Participant Questionnaires*, 2004 J. Disp. Resol. 229.

Task Force on Improving Mediation Quality, ABA Section of Dispute Resolution, Final Report (2008), *available at* http://www.abanet.org/dch/committee.cfm?com=DR020600.

Test Design Project, National Institute for Dispute Resolution, Performance-Based Assessment: A Methodology for Use in Selecting, Training and Evaluating Mediators (2005), *available at* http://www.convenor.com/madison/method.pdf.

Paula M. Young, *Take It or Leave It. Lump It or Grieve It: Designing Mediator Complaint Systems That Protect Mediators, Unhappy Parties, Attorneys, Courts, the Process, and the Field*, 21 OHIO ST. J. ON DISP. RESOL. 721 (2006).